Solid piggyback train rounding famous Horseshoe Curve #322 at Goldtree on the Santa Margarita Subdiv., the Southern Pacific's Coast Division on CTC territory.

RAILROADS

OF THE HOUR

S. Kip Farrington, Jr.

COWARD-McCANN, Inc.   New York

RAILROADS OF THE HOUR

Also by S. Kɪᴘ Fᴀʀʀɪɴɢᴛᴏɴ, Jʀ.

To

John M. Olin, chairman of the Executive Committee of the Olin Mathieson Chemical Corporation, sportsman, businessman and industrialist, who is a friend of the entire railroad industry.

CONTENTS

xi

xii

INTRODUCTION

It is axiomatic that the transportation system of a nation is one of its greatest strengths. The history of the railroads of our country is one of fabulous richness. Their story today, and the parallel story of our industrial growth, is a new and equally fascinating chapter in this history.

The nation's railroads have more than proved themselves in national emergencies and their extremely fine performance in World War II must never be forgotten. Their employees, men and women, met the challenge, not only in this country but in many areas overseas, just as they do in peacetime here. A sound and healthy railroad industry is most essential to the United States.

RICHARD M. NIXON
Vice President of
the United States of America

Washington, D.C.
August 8, 1958

FOREWORD

In the last ten years it has been my good fortune to personally inspect and travel over the railroads of thirty-seven foreign countries, some fifty-two properties in all. I was on these railroads with the officials, inspecting yards and facilities, riding business cars as well as passenger equipment new and old, locomotives in both freight and passenger service, electric, steam, and diesel, and the rear ends of freight trains when there were cabooses. After having the opportunity of viewing all their very fine railroads and territories, plus the tremendous job they accomplish with their tedious and tough operations and what they have to do it with, I am more thoroughly convinced than ever that rail transportation in the United States and Canada is the best and most luxurious in the world. Nowhere else on the earth are there so many passengers and so much freight on the move with such speed, such regularity, such safety, and such punctuality as on the North American continent.

Federal regulation of interstate commerce is constitutional and necessary. On the other hand, lawful commerce can be regulated to death. About seventy-five years ago the railroads were, or appeared to be becoming, a monopoly. They made their own rates and regulations. To protect themselves against political exploitation or to benefit themselves by political manipulations, they went into politics. In some states they came to dominate the government. Exacting "all the traffic would bear" was virtually the only rule that applied in fixing transportation charges.

Congress accordingly set up the Interstate Commerce Commission in 1887, putting the railroads under strict regulations. In the seventy years that have elapsed, conditions have drastically changed. Motor trucks, passenger buses, and airlines now compete with the railroads, and these newer modes of transportation are very largely subsidized through road-building and construction of airports at public expense, while the railroads continue to be subject to heavy taxation. This, along with continued regulation, puts them in a very adverse competitive position. Obviously the nation must have a country-wide railroad system. It is necessary to haul heavy freight in times of peace, for thousands of communities depend on the railroads. And we could not wage another war should there be a railroad breakdown. I have stated before that the American railroads won World War II for the United States. The proper reform ought to be plain enough. We need a national transportation policy that will utilize all the means of transportation—waterways as well as airlines, railroads as well as highways.

The obvious first step is to relieve the railroads of excessive Federal regulation or strangulation and to permit them to reorganize their structures and operate their services on a fair but self-supporting basis. It is not only the owners and employees of railroads that are affected by shrinking profits. It is everyone in every walk of life. The United States cannot be a healthy nation with sick railroads. The public is aware of this, and I believe it always will welcome accurate information on the subject. This information can result in an enlightened and elastic attitude toward today's railroads, an attitude that will, I hope, result in appropriate corrective legislative action. This is all any industry deserves—long overdue them, it is all the railroads ask.

If you do not believe the importance of this serious situation, look at the Russians and see how they are constantly improving their railroads and making sure they are kept busy and solvent.

So let's make this our motto: Always travel and ship via the railroads of the United States and Canada.

My one regret in writing this book is that it is not possible to include all the United States railroads in it. The great majority of them are definitely Railroads of the Hour.

It is a privilege to acknowledge and thank the publishers of *Modern Railroads* and *Railway Age* magazine for the help they gave me. The former is the finest railroad monthly in the world, and the *Railway Age* is, of course, by far the foremost weekly, considered by many to be the Bible of world railway publications. It cannot be stressed strongly enough that all who have this industry at heart, or even any interest in it at all, should read these two publications. And that goes for both sexes and all ages. I am indeed grateful to Olive B. Flannery for her work on the manuscript; and as usual I extend my deep appreciation to Richard H. Kindig for the outstanding photographs he made to be included in this volume. The work of Mr. Kindig is, as always, a great addition to the book.

S. KIP FARRINGTON, JR.

"Finning Out"
East Hampton, New York
October 1, 1958

RAILROADS OF THE HOUR

CHAPTER I

THE AMERICAN RAILROAD TIE

It may look like an ordinary, unimportant piece of wood, but without it and its hundreds of millions of identical companions, the railroad industry of the United States would never be able to provide the tremendous services that they do to the nation's travelers and shippers.

It's the lowly railroad tie—a chunk of unexciting-looking timber some eight or nine feet in length—that provides the important base flooring over which American industry delivers its people and its products.

There are about one billion crossties in use today throughout the country by Class I railroads alone, and they are accompanied by more than 24,000 miles of track that is supported by switch and bridge ties. If the ties in use by only one of the nation's major railroads were to be placed end to end, they would encircle the world twice.

Because railroad ties are so fundamental to operations, and because wood products represent the largest item in maintenance costs, the railroad industry is constantly engaged in scientific research aimed at advancing and improving its knowledge of wood preservation, in order to secure maximum length of service. Railroads maintain large, modern wood-treatment plants, where experimentation is constantly conducted, and where raw wood is treated to provide maximum resistance to weather, termites, and other destructive elements.

For the past fifty years or so, creosote, a coal tar derivative, has been the leading product used to impregnate wood for the manufacture of crossties. But modern research has brought forth a helping process: vapor drying, which is credited with reducing

1

wood-seasoning periods from a year or longer to only twenty-four hours.

Under the older process, the fresh cut, green wood ties had to be stacked and stored for seasoning. In addition to the disadvantage that this method required many acres of storage space, the length of the seasoning period depended to a great extent upon local weather conditions. However, under the new vapor-drying process, both of these negative conditions are completely eliminated.

There are today a handful of vapor-drying plants in operation in the United States, the first one having been put into operation at Somerville, Texas, in June, 1954. A cylinder 8 feet in diameter and 124 feet long is the heart of the new process; a complete cylinder charge consists of 750 ties, all of which are treated at one time.

Tram cars, specially designed in shape to conform with the diameter of the cylinder, are used to carry the freshly cut ties to the cylinder on standard-gauge track. The fresh wood is shoved into the vapor-drying cylinder, and the doors are securely locked and bolted.

The drying agent used is a xylene derivative, 5,000 gallons of it being pumped into the cylinder. This particular agent has been selected for the process because it has a very low boiling range that makes the vapor-drying process possible. When the temperature of the cylinder reaches about 250 degrees, steam is introduced into the cylinder. The steam performs two functions: it vaporizes the xylene-derivative drying agent, and it provides a method for vaporizing the natural moisture in the raw ties.

At this point in the process the natural moisture mixes with the vaporized drying agent, and the two are carried out of the master cylinder into a condenser, where they once again return to liquid form and where they are separated. The 750 ties in each cylinder load produce about 3,500 gallons of water, which is run off as waste; the condensed drying agent is claimed for re-use in the treatment of future batches of raw ties.

This process requires some twelve to fifteen hours (compared with the former method, which required twelve to fifteen months to accomplish the same result). Experience has shown that defective ties amount to an average of 5 per cent of each batch when vapor drying is used, as against about 30 per cent when conventional long-term air drying is employed.

A preservative, consisting of a mixture of 30 per cent creosote and 70 per cent residual oil, is then applied to impregnate the treated ties, right within the cylinder. This treating solution is forced into the ties at 180 degrees temperature, under a pressure of 175 pounds per square inch. At this temperature and under this pressure, it has been found that maximum penetration of the wood is accomplished, since higher pressures tend to break down the internal structure of the treated wood.

About nine additional hours in the cylinder are required for this permeating step, with the actual amount of solution retained in the ties largely controlled by the species of wood that is being used.

The vapor-drying process is the newest and most advanced in a series of processes that experts have evolved over the course of the years. Vast sums of money have been spent by the nation's railroads in experimentation, and the results of this huge effort have been to increase the life of ties from ten years to more than thirty years. Under vapor-drying techniques it is hoped that the life span of a railroad tie will become forty-five years. Any increase in the longevity of the many millions of ties used by the railroads, of course, means a tremendous saving, both in cost to the railroads and in the use of America's available timber.

While oak woods are mainly used for the manufacture of crossties, beechwood and hickory are increasing in popularity since the invention and application of the vapor-drying technique. About 77,000 ties of beechwood were turned out at Somerville during the last half of 1954, while some 3,500 experimental hickory ties were produced there during the same period. It was found that, while hickory has a tendency toward excessive checking and splitting during conventional air drying, it holds up excellently under vapor drying, and it is therefore likely to be used in greater quantity from now on.

Green ties flow into Somerville in a constant stream from East

3

Texas timber sources. Because vapor drying is still in its early stages, the plant's capacity for treating raw ties in this new way is not yet up to demand, and some air drying consequently also continues there. About half a million ties, therefore, are constantly stacked for air drying in an area that occupies about half of the plant's total space.

Before being treated in the vapor-drying cylinder, the raw tie is run through boring and adzing machines. It is cut to the required length and thoroughly inspected for checking or other possible defects. It is then adzed for uniform plate-bearing and is prebored with holes for spiking. As many as sixteen holes may be drilled, depending upon the weight of the rail under which the tie is scheduled to be placed.

Each end of the tie is then stamped with a code mark to provide complete identification. For example, one end of the tie might be stamped "O 9 131," indicating that it is made of oak, that it is 9 feet long, and that it has been bored for 131-pound rail. The other end of the tie might bear the legend "VZ S 54," which would show that it had been vapor dried, that it was treated with twelve pounds of treating solution per cubic foot, and that it was processed at the Somerville plant in 1954.

When air drying is employed, it costs the railroads about thirty-five cents to dowel each of the many checked and split ties that constitute some 30 per cent of the total batch treated. The damaged ties are sent to a doweling machine, which compresses the tie and inserts from two to four metal dowels at each end, thus making the tie usable for road service. Here, too, by cutting down on the percentage of ties requiring such corrective treatment, the railroads effect considerable financial saving.

The vapor-drying cylinders can be used, too, for other purposes than treatment of railroad ties. In fact, at Somerville, about one-third of the time during which the plant's three cylinders are operating is occupied with treating wood for other uses. Bridge lumber, piling, communication poles, track car setoffs, panel crossings, fence posts, crossing planks, and car decking are just a few of the wood products that are vapor dried and then treated with creosote and oil solution to provide a longer life span.

4

An additional aid to the process is provided by what is known as incising, which is a procedure that results in the cutting of slits one inch deep and one inch long at several points in a crosstie or other lumber product. A special incising machine is used for this procedure, which is employed primarily on gum switch, sawn oak, and some fir. These woods are difficult to impregnate with treating solution because of their low sapwood content, and the incisions allow the solution to penetrate more thoroughly into the lumber.

Considerable capital outlay is required to provide the special machinery needed by a railroad's wood-treating plant. For example, in addition to the vapor-drying cylinders and the incising machine already mentioned, a modern wood treatment plant requires a pole-peeling machine to strip off outer layers and knots so that a smooth-surfaced pole is ready for processing, storage tanks for the various solutions and agents, a cylinder control room, machine shops, power plants, chemical laboratories and their specialized equipment, machines to unload ties, lift trucks, cranes, and switch locomotives.

Attention must be paid, too, to the problem of protecting the valuable wood stockpile that is constantly being air dried. The ground must be continually sprinkled with special chemicals to prevent accumulation of grass and extraneous materials, and an elaborate fire prevention system must always be maintained.

Much experimentation has gone forward toward the use as crossties of other materials, such as steel and concrete, but no satisfactory substitute for properly treated wood has yet been discovered.

CHAPTER II

THE BANGOR AND AROOSTOOK

The Main Line of Maine

In relation to the density of the population it serves, no railroad in the country gives better or more complete passenger and freight service than the Bangor and Aroostook Railroad.

Compact, well maintained, and modern in every respect, it operates a total of 596 miles on its main line and branches, including 259 miles of main-line trackage and 337 miles on ten diverging lines. The Bangor and Aroostook has 1,500 employees, and its main line is laid with 110-, 112-, and 115-pound rails.

Completely dieselized with excellent Electro Motives, the Bangor and Aroostook owns and operates five G-P-9's and sixteen G-P-7's and two E-8 passenger diesels. The E-8's take care of the railroad's excellent passenger train: the Potatoland Special, which carries a through sleeping car from Boston.

All of the Bangor and Aroostook's diesels were built by the Electro Motive Company. The railroad also owns eight F-3's with 8 BL units, and eight switchers.

Bangor, with a population of 35,000, is the largest city served by the road. Next in size are Caribou with 12,000 people, Presque Isle with 11,000, Houlton with 8,500, Limestone with 8,000, Millinocket with 7,000, Van Buren with 6,000, and Fort Kent with 5,500.

The Bangor and Aroostook is completely radio equipped, with all diesels and cabooses having installations of this modern railroading aid to expedite the shipment of loads such as the 33,400 carloads of potatoes handled during 1957. The road's potato move represents its predominating traffic; it is followed by paper

6

and pulpwood, petroleum products, coal, fertilizer, lumber, frozen foods, grain and oats, and farm machinery, in that order. The fertilizer includes nitrates and phosphates that are loaded at the well-equipped seaport of Searsport.

During the summer months, when the potato move is not heavy in Maine, the Bangor and Aroostook leases out some of its diesel power to other roads that have heavy hauling demands at that time of year. Special reefers—1,350 of them—are all handsomely painted for the potato move, and an additional 2,500 box cars handle other commodities. Unusual dump cars, specially designed for pulp haulage, make use of side doors, and the road also maintains a group of other pulpwood cars.

Eight cars that were used as troop sleepers during the war years have been converted into fine all-steel cabooses.

The road has sixteen miles of single track under CTC and nine miles of double track from North Maine Junction to South LaGrange, and from that point to West Millinocket it maintains a twenty-eight-mile cutoff over which all manifest freight trains are operated, thus giving the Bangor and Aroostook a total of thirty-seven miles of double track over its main line. Heaviest grade on the line is 2.04 on a stretch between Greenville and Blanchard Shirley on the Greenville Branch. Ruling grade on the main line is 1.29, running north and south between Millinocket Summit and Sherman.

Excellent mileposts, well marked and painted rails, and snow equipment or flanger markers at every crossing and passing track characterize the road. There are speedboards all along the lines, and there are three dragging detectors in operation as well as rail-oilers at Millinocket Summit south to LaGrange.

Northern Maine is closer to Europe than any other point in the United States, and consequently probably rates as the number one defense area of the country. Because of the excellent service that this road can furnish, the government maintains two large and important air bases in this section, the Presque Isle Air Base for fighter and interceptor planes, and the Limestone Air Base, which handles B-52's and other large bomber planes.

One of the operational advantages enjoyed by a road of this

size but sometimes denied more extensive systems lies in the opportunity for close contact between top executives and staff members. The Bangor and Aroostook is fully aware of this, and conducts monthly "Meet the President" sessions. Every month forty employees of the road are brought into Bangor to spend half a day at a round-table conference in the directors' room with the road's officers. They are then taken to lunch, following which the afternoon is theirs to do with as they see fit.

Much that benefits both the road and its employees has come out of these meetings. The railroad has an excellent public relations department and publishes a top-notch bimonthly magazine, *Maine Line*.

Some of the nation's leading industrial companies are numbered among the shippers on the Bangor and Aroostook. They include a division of General Foods, located at Caribou, the American Thread Company at Milo, the Sherman Lumber Company at Sherman, the Great Northern Paper Company at Millinocket and East Millinocket, and the Fraser Paper Company at Madawaska.

Potential for the Bangor and Aroostook Railroad is tremendous, for the entire state of Maine, and particularly Aroostook County, are well suited for future industrial expansion. Manganese ore deposits are known to be abundant, and it is generally believed that in the not too distant future these will be opened and developed by the government. In addition, the area is inhabited by a population that is highly skilled and likes to work.

Two slate quarries are also located on the railroad's line, but the tremendous volume of white potato starch haulage represents one of the road's greatest operations. More than 65 per cent of this valuable product produced throughout the entire United States comes from Maine, with a total of some 40,000 tons being shipped annually to textile mills in the South and to paper mills along the eastern seaboard. Potato starch, the most versatile of all the starches, is in great demand, and its uses are constantly expanding.

Maine also has a well-developed agricultural industry, planting about 110,000 acres of grain each year as well as about 500 acres

8

of broccoli. But potatoes are the state's major crop. In fact, Aroostook County alone, served by this fine little railroad, grows more potatoes every year than are produced by any of the country's forty-eight other states.

That is why the Bangor and Aroostook's potato move, which will be described later in this book, is so important to this railroad, to its home county, to the state of Maine, and to the nation in general.

CHAPTER III

THE LACKAWANNA STREAMLINER

The Finest Daylight Train Between New York and Buffalo—Through Most Superb Scenery

At the turn of the century one of the most famous ladies in America was Phoebe Snow. The fact that she was an imaginary lady detracted not at all from her popularity, for Phoebe Snow was renowned in painting and poetry, in drama and song.

Dressed in immaculate white, which set off to perfection her auburn hair, always adorned with a corsage of dainty violets, Phoebe Snow was created to symbolize the cleanliness that accompanied travel on the Lackawanna Railroad. For in those days the Lackawanna was one of the very few railroads in the country that burned hard coal in its locomotives instead of the bituminous variety employed by most.

In one of the many advertisements of that day, bringing this virtue to the attention of the public, Phoebe Snow said:

> I won my fame and wide acclaim
> For Lackawanna's splendid name
> By keeping bright and snowy white
> Upon the Road of Anthracite.

For many years, however, Phoebe Snow disappeared from public notice, because the advent of two major wars compelled the issuance of government directives requiring all railroads to burn soft coal. But Phoebe Snow is back today, this time to lend her name to Lackawanna's No. 3, a diesel-powered, de luxe, ultramodern streamliner that traverses daily the shortest existing rail route from New York to Buffalo.

10

This beautiful train, named after a beautiful lady, reflects the very latest advances in modern railroad travel. All of its coaches, of course, are air-conditioned, with deep, inviting, relaxing seats whose comfortable sponge-rubber cushions recline at any desired position at just the touch of a button. Specially designed, extrawide baggage racks in each coach, running full length on both sides, make it possible to store all hand luggage, no matter how large, conveniently out of the passenger's way.

Wide panoramic-view windows combine with the easy-chair comfort of the Phoebe Snow's modern coaches to give every traveler a clear view of the magnificent scenic area through which the main line of the Lackawanna runs.

Special attention has been paid to the size and design of both the powder rooms and the men's lounges in these new coaches. Women passengers find a new luxury in the tastefully decorated and conveniently appointed powder rooms, which are finished in soft, quiet, relaxing pastel shades. Comfortable lounge seats, an abundant supply of both facial tissues and crisp towels within easy reach of each individual vanity table, and a separate "make-up" light over the mirror of each table are among the many appreciated features.

The men's lounge is equally well equipped. Next to each wash basin is a handy electric outlet for the passenger's electric shaver, while above it is a man-sized mirror, clearly lighted, to make shaving an easy and pleasant process. Two smartly upholstered lounge seats for those who desire to rest awhile over a cigarette are also part of the equipment.

A wonderfully unobstructed view of the magnificent Lackawanna territory is obtained from any of the deep-cushioned chairs in the Phoebe Snow's handsome, modern observation car. Luxurious appointments, a restful club-type decorative scheme, and a friendly atmosphere make the smooth-riding journey seem even shorter than it really is. Separated from the rest of the observation-lounge car by a high glass partition is a tavern section, with a refreshment bar and several cozily arranged small tables. Here, too, the traveler will find an original portrait of that famous lady, Phoebe Snow.

11

The westbound No. 3 carries a modern, all-private-room sleeping car between New York and Chicago, with connections made at Buffalo. The car has ten single roomettes and six double bedrooms, each a masterpiece of design and equipment, made with only the passenger's convenience and comfort in mind. Each room, whether single or double, has its own individually controlled heating and air-conditioning system, separate lighting controls, extra-length mirrors, spacious wardrobe and shoe lockers, and deep, sleep-inducing foam rubber mattresses.

The double bedrooms have private toilet annexes and are so designed as to make it possible for two of them to be combined into a family-style four-bed suite.

Similar cars are run on some of the Lackawanna's other all-night trains in addition to the Phoebe Snow. They will be found on night trains between New York and the Binghamton-Elmira-Buffalo area and between New York and Cleveland and Chicago.

The delicious homelike meals that have characterized Lackawanna service for so many years are, of course, to be found in the Phoebe Snow's spacious diner. Here too will the passenger find the bright, modern, panorama-type windows that permit him to take full advantage of the wonderful scenic areas lying along the Lackawanna's right of way. Gay draperies, soft lighting, sparkling white napery, and gleaming silverware all add to the luxurious picture of a meal aboard the Phoebe Snow's streamlined dining car.

But the Phoebe Snow, Lackawanna officials do not forget, is a train, not a hotel! Whatever may be added to the comfort and convenience of its passengers through the excellent facilities with which all its cars are equipped, its primary job is to get people where they want to go, quickly, safely, and smoothly. And Lackawanna's well-timed operations result in efficient travel conditions that bring No. 3 to its destination day after day on scheduled time, carrying its load of contented passengers.

Each day, for example, as the westbound Phoebe Snow glides smoothly to a stop at Binghamton, New York, the railroad's eager, well-trained service crews stand by. Their job: to keep the train on time, to hold it at Binghamton no longer than just three minutes while they perform the many tasks assigned to them.

In order that the Phoebe Snow may get under way again on schedule, almost twenty railroad men are kept busy doing their assigned tasks during that important three-minute span. As the train comes to a stop, two coaches that have been part of the train since it left its Hoboken terminus earlier in the day are cut out of No. 3. Traffic west of Binghamton is generally lighter than during the first stage of the run, and there is no need for these two streamlined coaches from this point west.

So a switch engine and its crew, which have been standing by for that purpose, take the last four cars off the train—the two extra coaches, the sleeper, and the observation-lounge car. The coaches are set out on a yard track, the switch engine returns the sleeper and the lounge car to the waiting train, air and steam lines are hooked up—and the switch engine's crew's job is done.

Meanwhile, as the cars are being hauled to the yard and back to the train again, up front the baggage and mail cars are being loaded and unloaded. In anticipation of the Phoebe Snow's arrival, all the mail and baggage and express shipments to be loaded at Binghamton have earlier been put on hand trucks at the station. The loaded trucks, as well as a group of empty ones, are lined up just where the mail and baggage cars will come to their halt. No time is lost in this vital operation of loading and unloading the train's commercial cargo.

While these operations are being carried out at both front and rear, car inspectors are working up both sides of the train, giving the Phoebe Snow's running gear a thorough check. While speed is an important factor in this operation, the Lackawanna will not permit it to take precedence over safety.

Water tanks in the dining car are being refilled while the train takes its three-minute service break, and a new train crew, which will carry No. 3 on to Buffalo, is taking over. The engine crew remains the same; it is the one that took over at Scranton, and it will continue on duty as far as Elmira.

The new conductor delivers the train orders and clearance to

13

the engineer on the powerful diesel, and by the time he has returned to the passenger coaches all the work has been completed —the inspection is over, the diner has been watered, the mail, baggage and express loads have been handled, two cars have been removed from the train, the air lines have been tested, and the passengers have debarked or boarded.

It is only three minutes since the Phoebe Snow came to a halt at Binghamton, and now, thoroughly and completely serviced, the modern streamliner starts to roll slowly out of the station to resume its quick, smooth, comfortable journey toward Buffalo.

On the Lackawanna's famous Phoebe Snow, "streamlining" is not only a design description; it is an operational procedure too.

CHAPTER IV

"THE SOUTHERN SERVES THE SOUTH"

Industrial Growth, Monument to the Road's Progressiveness

Since 1945 the Southern Railway System has invested more than $450,000,000 in a vast job of modernization that has included complete dieselization of the system, larger freight cars, more efficient freight classification yards, and a new signal and communications equipment. This program has proved a vital factor in enabling the railroad to live up to its famous slogan, "The Southern Serves the South," because the rapid industrialization of Dixie has placed added burdens upon the railway system.

Every single day the yards and terminals of the Southern dispatch some 475 freight trains and 118 passenger trains. With the exceptions of Nashville and Montgomery, the Southern Railway System serves every major city in the region; it is the nation's second-largest carrier of l.c.l. freight, while of the railroads that operate east of the Mississippi River it is third in total miles operated, fourth in passenger revenue, and fifth in freight revenue.

It operates more than 8,000 miles of road in thirteen states, in which there are located twelve major classification yards and twenty smaller ones. A modern network of communications keeps the general office at Washington in constant and immediate touch with outlying terminals in New Orleans, Cincinnati, Jacksonville, St. Louis, Memphis, Mobile, Charleston, and Norfolk.

15

The development of the industrial South has meant increased freight volume, of course, for the railroad system that serves the area. Chemical products from the Gulf coast and iron ore from South America represent new types of products that the Southern Railway System did not carry prior to World War II; but by and large, the increased tonnage has not meant any great change in either types of freight traditionally shipped or in its destinations.

The road's busiest lines are those that serve the major gateways to the North and the West—the Potomac yard in Virginia, Cincinnati, Louisville, St. Louis, and Memphis. Much traffic is also moved along those routes that serve the Gulf and Atlantic ports, with New Orleans in particular registering heavy traffic volume. In the area of Asheville-Knoxville-Chattanooga, local mine output is responsible for continuing heavy freight volume.

The Southern's Mobile division, between that city and Birmingham, and its St. Louis–Louisville division, which connects those two communities with the main line of the CNO&TP at Danville, Kentucky, have shown amazing growth patterns in the last few years. Industrial development of inland territory, which has characterized the South since the end of World War II, has been largely responsible for the freight volume growth on these two divisions. The railroad has aided this tendency by developing the St. Louis–Louisville division into a fast freight line in order to attract traffic through the St. Louis gateway to the West.

While freight volume has been increasing, the Southern Railway System has been keeping close watch on the economics of its local passenger operations. Some branches, where passenger traffic has virtually disappeared, have been abandoned, including a fifty-mile stretch between Rome, Georgia, and Gadsen, Alabama, while other marginally operated lines are constantly kept under scrutiny to determine their profitability.

Dieselization has resulted in tremendous operating gains for the railroad. Combined with the new yards and improved roadbed, it has helped to shorten through-train schedules. Time-freight schedules have been reworked to tie in with local and

16

Bangor & Aroostook Extra 501 south with solid train of new BAR reefers of latest design approaching Northern Maine Jct. Southern Div.

Bangor & Aroostook Extra 565 south with solid train of blue, white and red insulated boxcars with novel State of Maine products display.

Bangor & Aroostook #1 running around snowplow train at Presque Isle, Northern Div. in a typical heavy winter snowstorm. The BAR, like other railroads, has to pay its own money for snow fighting and removal.

Southern's fast thru freight #153 at Springfield, Va. on the Washington Div. This train operates between Potomac Yards and Jacksonville, Mobile, New Orleans and Memphis.

Lackawanna #3, the Phoebe Snow, premier day train between New York and Buffalo just after passing the point of the Delaware Water Gap along the Delaware River at m.p. 76 on the Scranton Buffalo Div.

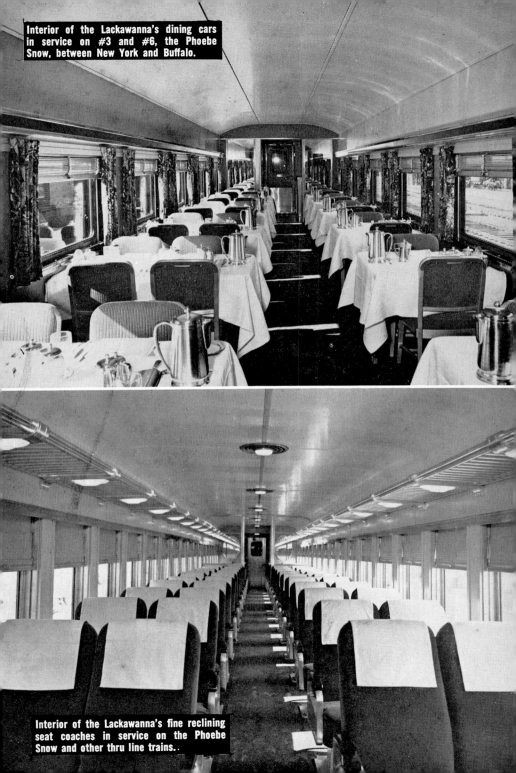

Interior of the Lackawanna's dining cars in service on #3 and #6, the Phoebe Snow, between New York and Buffalo.

Interior of the Lackawanna's fine reclining seat coaches in service on the Phoebe Snow and other thru line trains..

Observation lounge of the Lackawanna's Phoebe Snow looking towards the rear end.

Interior view of the observation lounge car on the Lackawanna's Phoebe Snow looking forward showing the attractive seating arrangements and the enclosed cafe.

Santa Fe #15, the Texas Chief, with diesel 45 nearing Washita Canyon in the Arbuckle Mountains along the Washita River on the 1st District of the Northern Div.

U.P. Extra 1456 east with 4-unit helper on the head-end and 1 GP-9 on rear end climbing Cima Hill on the 2.20 grade at Dawes, Cal. on the First Sub-div. of the California Div. with 105 cars. Photo by R. H. Kindig.

connecting trains, thus bringing improved service to many side-line cities and towns.

But in addition to helping the Southern Railway System move heavier trains at faster operating speeds, dieselization has effected great operating economies. For example, on the 631.3-mile run between the Potomac yard and Atlanta, it used to be necessary to change or service steam locomotives at eight individual points, all of which have now been eliminated.

Dieselization also means smoother train-handling, which in turn brings about less damage to cargo and less wear on rolling stock. It means, too, fewer trains to carry equal volume, resulting in less wear and tear on track and structures and consequently an easier task for the road's maintenance and repair crews.

Greatly improved classification yards have proved as important as dieselization as a factor in the Southern's upgraded postwar operations. All of the road's dozen major yards have been equipped with such modern devices as intercommunication and paging systems, flood-lighting, and elevated yard offices, while many also have power switches that save time for trains entering or leaving the yards. Then, too, air-brake charging equipment, installed at some of Southern's yards, materially reduces the time formerly required to build up brake-line pressure and to get trains under way.

Knoxville, Birmingham, Atlanta and Chattanooga boast ultra-modern "super-yards," with hump-retarder operations that have recorded their effects on the operations of the entire Southern Railway System. These four yards are equipped with the latest in push-button classification devices and are set up to permit the most complete blocking of all trains.

Improved communications and modern electronic office equipment have also added materially to the railway's operational efficiency in recent years. Centralized traffic control is now in effect on three segments of the busy "Queen and Crescent Route" between Cincinnati and New Orleans, while thousands of miles of new telephone and telegraph circuits have stepped up the capacity of the road's communications network.

The important Car Records office in Atlanta now uses IBM

17

equipment for fast, accurate, and complete control of freight cars wherever they may be along the line.

Industrial development of the South has also materially changed the road's passenger operations, with new emphasis now being placed on high-speed, long-distance, heavy-load operations, in place of the short-run local-branch operational activity that marked the road's passenger traffic prior to World War II. The diesel engine has here, too, been the vehicle for providing the road's passengers with improved service, while purchase of many new cars and renovation of old ones has acted to provide the Southern's travelers with better, faster, more reliable service.

Industrial Growth

Whatever benefits the South, whatever helps to develop the industrial growth and development of that area, also helps the Southern Railway System to increase its substantial volume of freight traffic.

Out of this relationship between the region and the carrier serving it has grown an important branch of the Southern's organization, its Industrial and Agricultural Development Department. This small group, composed of experts in the fields of endeavor that have marked the growth of Dixie, has been a tremendously important factor in the establishment of 2,375 new industrial plants and the enlargement of 1,207 others; in the location of 337 distribution warehouses along Southern's right of way; in the investment in one single year of about $1.7 billion in new plants and warehouses and in additions to existing facilities.

With its headquarters at Washington, the Industrial and Agricultural Development Department of the Southern Railway System maintains branch offices at Charlotte, Atlanta, and Birmingham. It consists of three general industrial agents, a general agricultural and livestock agent, and the staffs that assist them. It is their job to make industry and agriculture aware of advantages inherent in locating in the Southland in general, and specifically along the railroad's right of way. Prospects are constantly sought out, new sites are continuously sought—and the two must be brought together.

The experts making up this vital department keep in touch with large industrial organizations that are known to be planning expansion. They maintain constant contact with engineering companies, financial organizations, and other groups that might have advance information on such moves. They approach directly companies that, in their expert opinion, might profit by a move to the South.

To fill their responsibilities properly, the Department's experts must be fully familiar with all the important characteristics of the area served by the railroad. They must understand mineral, water, and agricultural resources; availability of labor; population characteristics, local tax structures; climate; facilities for recreation, culture, and education; proximity of raw materials; freight rates; and many other details. They must also be aware of the particular needs of any industrial group they approach in respect to all these factors.

And they must be tactful. . . . Their studies and their recommendations, while of maximum value to the company they seek to convince, must still not tend to give undue preference to any particular state or community within the vast area served by the Southern.

The business of nailing down a new plant or warehouse is a complex operation, so much so that in most cases, when the project is finally completed, it is almost impossible to assign credit for the job to any one agency. In many instances leads are furnished to the Department by state or local chambers of commerce or realty boards; sometimes information is handed on by some other department of the railroad; there have been cases in which purely personal contact resulted in the initiation of negotiations that have ultimately led to the movement of a major plant or warehouse.

Extensive national advertising on the part of Southern also plays a key part in this operation. It is designed to interest businessmen, in a very general way, in the industrial opportunities that are available in the South, and is therefore not intended to induce specific inquiries or leads. There are many examples on record, however, to indicate that an organization's initial interest in the Southland was aroused directly by such an advertisement of the Southern Railway System.

The Industrial and Agricultural Development Department carries out its tasks in a variety of ways. Sometimes it serves essentially as a liaison group, merely bringing together a prospect and a property owner, functioning only to the point at which the two major parties meet one another and pick up negotiations directly. Sometimes it does all of the important work before the primary parties are brought together, preparing and presenting to each information about the needs of the one—such as labor, utilities, raw materials, etc.—and the advantages offered by the other—local tax requirements, size and location of site, transportation facilities, etc.

The Department also has continuously available the services and aid of other key departments of the Southern Railway System. For example, the Transportation Department may be called upon to supply an automobile for inspection of a projected plant site by a prospect; or Maintenance of Way engineers may be requested to lend their expert advice about track layouts, clearances, and such matters. Emergency communications facilities may be sought from the railroad's specialists, and the Law Department may be called upon to facilitate title clearance and other legal papers.

The railroad has been instrumental in the development of a number of planned industrial districts that have sprung up along its right of way during the postwar years.

Largest of these is the Chamblee-Doraville Industrial District, located about ten miles from Atlanta, where more than $75,-000,000 has been invested in industrial plants, new highways, housing, and public utilities. It was started in 1945, and since that time about twenty-five companies—most of them nationally known—have either built warehouses or distributing facilities here or have acquired sites on which they will shortly undertake such construction. There are a few light manufacturing operations carried on in the development too.

The Southern Railway System has been active in the development of this area, not only through the work of its Industrial and Agricultural Development Department but also through the necessary construction of new and additional trackage and equipment that serve the area.

Usually the railroad avoids actually acquiring the land for such developments in its own name and contents itself with aiding others who act as the principals. However, there are some industrial development sites in the Southland that are built upon land owned outright by the railroad, although in most such cases the property had been acquired by Southern many years ago for some other purpose.

Among these are the 100-acre Peachtree-Piedmont Industrial District, also located near Atlanta; the 125-acre area at Paris, five miles north of Greenville, South Carolina, and one near Columbia, South Carolina. Also there are the Kinsler Development Area of 500 acres and the Fairground Development Area of 1,000 acres, both of which are also near Columbia; the Camp Croft Area, 1,100 acres in size, near Spartanburg, South Carolina; two smaller tracts near Greensboro, North Carolina; and a 58-acre tract not far from Louisville and near Cincinnati, the Kenton Lands Industrial District, Erlanger, Kentucky and extensive holdings at Huntsville, Ala., and near Citico Yard at Chattanooga.

The area served by the Southern Railway System still contains vast acreage that can be developed into similiar industrial districts as future needs dictate.

Industrial developments of major size—those requiring capital investment in excess of $500,000—compose only 16 per cent of the new industries that have located along Southern's right of way since the end of World War II. Yet some extremely large operations have been brought into Dixie as a result of the work of the railroad and its Industrial and Agricultural Development Department.

Among the larger ones are a $225,000,000 General Electric

21

appliance factory near Louisville; a $150,000,000 Kaiser Aluminum & Chemical Company aluminum plant at Chalmette, Louisiana, near New Orleans; a $50,000,000 Celanese Corporation plant at Rock Hill, South Carolina; and a $50,000,000 newsprint mill constructed at Calhoun, Tennessee, by Bowater Southern Paper Corporation.

The existence of plants like these and the development of industrial districts have proved important factors in the Southern's record of achievement. The road's freight tonnage has more than doubled since 1939. While much of this great increase results from the growth of the area the railroad serves, it must not be forgotten that the aggressive and forward-looking activities of the Southern Railway System itself have been a tremendous factor in the growth of Dixie as an important industrial area of the nation.

CHAPTER V

THE SANTA FE

The New Line to Dallas and the Modern Texas Chief

The famous rivalry between the neighboring Texas cities of Fort Worth and Dallas has been given a brand-new twist.

For many years—ever since 1887, in fact—Fort Worth had been able to boast that it lay along the main line of the Santa Fe railroad while its rival community did not. Passengers to Dallas from Chicago, for example, riding the road's Texas Chief, were required to get off at Fort Worth and take a bus the remaining thirty-five miles to their destination.

Freight in and out of Dallas also had to travel a roundabout route. A branch line of the Santa Fe ran from Dallas southwest to Cleburne, where cars were then switched onto main-line freight trains running north through Fort Worth.

But all that is changed now. Since December of 1955 the Santa Fe has had direct connections with Dallas via fifty miles of brand-new trackage that the line constructed and opened within a period of about two and one-half years. Now the southbound Texas Chief, en route to Dallas from Chicago, branches off to the southeast at Dalton Junction, proceeds through the towns of Denton, Lewisville, and Richardson, and joins the old Cleburne-Dallas-Paris branch line at Zacha Junction to run directly into the Santa Fe's Dallas yards.

It was an undertaking that cost the railroad $7,000,000. But then President Fred G. Gurley of the Santa Fe has estimated that during its first five years of operation the new trackage will move some 55,000 freight cars in and out of Dallas, bringing in total revenue of about $20,000,000. Passenger operations, too,

23

will benefit; during the same five-year period, the road's passenger traffic manager foresees a total of close to 350,000 passengers, who will purchase tickets worth a total of more than the $7,000,000 spent on the new line's construction.

The size of this great project—it represents the longest section of track laid down anywhere in the United States during the past twenty-five years—can be judged by picturing a freight train more than six hundred miles long filled with the dirt and rock that had to be moved during construction. More than 3,500,000 cubic yards of earth were removed to provide for such factors as twenty-two major grade separations and waterway structure approaches. A steel and concrete bridge had to be built to span the Dallas Expressway and the Southern Pacific's right of way. The largest of three such spans along the route, it is 590 feet in length.

There are 179,000 ties along the new line, which alone, at three dollars per tie, represent an outlay of more than half a million dollars. Rail is 110- and 112-pound, 15,000 lengths of it in the 48.6 miles of new trackage. Even the 716,000 spikes that firmly hold the rails to the ties cost more than $57,000. The road consumed about 2,600 cubic yards of ballast per mile, for a total of 143,000 cubic yards. Cement, too, proved to be a big item, for it took 18,000 cubic yards of concrete to build the culverts, grade separations, and boxes needed. About 1,800 tons of structural steel went into bridge beams and girders, and an additional 1,201,745 pounds of reinforcing steel was also used.

Although no new engineering problems were encountered in building the line into Dallas, several unique factors had to be considered. For one thing, in building grade separations over highways, allowances had to be made for future widening of those roads for the heavier motor traffic expected in future years.

The project has been called a miracle of modern engineering and construction. The new technique involved the construction of bridges even in advance of road grading, so that the entire fifty-mile run was defined by a series of concrete bridge piers and abutments of various sorts that jutted out above the Texas terrain even before grading was started.

Steel structures of bridges were completed in off-the-job locations, trucked to their proper sites, and erected with cranes operating from the ground. As a result of this unusual approach to the job, there was never a time when a track-laying crew had to suspend operations to wait for a bridge to be finished. The bridges were all in place waiting for the trackage to be laid.

Actual construction of the line was completed in about thirteen months, with the balance of the two-and-one-half-year period being devoted to ICC hearings, legal manipulations, and acquisition of property for the right of way. Nearly eighty pieces of heavy grading and earth-moving equipment were employed in the construction of the line. To push it through on time, in accordance with the schedule set by the ICC, Santa Fe officials resorted to much night work, during which powerful floodlights, mounted on portable towers that could be moved along from night to night with the progress of construction, were used to illuminate the construction area.

General direction of the construction project was in the capable and experienced hands of T. A. Blair, chief engineer for the entire Santa Fe system, and W. T. Donoaho, chief engineer of the Gulf, Colorado & Santa Fe railroad.

From the very inception of the plan for the new line, a soil-testing headquarters in the Denton office of the GC&SF proved an important factor. Much of the material for embankments was either accepted or rejected on the basis of constant tests conducted here, some 350 samples of various kinds of earth having been analyzed during the construction period.

Soil tests were made at least every thousand feet along the entire right of way; core tests were made to a depth of ten to fifteen feet along most of the line's route, and deeper samples were drawn and analyzed wherever bridges were to be constructed.

Principal objective of all this testing was to determine what engineers call curves of wet and dry destiny. By plotting curves based on information learned through testing soil samples, it is possible to calculate just how much water in gallons per cubic yard the contractor must add in order to compact the material up to specifications.

One step in this complex testing procedure was conducted by dropping a hammer twenty-five times from a height of one foot to determine compaction qualities. Another specified the soil's moisture content through baking in an oven.

Through these tests it was possible to tell the contractor that, moving southward along the new line, blow sand could be used from Dalton Junction to Denton Creek for bank stabilization, sandy gravel from there to Lewisville for topping material, and easily crushed native limestone from that point on to Zacha Junction.

It was the changing pattern of business conditions in Texas that led the Santa Fe road, on July 9, 1953, to file a petition with the ICC requesting permission to build new trackage that would open a front door to Dallas. When the line originally hooked up the GC&SF with the old AT&SF back in 1887, cattle was king in Texas and Fort Worth was its center. But within the past fifteen years or so Dallas began to outstrip its neighbor in population, industrial activity, employment, and total business revenue. As a result, the city itself began raising a demand for better, more direct railroad service for both passengers and freight shipments.

Originally it was proposed that thirty-eight miles of new trackage be constructed from Santa Fe's main north-south line near Sanger to Addison, where arrangements were to have been made to obtain trackage rights along the Cotton Belt right of way from Addison into Dallas.

However, the community of Denton, which for nearly seventy years had been attempting to influence Santa Fe officials to construct a direct line to Dallas—which would serve their town as well—immediately began efforts to change the course of the newly proposed trackage. The nearby town of Lewisville also joined the campaign, and the chambers of commerce of both communities, plus local newspapers, began all-out efforts to accomplish their objective.

After several meetings, Santa Fe officials agreed to conduct a survey of the route proposed by Denton and Lewisville officials, and at about the same time various civic bodies entered petitions

26

with the ICC, calling for a change of the Santa Fe's originally announced plans.

Finally, following a series of hearings in Dallas and Washington, the Commission issued a ruling authorizing the railroad to build its new line via Denton, pointing out that "the record shows that Denton is part of an expanding industrial area moving northward from Dallas and Fort Worth in a triangular area toward Denton."

This authorization was issued on August 6, 1954. The ICC certificate directed that the new line be begun on or before November 1 of that year, and completed no later than December 31, 1955.

Here was a tremendous task for the Santa Fe to accomplish in just a little more than one year. Despite difficulties of acquiring right of way and in the face of unusual weather conditions, the first Texas Chief out of Dallas directly to Chicago over the new trackage left the Dallas Union Terminal at 1:15 P.M. on December 5, 1955.

Full-scale construction, of course, was not possible until complete right of possession to all land upon which to build the railway had been obtained. This was not finally accomplished until April 15, less than eight months before the first train was to run over the new trackage! But the energetic operations of J. P. Cowley, then vice-president and general manager of the Santa Fe's Gulf Lines, under whose direction this important work was undertaken, solved the myriad problems that were encountered.

While this work was going on, preliminary construction was accomplished, mainly along the north end of the new line. Then abnormally heavy rains interfered with the scheduled progress. By the first of June, 1955, however, grading was 25 per cent completed, more than 500,000 cubic yards of earth had been removed, more than two miles of track had been laid, and concrete substructures on four important bridges were an average of about 60 per cent complete.

But the line was pushed through according to plan, and Dallas business and civic leaders hailed the Santa Fe and its new Texas Chief at December 5 ceremonies.

The railroad returned the Texans' salute by providing a streamliner that is "typically Texas" in its interior design.

After a thorough study, W. J. Rodgers, passenger traffic manager of Santa Fe's Gulf Lines, told the delighted Texans that it had been decided to use materials "in a modern fashion representing the present-day thinking of the people in the Dallas-Denton area, as illustrated by the modern buildings that are being constructed there."

A hand-made copper frieze extending the full length of both wall surfaces is an outstanding feature of the new Chief's dining car. The design illustrates, in modern fashion, foliage and animals of the Lone Star State, the bluebonnet, which is the Texas state flower, and the Lone Star itself.

Burnt orange, tan, and copper are the predominating colors in this unusually handsome diner, with frosted walnut being used on table tops, window capping, and buffet.

Matching the color scheme of the diner is that of the lounge car. The curved bar front consists of a hand-hammered copper plaque, illustrating modern buildings, a cowboy, oil wells, foliage, and the famous Santa Fe diesel, appearing as it rounds a corner of the car representing the Santa Fe's progress into Texas. In back of the bar there is a hand-made leather plaque depicting the Lone Star surrounded by cattle brands of the most outstanding ranches in the state.

Directly across from this, the bulkhead is decorated with a free-flowing frosted walnut design on which is mounted a hand-hammered copper plate illustrating cowboys gathered around a campfire.

In both the diner and the lounge car, the carpeting features a prickly-pear design.

The interest of Denton's civic and business leaders in urging the Santa Fe to construct its new line through their community is easily understandable, for the history of the Southwest demonstrates that wherever the Santa Fe touches a city or town, business expansion and success have followed. The area was only sparsely settled when the railroad first began to lay its lines through that territory in the era following the Civil War.

As time went on, the Santa Fe, aided by its own industrial and agricultural experts, helped farmers and communities develop the tremendous potential. Today it continues this type of development activity, but with a new emphasis that reflects mid-twentieth-century America.

The railroad, during the period 1946 to 1952, located more than 3,000 permanent industries along its right of way, representing an investment of billions of dollars and totaling gross revenue of about $150,000,000. In that same seven-year stretch about 1,050 industries that already existed along the line expanded their operations, increasing the value of rail traffic by some $40,000,000 each year. Thus the advent of a new line means increased revenue for the railroad and tremendous industrial expansion for the communities that lie along its trackage.

The Santa Fe itself has already established two industrial development tracts in Dallas—a 320-acre tract in the southwestern part of the city along the old Cleburne branch line, and now a 211-acre section in Dallas' northeast section where the new line enters the city.

Denton, therefore, clearly visualizes itself as the apex of the new industrial triangle, of which the other two points are Fort Worth and Dallas. It foresees that the railroad's new facilities and time-saving service to and from Chicago will encourage new industries to locate in and around the Denton area. "The Santa Fe," says the Denton *Record-Chronicle*, "is due to make Denton great."

A new passenger station and a new freight station have already been built there by the Santa Fe. And in Dallas a new suburban passenger station has been constructed where the line comes into the northeast side of the city.

The new line, coming directly in from the north and avoiding the long trek through Fort Worth, down to Cleburne, and up northeast again, will save shippers up to seventy-two hours in some cases. Santa Fe officials believe that this fact alone will serve to open up thousands of acres of industrial areas north of Dallas toward Richardson, Lewisville, and Denton.

In 1950 the population of Dallas County was estimated at

614,799; by 1954 it had grown to 725,000; and forecasts of 1,250,000 people resident there by 1980 are freely heard.

So the handsome new daily Texas Chief, hauled by its triple-unit diesel, will combine with new freight runs and suburban trains to add to the glory and industrial development of the Dallas–Fort Worth–Denton triangle, as a fifty-mile length of new track opens new opportunities for the Santa Fe, the area's businessmen, and its suburban residents alike.

CHAPTER VI

UNION SWITCH & SIGNAL

CTC and New Cab Signals

Centralized traffic control systems have become an accepted part of the American railroad scene. So far, however, their use has been limited to areas of relatively heavy traffic.

But with the recent development of a new signal system by Union Switch & Signal, it is now expected that the use of CTC will be greatly expanded, since the arrangement makes it possible to install CTC profitably along lines where lighter traffic is the rule.

CTC, of course, permits handling large sections of a railroad, or perhaps even an entire railroad, from one central point. Here a dispatcher, using a miniature model of the tracks under his control and a series of lights, can watch over the movement of all trains in the area assigned to him.

Until now, however, marginal operations—that is, those where fixed costs tend to offset small profits resulting from light traffic —have not been able to afford the capital outlay needed to install new CTC equipment. The new Union development, it is anticipated, will now permit improved operations on light-traffic lines. This will mean an increase in track capacity, a reduction of operating expenditures, and a speeding up of the movement of freight all along the line from shipper to consignee.

The new system fully complies with the standards of Interstate Commerce Commission regulations as well as with the Association of American Railroads code, and it is said to be comparable in operational costs with the traditional timetable-and-train-order method of controlling traffic through block systems.

Here are the basic features of the new CTC system for light-traffic lines:

1. Each controlled siding has a power switch and the normal complement of three signals at one end only. Where meets and passes are scheduled, trains will generally enter the siding from that end.

2. A spring switch, coupled with a dwarf signal, is set up at the other end, which is intended to be used only for leave-siding moves.

3. There are approach signals established in advance of the two main-line controlled signals; these are located at the power-switch end of the siding, at no less than normal braking distance from the controlled signals.

4. The block thus established extends from one power switch location to the next power switch location.

5. No following moves are entailed, since these signals can be displayed to authorize entry of only one train at a time into the block.

6. However, the railroad's own traffic conditions can be taken into account when the system is set up, so that power switches may be established at alternate ends of adjacent sidings if the traffic pattern demands it.

Among the many advantages provided by this new light-traffic CTC system can be counted the fact that it provides complete track circuit protection for all main-line moves, that sidings are not track-circuited, that all main-line moves continue to be made under signal direction and protection, and that electric switch-locks may be installed as required.

In addition, it is always possible to expand the system, whenever the railroad's executives think it advisable or necessary, to include a "take siding" aspect at that signal which is located in advance of the spring switch. At any time, too, the system can be expanded to become a full-scale CTC installation by setting up power switches at both ends of sidings and adding automatic signals to permit following moves.

Another recent Union Switch & Signal development that is

helping to service freight traffic more safely and faster despite poor visibility weather in classification yards is the new CY inductive cab signal system.

Essentially, this is a setup that makes it possible for a yardmaster to control as many as four switch engines in his yard simultaneously, simply by operating toggle switches. A four-unit light post and a bell in the cab of each locomotive serve to keep the yardmaster's instructions in front of the engineer. The system puts the signal in the cab, where it can always be visible to the engineer despite rain, snow, fog, curved track, or any other adverse conditions.

The four lights on the compact unit within the cab are used to direct the engineer to carry out any one of that number of directions: approach hump, hump, back up, stop.

A change in signals to the cab, called to the engineer's attention by an automatic single stroke on a special bell to which the system is hooked, are carried from wayside to locomotives by inductive coupling between a modulated carrier current and a weather-proof receiving coil mounted on the locomotive. A pole line running parallel to the tracks supports an elevated wire that conducts the modulated carrier for operation of the signals.

In the yardmaster's office, equipment consists of a power supply unit, an audio oscillator unit, and a carrier modulator unit, all mounted on a standard communications rack. Interference is virtually eliminated through the use of a coupling unit that serves to block other frequencies.

No motor-generator set is required, since power for the equipment is supplied directly from the sixty-four-volt locomotive battery. By merely moving a channel-selection switch in the cab to the "off" position, the entire locomotive equipment may be de-energized when not in use.

Employing the same basic principles of induction that make possible the operation of the CY cab signal system, Union Switch & Signal has brought forward Identra—an important step in railroad automation.

Developed primarily for use where trains operate on close

33

headway, this new Indentra system enables trains to register their identity at the same time as they notify a control operator of their location. Together with other available equipment, the new device can be used to provide such services as automatic route line-up and automatic announcing systems.

With the Identra system, a block is no longer merely occupied —it is, in effect, occupied by a specific train, whose identity can be made known to a control operator or flashed automatically on an illuminated sign.

One feature of the new system is that no source of energy or electrical equipment is required on the train itself. Only an inert tuned coil is carried on the train, and it is mounted in such a manner, either on the locomotive or on any car, that it inductively couples with a wayside coil when passing a given location where the coil is stationed. It is also easily possible to change identity of the tuned coil when desired.

At the wayside point, the stationary coil is also mounted so as to couple inductively with the coil on the passing train. Electronic equipment is housed in an instrument case at the wayside point, and the fixed-position coil is connected to it by means of a short cable. Consisting of a power-supply unit, an amplifier unit, and a frequency-selector network unit for each identification frequency, this equipment serves to energize a relay as the train passes; a signal is consequently sent forward to the control tower, automatic sign, or switch point, where routing can be automatically set.

The electronic equipment, heart of the system, is mounted at the wayside point in a shockproof rack and amply protected, so that the Identra system can operate at all train speeds in any kind of weather.

Another device developed by Union Switch & Signal to make it possible for the railroads to enjoy the benefits of modern electronic progress is the type EL cab signal equipment.

Designed to retain all the features of the company's earlier and heavier type E equipment, this new unit is 47 per cent lighter, 53 per cent smaller, and about 30 per cent lower in initial cost. The company maintains that despite the savings in weight, size, and cost, the new equipment does not sacrifice any of the larger unit's reliability, safety, or ease of maintenance.

Embodying latest design principles, the type EL is able to achieve these advantages, in part, by using junction-type silicon transistors instead of the more traditional vacuum tubes in its amplifying unit. It is believed that this marks the first use of the transistors of the silicon type in cab signaling equipment.

Grain-oriented silicon steel strip—noted for its features of high permeability and low loss—has been used for the cores of all transformers and reactors in the unit. Modern-design capacitors, approximately one-third smaller than the type previously used, are employed for tuning decoding circuits.

Vibration and shock to the unit have been reduced to a minimum through mounting it on an L-shaped resiliently supported shelf. An adjustable guide bar at the top of this shelf engages two vertical pins, an arrangement that both prevents tilting and facilitates removal of the shelf for maintenance and inspection purposes.

Thus, through the extension of basic automation and electronic principles, embodying the usage of the latest scientific improvements, equipment is constantly being developed to make it possible for all railroads—not merely the largest—to use devices that make for speed, safety, and economy. All this not only is in the interest of the railroads themselves, but helps to bring improved service to the shippers and travelers of America, constantly making available to them faster, safer, and more economical transportation of people and of goods.

CHAPTER VII

UNION PACIFIC

More Than a Railroad—Vacation Resorts, Ore Move, Farm Scholarships, Trailer-on-Flat-car Freight

The varied and ramified operations of a modern American railroad are nowhere more clearly exemplified than in the widespread operations of the Union Pacific. Its right of way running through areas marked by some of the country's most breathtaking scenery, the UP maintains a subsidiary company, the Utah Parks Company, which operates a year-round cafeteria camp center in Zion National Park; it transports thousands of carloads annually of the West's important iron ore; it awards agricultural scholarships to deserving students in the eleven states through which the railroad runs; it operates and continues to expand an important piggyback freight service for its shippers.

These manifold activities—recreational, educational, and commercial—are an outgrowth of UP's historic role as a vital factor in the opening of the great West and in the building of America.

Each summer the Union Pacific sponsors low-cost all-expense tours from Chicago to the Utah national parks, Zion and Bryce Canyon. One of the UP's finest streamliners carries its passengers to Cedar City, from which point the railroad's sightseeing bus fleet takes the visitors to Cedar Breaks National Monument, to Kaibab National Forest, and to sections of the two great parks most sought out by sightseers.

Perhaps nowhere else in the entire world has nature created such colorful, rugged, weird beauty with such great strokes of her ever amazing brush. At Zion National Park, for example, the

36

Virgin River's swirling waters have over millions of years carved the startlingly colored Zion Canyon out of the towering beds of Navajo sandstone. Unbelievable sculpture in vivid vermilions, yellows, and blues is the result that the visitor has unfolded before his awe-struck vision. Far back in the canyon, where the walls taper off to form narrows, one finds the well-named Mystic Temple of Sinawava, enclosed by a natural amphitheater of trees and sheer rock walls. A profusion of highly colorful flowers, ferns, and trees offers a glorious color contrast to the brooding dark red hues of the temple itself.

Through Zion National Park there are twenty miles of improved roads affording visitors a succession of magnificent scenic views. In addition there are some twenty-six miles of trails available solely to hikers and horseback riders, where guides may be hired and horses rented. The Zion–Mount Carmel highway, world-renowned as an outstanding feat of engineering, is constructed inside a solid cliff for a full mile, and from six different galleries broken out through the face of the cliff the visitor views a succession of magnificent breath-taking scenes.

Even the names that have been given to the scenic wonders of Zion National Park are themselves exotic and exciting: the East and West Temples, the Altar of Sacrifice, Angel's Landing, the Three Patriarchs, and the Great White Throne, which rears its magnificent head some 2,500 feet above the valley floor. The Virgin River falls from fifty to ninety feet each mile of its course and erodes about three million tons of rock each year; in railroad terms, this is equivalent to an average of 180 carloads each day!

Zion National Park embraces about 135 square miles, and was so named by its pious Mormon discoverers and explorers whose deeply religious nature made them reverently aware of its heavenly tranquility. The Altar of Sacrifice, named by the same Mormon pioneers, derives its title from the blood-red quality of the rock that stains the pure white mass of the two-thousand-foot sides of sheer stone. The Great White Throne, perhaps the most famous of all the natural wonders within the borders of Zion National Park, is a miracle of color combinations. Set on a carpet of rich green, crowned by the unique deep, vivid blue that characterizes the Utah sky, the rocks ascend from a base of warm-hued mahogany through a series of delicately tinted pinks into pinnacles of pristine white capped with green pines.

Bryce National Park, also served by the Union Pacific, is a tremendous bowl of horseshoe shape that has been cut by erosion from the pink cliff formations that surround it. It is about two miles wide and three miles long, and its majestic rim is eight thousand feet high. It strikes visitors as a veritable fairyland with its brilliant and bewildering variety of sculptured sand shapes alive in rich, glowing colors. Throughout there are statues of famous people, spires, minarets, cathedrals, castles, bridges, and a host of naturally formed shapes that defy human description.

What is no doubt the understatement of all time has been attributed to Ebenezer Bryce, the Mormon pioneer who discovered the amazing area and who was the first man to settle there. He is the only man for whom any of our great national parks has been named, and in 1928, when the park was officially established and named for him, the old man said, in response to a request for a statement from him, "I remember it was a bad place to lose a cow."

Visitors have been advised to view the canyon from the west rim in the morning and from the east rim in the afternoon, since the most rewarding views can be obtained by placing the weird formations between the sightseer and the sun. There are horseback and foot trails running along the rim of the canyon in both directions from Bryce Lodge, a modern inn of rustic design surrounded by cabins nestled among the area's pine trees.

An additional feature of the Union Pacific's tour of the scenic wonderlands of Utah is found at Cedar Breaks National Monument, a series of vast chasms eroded to a depth of some two thousand feet and encompassing a total area of about sixty square miles. Thousands of unusual natural forms, reflecting every color imaginable, are found within its boundaries. Nearby, UP maintains a handsome, comfortable, forest-set inn, Cedar Breaks Lodge.

Then of course there is still Sun Valley, Idaho—tops in winter sports, unsurpassed for spring, summer, and fall vacations.

But the service the Union Pacific offers to America's vacationers each year in transporting them to the scenic wonderlands of the West is only one facet of the railroad's vast operation. In Utah there are found not only breath-taking vistas but commercially important iron ore as well, and it is the UP that is called upon to move this vital product from its source to areas where it can be fabricated into products needed and wanted by modern man.

In the state's Iron Mountain district the railroad loads ore at Iron Mountain and at Desert Mound for the Columbia Iron Mining Company, at Iron Mountain and at Comstock for the Utah Construction Company, and at Iron Springs for H. L. Beatty. In 1957 the UP moved a total of 72,802 carloads of iron ore, ore fines, and sinter to various points. Included in this total were 51,076 carloads of ore to Geneva and Ironton, 16,569 carloads to Minnequa, 2,601 to Fontana, 110 to the Missouri River and east, 2,119 to Long Beach, California, for export purposes, and 59 carloads of ore fines and sinter to Geneva and Ironton.

Ore fines are screenings that are obtained from the ore that comes from the Iron Mountain district, while sinter is described as the lumps that are in turn made from the fines.

In 1921, when the late Carl Gray had but recently become president of the Union Pacific Railroad, he began to investigate the educational opportunities that existed for farm youth in the area served by the road. Through his efforts, UP then developed a scholarship plan that today serves to encourage young people to further their education in agriculture. This is a public service that has contributed much to the renown of the railroad throughout the eleven states in which its trains serve passengers and shippers alike.

The original scholarship plan, undertaken on an experimental basis, offered a $100 award in each county in Nebraska served by the UP on the basis of work done by farm boys and girls in 4-H

Clubs. Within a year the plan had proved so successful and was so well received that Mr. Gray made arrangements to extend it to Kansas, Colorado, Wyoming, Nevada, Utah, Idaho, Oregon, Washington, Montana and California.

By 1926 these scholarships were firmly established and were then made available to high school vocational agricultural students in all those states. Originally known as the Union Pacific scholarships, the awards were renamed in 1939 in honor of Mr. Gray and are today called the Carl Raymond Gray scholarships.

Under the rules set for judging to whom the awards will be granted each year, high schools to which the plan applies must be located in counties served by the Union Pacific Railroad and must have an established vocational agriculture department in existence for at least two complete years. The award must be used within the same state in which it is granted, at a state college or school of agriculture, or for agricultural engineering, agricultural education, forestry, or veterinary medicine when such courses are given in a school that is part of the state agricultural college.

The railroad itself does not take any active part in the judging; in each county a committee of three is set up, consisting of two members named by the state supervisor of vocational agriculture and a third named by those two persons. The committee, subject to the review and approval of the state supervisor, makes its choice from among the county's high school students based on the supervised farming program engaged in by the applicant, his scholastic standing, and such qualifications as character, interest, leadership qualities, and community and extracurricular activities. When qualifications of several applicants are so high as to make the choice a difficult one, the UP authorizes the state supervisor to make his selection from among the members of the senior class or from among those applicants who have been out of high school for not more than one year.

With only very special exceptions permitted, the winner must be chosen from among the top one-third of his class insofar as his grades are concerned.

Each applicant must submit to the county committee a standard application form containing a summary of his personal history, his supervised farm work, his community and extracurricular interests, awards he may have received previously, and a listing of any publicity received as a result of his work. He must also send the committee a picture of himself and of the project he has engaged in, as well as a transcript of his school grades, signed by his principal or superintendent, a story of at least five hundred words describing his project, and letters of recommendation from educational, civic, and religious leaders.

After review by UP, the winners and alternates are officially announced by the state supervisor of vocational agriculture. In addition to providing the $100 scholarship to each winner, the Union Pacific transports each successful applicant on one round trip between his home and the college he has chosen to attend, provided that travel is made by UP facilities and that it is limited to points within the borders of a single state.

The railroad makes no payment directly to the students who are selected, but instead pays the college the amount of the scholarship award upon receipt of a certification of enrollment sent to UP by the college authorities.

Progressive in its operating policies as well as in its community relations program, the Union Pacific is one of the increasing number of railroads that are offering shippers the advantages of trailer-freight, or piggyback, service.

In 1953 UP began an experimental TOFC operation between Los Angeles and Las Vegas, which proved so successful that within four months it had been extended to the Salt Lake City area. During the first month of original service, only nine trailer loads were carried; today UP runs 145 specially equipped flatcars and a total of 216 trailers, some of which are fully insulated vans.

The insulated vans furnish important protection to their contents during extremely hot or cold weather; studies are still in progress to determine the best methods for refrigerating perishables, with both dry ice and mechanical refrigeration being tried out under day-to-day operating conditions.

UP TOFC operations now cover some 2,500 miles of rail line. In addition to the original run, trailer-freight service is now available to shippers to major communities in Utah, Idaho, Nevada, Oregon, Washington, Wyoming, and points on the Southern Pacific Railroad through interchange at Wells, Nevada, Ogden, Utah, and Portland. In its eastern district UP participates in through TOFC service between Chicago-St. Louis and Denver, by means of interchange with the Milwaukee Railroad at Council Bluffs, Iowa, and with the Wabash line at Kansas City. Between Omaha and Kearney, Nebraska, the line handles trailers owned outright by its shippers, but elsewhere the traffic is restricted to UP-owned vehicles.

Some of the railroad's flatcars have been specially equipped with stakes and sideboards; handling steel from Geneva to the West Coast, these flats are then used to transport roofing materials, machinery, lumber, and pipe on the return journey. Other eastbound products consist of a great variety of items, including canned goods, paper products, crude rubber, floor tile, and appliances. On the westbound run trailers may be loaded with powdered milk, butter, cheese, various chemicals, and several different kinds of steel products.

The service has been responsible for a full one-day improvement over previous freight schedules between southern California and the Nevada-Utah-Idaho area, and records show that the time advantage increases with the distance the merchandise is shipped. From the West Coast, schedules provide for first-morning delivery at Las Vegas, second-morning arrival at various points in Utah, and either second-morning or later in the second day delivery at several Idaho yards. Out of Portland, first-day delivery is effected to the Boise-Nampa area, with delivery the next day in Twin Falls, Pocatello, Idaho Falls, and Salt Lake City.

Each day an average of about a dozen trailers leaves Los Angeles and about eighteen are driven off incoming flatcars at this same southern California terminal. The railroad has adapted both 42-feet and 52-feet flatcars for its expanding trailer-freight service.

This, then, is the picture of a modern American railroad, active on a host of fronts simultaneously. Providing pleasant, unique vacation atmosphere for its passengers as well as sturdy, reliable, fast-moving equipment for the transportation of the nation's goods, and educational opportunities for the younger generation living in its service territory, the Union Pacific Railroad is growing and moving ahead with America.

CHAPTER VIII

CHICAGO GREAT WESTERN

A New Look and Fine New Railroad, Probably This Country's Outstanding Rehabilitation Job

The Chicago Great Western Railway operates in the states of Illinois, Iowa, Minnesota, and Missouri, with short segments in Nebraska and Kansas, all of its 1,470 miles of road being in a highly developed agricultural country. The total mileage of all main, auxiliary, and yard tracks is 2,116 miles.

The distances over the principal lines are as follows:

	Miles
Council Bluffs–Chicago	504
Council Bluffs–Minnesota Transfer	348
Minnesota Transfer–Chicago	431
Kansas City–Chicago	595
Kansas City–Minnesota Transfer	535

To gain entrance to its four major termini, the Chicago Great Western uses the rails of:

The Union Pacific	Council Bluffs to Omaha and South Omaha
The Great Northern	Saint Paul to Minnesota Transfer and Minneapolis
The Missouri Pacific	Leavenworth to Kansas City
The B.&O.C.T.	Forest Park to Chicago

Oelwein, Iowa, is the hub of the railroad, with main lines radiating in four directions; east to Chicago, north to the Twin Cities, south to Kansas City, and west to Council Bluffs and Omaha. It is also general office headquarters for the Operating,

44

Mechanical, Engineering, Accounting, and Purchasing Departments.

On the Chicago Great Western Railway there are eight terminal yards and nine intermediate yards.

The new train yard at Oelwein consists of eight receiving tracks and twenty-two classification tracks with a capacity of 2,586 cars; including the rip, shop, team, and other auxiliary tracks, it has a total capacity of 3,350 cars.

Radio is used extensively throughout Chicago Great Western territory to provide a modern and efficient transportation machine. Eighty-seven Diesel units, forty-five cabooses, thirty-three land stations, and thirty-six autos and trucks for official and service use have been equipped with two-way radio. Radio enables crews of moving trains to contact other trains and wayside stations, increasing safety and reducing delays.

A teletype system connecting all major terminals with the Central Service Bureau at Oelwein enables them to have complete consists of trains in advance of their arrival at terminals, so that switching of trains can be programed immediately upon their arrival.

The Service Bureau also makes out daily passing reports which are sent to all traffic offices, both on and off line, for use in tracing car movements and for general information to patrons concerning traffic in which they may be interested.

Since 1954, all accounting, including car records and payrolls, has been handled by IBM machines.

The Chicago Great Western Railway became fully dieselized in September, 1949, and was the first railroad in its territory to achieve that status.

Among the important improvements that have been made since 1947 are:

The completion in September, 1949, of the conversion from steam to diesel locomotives.

The construction of longer passing tracks capable of handling the longer trains made possible by diesel power.

The rehabilitation of the terminal facilities at Oelwein, including the rebuilding and enlargement of the train yard, storage, and repair tracks, and construction of new Diesel shop, freight house, passenger station, office buildings, ice plant, car shop, yardmaster's tower, radio control station, and intercommunication system.

The erection of seventeen new depots.

The completion of new freight and passenger buildings at Des Moines, Saint Joseph, Kansas City, Fort Dodge, Council Bluffs, Roseport, and Marshalltown, and of new freight-house facilities in the East Minneapolis yard and at Austin, Minnesota.

The rehabilitation and enlargement of the yards at East Minneapolis, South Saint Paul, and South Des Moines.

The installation at Oelwein of fuel-oil storage tanks of 3,000,000 gallons capacity, providing approximately ninety days supply of diesel fuel.

Also at Oelwein, the completion of an ice-manufacturing plant of 62.5 tons per day capacity, with a mechanical car-icing machine.

Expansion and rehabilitation of the terminal yards at Kansas City, Missouri, Council Bluffs, Iowa, and Austin, Minnesota.

They have three Cline truck cranes stationed at Oelwein, Saint Paul, and Council Bluffs for emergency service in yard and on line. These trucks have an over-all length of 28 feet 1¾ inches and wheel base of 20 feet 7 inches, and are equipped with dual wheels front and rear, two-way radio, an air compressor, a twenty-five-ton crane with a twenty-five-foot collapsible boom, power steering, and air brakes. They are also equipped with two one-hundred-ton air jacks in addition to necessary cables, blocking, and acetylene outfit, as well as other items for quick repairs; and they can carry a complete freight-car truck for replacing one that has broken down.

46

NEW FREIGHT EQUIPMENT PURCHASED

Year	No. Units			Cost
1947	500	Box—40'6" x 10'	100 M capacity	$ 2,006,959
	25	Covered hoppers	140 M capacity	120,431
1950	600	Box—40'6" x 10'	100 M capacity	3,204,072
1951	300	Gons—50'	140 M capacity	1,725,348
	150	Flats—53'6"	100 M capacity	851,055
1955	10	Covered hoppers (roller bearing)	180 M capacity	92,545
	17	Tanks—19,000 gal. capacity (roller bearing)		203,738
	15	"C" compartment box converted—40'	100 M capacity	29,600
	10	"DF" box converted—40'	100 M capacity	18,201
	10	Steel cabooses (roller bearing)		165,270
	50	"DF" insulated box—50'	140 M capacity	638,000
	50	Covered hoppers (roller bearing)	140 M capacity	425,000
	10	Tanks—19,000 gal. capacity (roller bearing)		110,000
	100	Auto box—50'6"	100 M capacity	955,000
	100	Hoppers "triple door" (roller bearing)	140 M capacity	768,833
	25	Airslide hoppers (roller bearing)	140 M capacity	304,500
	200	Box—40'6"	100 M capacity	1,468,000
			Total cost	$13,086,552

47

CHAPTER IX

NORTHERN PACIFIC

New North Coast Limited—A Scenic Route Through the Northwest Over a Superlative Roadbed

Chicago to Seattle—this is a journey the very names of whose two terminal points conjure up a romantic picture of American history, scenic wonders, agricultural production, and industrial activity.

And the Northern Pacific Railway has made it possible for the traveler on NP's famous North Coast Limited to enjoy to the utmost the trip between these two great cities. The sleek, smoothly gliding green streamliner that traverses some of the nation's most fabulous countryside is equipped to make the entire journey a sheer delight for every passenger.

The 2,446-mile route that is traversed by the North Coast Limited's vista-dome cars, all-room Pullmans, and comfortable reclining seat chair cars has hardly begun, and the passenger has barely had time to admire the thirteen-car train and its silvery two-unit diesel, when the streamliner brings its travelers to Savanna, Illinois—just two hours out of Chicago. Here the streamliner, which was headed west, turns north as it encounters the mighty, the historic, the romantic Mississippi River.

Majestic bluffs alive with wild foliage line the banks of the river as the train runs its three-hundred-mile course on the way to Saint Paul. Having left Chicago promptly at 11:30 A.M., the North Coast Limited offers its passengers the thrill of having their first meal aboard while tracing the banks of America's most famous stream. And what a luncheon it is, too—such items as chilled apple juice, grilled lamb chops, relishes, buttered green

Chicago Great Western #90 crack Omaha-Chicago fast freight which carries the meat, perishables and other expedited items crossing the Des Moines River at Ft. Dodge, Iowa on Council Bluffs Dist., Minn. Div.

Northern Pacific #25 new Vista-Dome North Coast Limited west of Missoula, Mont. on the Sixth Subdiv. of the Rocky Mt. Div.

View of Vista-Dome and high level seating arrangements in both coach and sleeping-car domes on new Northern Pacific North Coast Limited built by Budd.

Deluxe reclining seat coach on Northern Pacific's North Coast Limited with MP gold spike mural in background. Built by Budd.

New Northern Pacific dining cars for North Coast Limited. These cars seat 48 persons, 32 in the main center section, and 8 each in two glass partitions (banquettes) built by Budd.

General view of lounge portion of the Lewis & Clark Traveler Rest car on Northern Pacific's North Coast Limited. Simulated rawhide with painted murals adorn the walls and ceiling. Comfortable chairs and settees seat 30 people.

The Blue Streak near Rison, Arkansas, on the Pine Bluff-Texarkana Subdivision.

Lehigh & Hudson crack fast freight #32 from the Lackawanna connection at Port Morris west of Warwick, N. Y. headed for Maybrook and New England points. Note this fine road's well marked and excellent track.

C & O #1, the westbound George Washington, meeting a coal train and manifest freight train at Russell, Ky. Russell Div.

C & O train ferries S.S. Spartan in foreground and S.S. Badger off Manitowoc during trial runs of Badger.

Night loading aboard Chesapeake & Ohio train ferry SS. Spartan at Ludington, Mich.

SPARTAN

Centralized Traffic Control board located at Pine Bluff, Ark., which controls movement of trains between Illmo, Mo., and Texarkana. Ark-Tex.

The main shops and headquarters of Mechanical Department are located at Pine Bluff, Arkansas. Photo is interior view of structure where road diesels are serviced and light repairs made.

Santa Fe yard diesel switching cars into Republic Carloading and Forwarding freight house at Santa Fe's new Corwith freight terminal at Chicago.

DALTON - JCT.

Santa Fe #16, the Texas Chief, passing Dalton Jct., Tex. where the new Dallas Line leaves the Main Line. This is CTC territory on the Second Dist. of the Northern Div.

Lackawanna HB-9 coming around the Port Morris lead with L & H New England connection bound for East Buffalo. Its consist is restricted to box and refrigerator cars and is authorized to operate at 60 miles an hour. Hauled by 2 Fairbanks Morse Trainmasters.

Lackawanna #47 at Stroudsburg, Pa. deadheading milk cars to Binghamton. This road gives fine service to the dairy farmers along its line and #44 is the premier eastbound milktrain of the road.

Southern Railway #48, the Southerner, deluxe streamliner, between New Orleans and New York via Birmingham and Atlanta running over the Birmingham Div.

Southern Pacific Extra 6301 west coming out of the snowshed at Crystal Lake, Cal. on the Mountain Subdiv. of the Sacramento Div. Here the Southern Pacific combats one of North America's heaviest snowfalls every year at their own expense even though the snowfall is up near the top of the poles. Note way snow has been cleared leaving room to dispose of next fall.

Southern Pacific's new type of CTC control center developed by Union Switch & Signal Co. at Tucson, Ariz. headquarters of Tucson Div. This board controls 125 miles of track between Lordsburg, N.M. and Mescal, Ariz. on the Bowie Dist. of Tucson Div. This new control center provides means for concentrating control of traffic into a center small enough for one dispatcher to control many more miles than he is now capable of handling. This is possible because the track diagram is miniaturized and controls concentrated in center of desk so that dispatcher may remain in one position while operating entire center. This CTC installation will make it possible to remove sidings at Benson, Tully, Manzoro, Ariz. and Mondel, N.M. 14 others will be extended to a minimum length of 9,000 ft. each and longer sidings will be put in near Dragoon, Ariz. and Steins, N.M.

Southern Pacific #10, the Shasta Daylight, running through some of the nation's most beautiful country as it passes Odell Lake, Oregon on the Springfield Subdiv. of the Portland Div.

U.P. diesel #905 rebuilt to E-9 arriving at Denver with #10, the crack domeline City of St. Louis, shown turning on wye. Rear of train under bridge at left. First Sub-div. of Wyoming Div. Photo by R. H. Kindig.

U.P. #103, the City of Los Angeles, climbing Sherman Hill on the 1.55 grade at Granites, Wyo. with 15 cars on the Second Sub-div. of the Wyoming Div. Photo by R. H. Kindig.

New Chicago Great Western Yard at Oelwein, Iowa snapped from the modern yard tower.

Chicago Great Western's new up-to-date car icing facility and ice plant at Oelwein, Iowa.

peas, Parisienne tomatoes and NP's famous big Idaho baked potato! All followed by a delicious portion of strawberry shortcake topped with whipped cream.

Out of Saint Paul, No. 25—as the North Coast Limited is known—replaces its Burlington road locomotive with a new three-unit diesel and a full Northern Pacific crew. From here to its West Coast destination it's all Northern Pacific as it sweeps upgrade on a long curve to give its lazily reclining passengers a grand view of downtown Saint Paul, the state capitol building, and the stately Summit Avenue Cathedral, then across historic Stone Arch Bridge and into Minneapolis, where No. 25 again comes to a halt to load more passengers for the westward journey.

While the passengers relax to the accompaniment of music coming over the streamliner's public address system, the train speeds through the gathering dusk across Minnesota's famed prairie land. Night has fallen by the time the North Coast Limited reaches Staples, where a connecting train from Duluth awaits the transcontinental speedster's arrival.

When the sun next arises, the travelers witness the glowing beauties of Montana, through which state the NP route runs for almost eight hundred miles. Prairie and plain mark its eastern boundaries; but when No. 25 reaches the western half of Montana—a traversing that takes a full span of daylight—its travelers are in a land of fantastic mountain peak, jagged sky line, and rugged plateau. As the North Coast Limited enters Montana, its rails carry it through the valley of the Yellowstone River, whose historic waters it follows for some 341 miles.

This day's journey offers the passenger a course in American history, for it was through this very country and along the banks of this same Yellowstone River that Lewis and Clark worked their way back from their great expedition in 1806. Now the train speeds through the hamlet of Pompeys Pillar, where the keen-eyed can see a huge oval rock into which Clark's name was long ago cut into the stone. Here the NP has protected the inscription by erecting a metal screen about it.

But the North Coast Limited itself offers the voyager an un-

49

paralleled opportunity to refresh his memory and to brush up on historical lore. For right in the midst of its thirteen-car consist is the unique Lewis and Clark Traveler's Rest Car.

Designed in the contemporary manner to fit the needs of the present-day traveler, by world-famous Raymond Loewy, the car nevertheless is fitted out to capture all the atmosphere of the old, rugged, untamed West.

The very name of the car, "Traveler's Rest," is a reference to an entry in the Lewis and Clark log of their expedition; it was the name given by the famous explorers to a camp site in what is now western Montana, where they and their intrepid party rested on both the original westward trek and on the return journey as well.

The upper walls and ceiling of this truly fascinating railroad car are finished in a light beige color and with a material that simulates the traditional old buckskin of the West. Cross-stitching at the seams helps to carry out this clever illusion. Colorful murals, the work of Chicago's Edgar Miller, depict known events that took place at varying intervals during the Lewis and Clark journeys, and there is a large wall map that traces the actual route of the two great explorers. Paintings of Indians and of the various wild animals that abounded throughout the region at the time of the explorations are spotted throughout the car and help to complete its frontier atmosphere.

There are reproductions of historic documents that pertain to the expedition and a Harper's Ferry flintlock rifle, as well as a pipe of peace, to complete the pioneer Western feeling. Booklets within easy access of each passenger tell the story of the car and of the history and romance that it symbolizes, while attractive stewardess-nurses are prepared to help the younger travelers learn something of the historic country through which their modern train is smoothly and speedily carrying them.

Oil refineries, stockyards, and acres of sugar beets tell the NCL's passengers about mid-morning that they are pulling into Billings, where famous Calamity Jane once sold souvenirs at the old railroad depot. The community itself, appropriately, was named after an early president of the Northern Pacific Railway.

West of Billings now, and No. 25 begins to climb on its journey toward the Continental Divide. Ahead, readily viewed from the vista domes, can be seen the exciting panorama of the snow-capped Rocky Mountains. As the train makes one particular turn, there is a tantalizing glimpse of Granite Peak, Montana's highest, 12,850 feet above sea level.

The meticulous attention that NP pays to its roadbed is never more greatly appreciated by its passengers than in this winding, hilly terrain. Between Greycliff and Livingston the ride becomes unbelievably quiet and smooth as No. 25 slides along on a forty-three-mile stretch of welded rail.

Some passengers get off at Livingston, to take the Northern Pacific's scenic bus trip through Yellowstone National Park. They will return at a later time to pick up another day's North Coast Limited. Meanwhile, the train continues its inexorable climb until it reaches the Bozeman Tunnel, three thousand feet long. Then it rolls downward through the valley if the Gallatin River to Logan.

But now the climb starts again, this time more sharply. The streamliner snakes one way and then another till it reaches a height of 6,356 feet, the highest point achieved by any of the northern transcontinental roads. Reverse curves, horseshoe curves, and grades up to 2.2 per cent give the passengers a series of thrills.

Leaving the newly named Daylight Tunnel at the height of the Continental Divide, the vista domes afford a glorious view some ten miles across Silver Bow Valley. Here there is a sheer drop of one thousand feet on one side of the track.

Down the ledges goes the North Coast Limited, and into Butte, America's copper capital, where for every mile of city street there are said to be ten miles of mining tunnels. Now the roadway levels out and No. 25 zooms at a smooth seventy miles per hour into Garrison, where a branch line from Helena meets the main track. And eight miles farther on, the limited speeds past Gold Creek, where the last spike was driven on September 8, 1883, to mark the completion of the transcontinental railroad. It was an event that took place in the presence of General Grant

51

and many other notables of the time, and a dignified white board sign now marks the spot.

While the travelers are enjoying dinner, No. 25 pulls into Missoula. Here, for the second time that day, the streamliner gets a complete window-washing, the first having taken place that morning at Billings. A movable high platform is wheeled alongside the dome cars, and while one man scrubs the glass blisters on the upper deck, others spray the lower windows.

As darkness falls once again, the train glides gently out of the station and begins another climb over the third and final range of the great chain of Rockies. Into Idaho by moonlight, and the travelers see the mystic beauty of Lake Pend Oreille.

Now a final night of restful, relaxing sleep, up at six and the gorgeous ride down the Cascades after coming over historic Stampede Pass and through the tunnel, and at 8:00 o'clock the following morning, No. 25 pulls into Seattle, largest city in America's burgeoning Pacific Northwest.

It has been a journey of thorough delight. History, romance, good food, comfort, speed, and safety have all combined to give Northern Pacific's customers an ideal trip.

CHAPTER X

THE SAINT LOUIS SOUTHWESTERN OR COTTON BELT

Crack Fast Freight Service, Piggyback, and CTC

One of the major operational problems faced by every railroad involves the maximum efficient use of its power units to bring its trains through on schedule, while at the same time keeping to a minimum the amount of time during which its locomotives are side-lined for servicing or just waiting to pick up consists.

The Cotton Belt railroad—officially the St. Louis Southwestern Railway—running three basic manifest schedules daily, plus additional sections as required by traffic volume, in each direction between East St. Louis, Illinois, and destinations or connections in Northeast Texas, provides an excellent example of how such schedules can be worked out to provide maximum speeds without greatly affecting tonnage haul per power unit.

Southward, the Cotton Belt runs the Advanced Motor Special, the Blue Streak, and the Motor Special out of East St. Louis each day. The Advanced Motor Special leaves the southern Illinois terminal at 10:30 A.M. and travels the 752 miles to Corsicana, Texas, where it connects with the Southern Pacific, by 5:30 the following morning. A Dallas-Fort Worth connection puts traffic into Dallas by 10:00 A.M. and into Fort Worth by 10:30 A.M. the first day after departure from East St. Louis.

The Blue Streak departs from East St. Louis at 9:30 each night. A connection leaves Memphis at 11:59 P.M., and the two units are consolidated at Pine Bluff, Arkansas, which is the approximate geographic center of the railroad's freight operations. The combined consist arrives at Shreveport, Louisiana, a distance of 583 miles, at 5:30 P.M. the next evening; at Corsicana, Texas, a distance of 752 miles, at 3:40 P.M. that same afternoon; at Dallas, a total distance of 743 miles, just before midnight that night; and at Fort Worth, a distance of 761 miles, at 3:00 A.M. the second morning.

The Motor Special follows the Blue Streak out of East St. Louis by one and a half hours every evening, departing at 11:00 P.M. It also connects with a Memphis-originated train at Pine Bluff, arriving the second morning at Shreveport at 3:45 A.M., and at Corsicana at 5:10 P.M. the first day.

Southward, both the Blue Streak and the Motor Special operate on coordinating schedules with Southern Pacific lines and the motive power of the two companies is pooled from Pine Bluff to San Antonio, Texas, and return. Power units hauling these trains on the round trip of 1,260 miles require no mechanical attention other than the addition of fuel, water, and sand. This is true also of two northbound freights traversing the same route, the Imperial Valley and the Colton Block. The four units also run the round trip of 796 miles between Pine Bluff and East St. Louis in about thirty hours, again without any mechanical attention beyond the normal addition of fuel, water, and sand.

To make this schedule function at highest efficiency with a minimum use of diesel units required extensive study and experimentation on the part of Cotton Belt officials. In addition, the problem of seasonal flunctuations in freight volume had to be taken into account when these schedules were worked out.

Because Pine Bluff is so strategically located in relation to its freight operations, the railroad has been able to set up its freight power in a pool operating out of that center. All inspection, maintenance, and repair operations on the road's freight diesels are performed there.

A check indicated that in some districts power units were subjected to uneconomical waits at some terminals because of a spread between arrival and departure times. Where this was found to be true, the Cotton Belt assigned general-purpose units to those through freight schedules in order to make use of

54

the power during lay-over periods to handle switch engine shifts and turn-around runs out of the terminal, and yet return in time to take the through freight out on schedule.

In some cases this decision resulted in releasing several power units that had previously been used on switch engines and turn-around jobs. For example, the Blue Streak is operated with two general-purpose diesel units. When the freight arrives in Dallas at 11:59 each night, the two units are separated; one pulls a run from Dallas to Addison and return, getting back to Dallas at 6:00 A.M. This makes it available for switch duty in the Dallas yard until 7:25 that night, at which time it is reassembled with the other unit to haul the daily 7:55 freight out of Dallas to Texarkana, arriving at Texarkana by 8:00 the following morning. At this Texas-Arkansas border community one of the units is again detached and is used to power a turn-around local operating from Texarkana to Redwater Ordnance Plant. This is a round trip of only twenty-six miles, which is made in plenty of time for the unit to return to Texarkana in order to be reassembled as part of the two-unit power plant that hauls the next Blue Streak from Texarkana to Dallas.

With this arrangement, Cotton Belt is able to use only two diesel units to protect 386 through freight miles, a short turn-around through freight schedule for 28 miles, a 26-mile operation out of Texarkana, and about twelve hours of switch service at Dallas.

At Waco the railroad uses only three engines to work four switch-engine shifts and to operate four turn-around locals out of the terminal there each day, providing a utilization of 90 per cent. A recent check indicated that through freight operations are averaging 12,000 miles per month for each power unit; this comes to 3,652 gross tons per train, with an average of 0.93 gross ton miles per horsepower.

The seasonal flunctuations on the Cotton Belt freight lines varies no more than 10 per cent to a maximum of 20 per cent. To avoid the wasteful storing of power units during these less busy times, the railroad has scheduled its maintenance program so that annual inspections and general repair operations take place during those periods. Units can then more easily be spared from operations, and the Cotton Belt is also thus assured that all its power units will be available for maximum service and in tiptop operating condition when the peak periods arrive.

At the Cotton Belt's centrally located merchandise transfer station at Pine Bluff, Arkansas, which is operated on a twenty-four-hour basis every day of the year, the railroad also performs transloading of carload freight. Transloading permits direct delivery to two or more destinations of portions of an original carload shipment. Thus, consolidated carloads moving via Cotton Belt may be transloaded at Pine Bluff into two or more individual cars destined to different points in the Southwest and California.

Piggyback

The Cotton Belt railroad, like other farseeing roads throughout the country, has also begun to develop its trailer-on-flatcar or piggyback service as a convenience to its customers.

As far back as 1930 the road began to experiment with this type of service, perhaps one of the very first tryouts of this system anywhere in the country.

The road was ahead of its time, however, and after a brief trial period abandoned the new service. However, twenty-five years later Cotton Belt instituted the first piggyback service offered by any railroad between St. Louis and points in the Southwest.

Reinstituted on June 14, 1955, the new service is being continually expanded as more and more connecting lines indicate a willingness to join them in establishing interline piggyback service. The Cotton Belt has constructed loading and unloading ramps for trailers at East St. Louis, Jonesboro, Memphis, North Little Rock, Pine Bluff, Camden, Texarkana, Dallas, Fort Worth, Lufkin, Waco, Tyler, and Shreveport.

The road has established a subsidiary, Southwestern Transportation Company, which owns all the trailers involved. SWT trailers are leased by the railroad from its own trucking subsidiary for piggyback service.

Ample flatcar space has been assured by means of conversion of one hundred of the railroad's conventional cars to trailer-on-flatcar service. Special equipment, consisting of tie-down gear and brackets and staggered hinged-brackets at either end of the cars, has been installed on eighty 42-foot cars. Modern type retractable hitches, for tie-down purposes, have been installed on twenty of the railroad's 53-foot 6-inch flatcars.

The service, typical of piggyback operations, offers the shipper the convenience of door-to-door pickup and delivery without loss of time or extra labor charges for unloading and reloading at each end, and provides him with reliable, fast, all-weather shipping schedules. The same precise tracing service that Cotton Belt has always offered its conventional rail freight customers is also available to those using the new trailer-on-flatcar method of shipping their products.

CTC

Further evidence of the Cotton Belt's progressive, forward-looking operational policies can be found in its 628 miles of track that are now equipped for centralized traffic control. With the exception of isolated sections totaling no more than 17.8 miles, the entire right of way of the railroad is single-track main line. Prior to introduction of CTC, train movements were authorized by timetable and orders, with no automatic signaling in service.

But a heavy increase in main-line traffic during the early years of World War II brought about a necessity for getting trains over the road in a shorter time, so two very important decisions were made by the railroad's management.

These were: first, not to attempt to construct a second main

57

track, but rather to secure increased capacity on the existing single line; and second, to improve the single track by installing a system of centralized traffic control, complete to power switch machines and to signals that would authorize train movements.

A total of 47 miles of track was placed under CTC operation in 1943 between Illmo and Dexter, Missouri, this section being where traffic had shown the heaviest increases and therefore the greatest need for this new system. Next came a 152-mile stretch between Pine Bluff and Texarkana, where the line crosses four major rivers and encounters grades up to 1.17 per cent as well as curves as great as 4 degrees. This section was completed in 1947.

Shortages of men and materials during the critical postwar period held back some of the planned work, but in 1952 installation operations were resumed, this time on the 68-mile stretch north of Pine Bluff to Brinkley, Arkansas. A year later the 84 miles from Jonesboro to Dexter were under CTC, and in 1954 the Texarkana-Dexter stretch was completed with the installation of CTC operations between Jonesboro and Brinkley. Since that time, centralized traffic control on the Cotton Belt has pushed southward and now extends as far as Corsicana.

Headquarters for this operation are set up in a new brick building at Pine Bluff, where two machines do the entire job of controlling train movements all the way from Illmo, just south of St. Louis, to Texarkana; Illmo to Brinkley, 206 miles, is controlled by one machine, and Brinkley to Texarkana, 220 miles, by the second. The CTC operations between Texarkana and Corsicana, 202 miles, are controlled by one machine located at Tyler.

Along with these installations, basic changes were made in strategically placed sidings. Where it had been decided that sidings were to be equipped with power switches and signals, they were lengthened to provide capacities of from 120 to 250 cars. Short sidings, which under the improved control system would not be used for meeting or passing trains, were either ripped up or converted into spur track, which now serves industrial plants or the railroad's freight houses. Those main-track switches with hand-throw stands that remained in service were equipped with electric locks that can be controlled by the distant dispatcher.

Lap siding layouts, previously used to hold two trains while a third passed by, are no longer needed under CTC. Where they existed, the tracks were thrown to connect the old sidings through into one long siding.

There are two heads to each station-entering signal on the Cotton Belt's CTC set up. The red-over-yellow aspect is displayed when a power switch is reversed to permit a train to enter an unoccupied siding. If that siding is already occupied by a train headed in the same direction, the signal will show red-over-lunar, but if the train already on the siding is headed in the opposite direction, the signal cannot be set to display an entering aspect.

Some special signaling features were designed and built into the Cotton Belt's CTC to provide for unique features of the road's operation. Half a mile north of the Jonesboro station, for example, there is a double location of "holdout" signals under the dispatcher's control. When he sets these at the stop aspect, the dispatcher sets up a switching zone in the Jonesboro industrial area, permitting a local freight or switch engine to use the main track, service industries in the area, and then get into the clear.

While this activity is being undertaken, it is possible to make a line up for a southbound freight to depart from Brookland, eight miles north of Jonesboro, and to begin its journey southward. Then, when the local freight or switch engine leaves the switching area, the southward holding signal is cleared for the through freight by the dispatcher and it can continue without delay.

The CTC installation on the Cotton Belt was planned and set up under the direction of the road's signal engineer, B. J. Alford. The Union Switch & Signal Division of Westinghouse Air Brake Company was the supplier of all major items of signal equipment.

TELETYPE SWITCH LIST BSM

CB MC
       PINE BLUFF FEB 7 1955
ALL TEXARKANA
CB 47 SOUTH
BSM SP 300-500-312 BARFIELD 2012 267 2/7 1020 AM 58-4-
    2457 419
FAIRLANE 4 80 BUSINESS CAR 547
ARTX 28310 R 47 SPUDS 584 CPS
GATX 17332 T 24 MTY 547
GATX 37646 T 24 MTY 547
GATX 61807 T 24 MTY 547
PLE 22147 B 40 MDSE 1 612 ACME STOP 621
PRR 59540 B 40 CABTS 347
NATX 7223 T 24 MTY 547
CO 14573 D 42 SOAP L 612
SP 104275 B 42 MILK 677 MKT AUSTIN STOP 547
RDG 107946 B 40 MDSE D 696 GCSF TEMPLE ACME STOP
    677
CO 14021 B 42 PIPE 677
PFE 44768 R 59 BEER 677
RBNX 80381 R 56 BEER 677 VC
SPS 12592 B 40 MDSE 621 SP SAN ANT ACME 671243
CN 520575 B 40 MDSE SAME LAREDO
PRR 65506 B 40 MDSE SAME ANAHEI MACME 6E2564
CBQ 15235 B 40 MDSE SAME SAN DIEGO ACME 6E2564
DLW 45672 B 40 MDSE SAME SAN DIEGO ACME STOP
    PHOENIX 6E2564
WAB 48120 B 40 MDSE SAME C CHRISTI ACME 672543
IC 40285 B 40 MDSE D 671243 SAN ANT ACME
BAR 5438 B 40 MDSE SAME SAN DIEGO ACME 6E2564
SSW 37884 B 40 MDSE SAME SAN DIEGO ACME 6E2564
SSW 38012 B 40 MDSE SAME TUSCON ACME 6E2564
SSW 38777 B 40 MDSE 6 7 2543 SAME AUSTIN
PFE 67774 R 40 MDSE 6 E 2564 SAME EL CENTRO ACME
LN 99492 B 40 MDSE SAME LAREDO STOP SAN ANT ACME
    672543
SSW 32939 B 40 MDSE SAME BURBANK ACME 6E2564

WP 20224 B 40 MDSE SAME AUSTIN ACME STOP SAN ANT
    672543
NH 31488 B 40 MDSE C CHRISTI ACME ((621SP)) 672543
CO 18875 B 40 MDSE SAME PHOENIX 6E2564
RDG 108483 B 40 MDSE SAME SAN DIEGO ACME 6E2564
LV 62841 B 40 MDSE SAME LOS ANGELES
SSW 36704 B 40 MDSE SAME 6E2564 PASADENA ACME
CRIP 26151 B 40 MDSE D 6 7 2543 621 SP LAREDO ACME
ELS 8014 B 40 MDSE SAME SANTA BARBARA ACME 6E2564
CS 1207 B 35 MDSE L 612 TERM
SLBM 18564 B 40 MDSE L 612 TERM
SF 17750 B 50 MDSE L 612 ACME
NP 24425 B 41 B GDS C 590 SP L 612
IGN 14362 B 42 RUBBER C 635 TP BELLEMONT
ERIE 90431 B 31 F BRD C 635 FWD LUBBOCK
GN 20664 B 40 LADDERS 419
WAB 85053 B 36 MACHY 419 KCS K 452
NYC 72121 B 75 LIQUORS C 590 SP L 612
PLE 47421 B 45 PIPE L 612
NYC 104462 B 38 RODS L 612
PRR 573559 B 41 PIPE SAME L 612
PRR 345989 G 55 PIPE 480
CBQ 33358 B 40 SUPPLIES D 589
NH 31027 B 40 MDSE C 635 ACME
CN 533692 B 40 MDSE D L 612 ACME
CN 484167 B 40 MDSE L 612 ACME
ARTX 26087 R 40 MDSE L 612 ACME
MP 47803 B 40 MDSE L 612 ACME
DH 19215 B 40 MDSE C 635 FWD W FALLS ACME
GMO 26346 B 40 MDSE D L 612 SP WAXAHACHIE ACME
    STOP L 612
SOU 10176 B 40 MDSE C 635 ACME
GMO 26324 B 40 MDSE L 612 ACME
RDG 101251 B 40 MDSE L 612 ACME
SSW 46170 B 40 MDSE 480 PMP PARIS ACME STOP 419
INSERT BETWEEN CBQ 33358 AND NH 31027 AS 51st CAR
    INTRAIN
CGW 5009 B 32 BEDS L 612

J R TUCKER.........1135 AM

RUN OF BSM

E. St. Louis	to Pine Bluff—	10′39″
″	to Shreveport—	16′53″
″	to Sherman—	25′23″
″	to Dallas—	24′43″
″	to Corsicana—	23′08″
″	to Waco—	29′53″

CONDENSED FREIGHT SCHEDULES

WESTBOUND

TO WEST COAST		AMS	BSM	MS
East St. Louis	lv	10:30 am-0	9:30 pm-0	11:00 pm-0
Memphis	lv	10:00 am-0	11:59 pm-0	11:59 pm-0
Pine Bluff	lv	9:00 pm-0	7:25 am-1	9:20 am-1
Texarkana	lv	12:30 am-1	10:55 am-1	12:40 pm-1
Tyler	lv	3:55 am-1	2:05 pm-1	3:45 pm-1
Corsicana (SP)	lv	5:50 am-1	3:55 am-1	5:25 pm-1
San Antonio	lv	1:45 pm-1	10:45 am-1	12:15 am-2
El Paso	ar	5:30 am-2	1:45 pm-2	3:10 pm-2
El Paso	lv	8:00 am-2	3:45 pm-2	5:00 pm-2
Phoenix	ar	5:00 am-3	6:00 pm-3	6:00 pm-3
Los Angeles	ar	10:00 am-3	1:00 pm-3	2:30 pm-3
San Francisco	ar	9:00 pm-4	9:00 pm-4	9:00 pm-4
TO RIO GRANDE VALLEY				
East St. Louis	lv	—	9:30 pm-0	11:00 pm-0
Memphis	lv	—	11:59 pm-0	11:59 pm-0
Pine Bluff	lv	—	7:25 am-1	9:20 am-1
Texarkana	lv	—	10:55 am-1	12:40 pm-1
Tyler	lv	—	2:05 pm-1	3:45 pm-1
Corsicana (SP)	lv	—	3:55 pm-1	5:25 pm-1
Corpus Christi	ar	—	11:00 pm-2	11:00 pm-2
Laredo (TM)	ar	—	9:00 am-3	9:00 am-3
Brownsville(SP)	ar	—	7:30 am-3	7:30 am-3
TO HOUSTON— NEW ORLEANS				
East St. Louis	lv	—	9:30 pm-0	11:00 pm-0
Memphis	lv	—	11:59 pm-0	10:00 am-1
Pine Bluff	lv	—	10:00 am-1	7:30 pm-1
Shreveport	ar	—	5:30 pm-1	3:45 am-2
Houston (SP)	ar	—	5:00 am-2	6:00 pm-2
New Orleans (SP)	ar	—	3:30 am-3	—
TO DALLAS— FORT WORTH —WACO				
East St. Louis	lv	10:30 am-0	9:30 pm-0	11:00 pm-0
Memphis	lv	10:00 am-0	11:59 pm-0	11:59 pm-0
Pine Bluff	lv	9:00 pm-0	7:25 am-1	9:20 am-1
Texarkana	lv	12:30 am-1	10:55 am-1	12:40 pm-1
Dallas	ar	10:00 am-1	11:59 pm-1	11:59 pm-1
Fort Worth	ar	10:30 am-1	3:00 am-2	3:00 am-2
Waco	ar	5:00 am-2	5:00 am-2	5:00 am-2

EASTBOUND

FROM WEST COAST		Colton Block	Yuma Block	Arizona-Mexican Block
Los Angeles (SP)	lv	1:30 pm-1	—	—
Colton	lv	11:59 pm-1	—	—
Yuma	lv	—	7:00 pm-1	—
Phoenix	lv	—	—	4:00 am-1
Nogales	lv	—	—	3:00 am-1
Tuscon	lv	8:20 pm-2	—	—
El Paso	ar	7:30 am-3	12:01 am-3	4:00 am-2
San Antonio	ar	7:30 am-4	3:30 am-4	3:30 am-3
Corsicana (SSW)	lv	7:15 am-4	4:00 am-4	4:00 pm-3
Tyler	lv	8:45 pm-4	5:30 pm-4	5:30 am-3
Texarkana	lv	12:30 am-5	11:15 am-4	11:15 am-3
Pine Bluff	ar	6:35 am-5	4:30 am-5	4:30 am-4
Memphis	ar	7:00 pm-5	7:00 pm-5	7:00 pm-4
East St. Louis	ar	8:00 pm-5	8:00 pm-5	8:00 pm-4

FROM TEXAS		Rio Grande Valley Block	130-218-18	No. 18
Edinburg (SP)	lv	6:00 am-1	—	—
Laredo (TM)	lv	1:00 am-1	—	—
Houston	lv	2:30 am-2	3:10 pm-1	—
Shreveport (SSW)	lv	2:30 pm-2	5:00 am-2	—
Fort Worth	lv	—	—	7:25 pm-0
Dallas	lv	—	—	7:55 pm-0
Tyler	lv	—	—	7:30 pm-0
Texarkana	lv	—	—	5:15 am-1
Pine Bluff	lv	10:30 pm-2	2:30 pm-2	2:30 pm-1
Memphis	ar	7:00 am-3	7:00 pm-2	7:00 pm-1
East St. Louis	ar	12:01 pm-3	6:35 am-3	6:35 am-2

CHAPTER XI

LEHIGH & HUDSON

One of the Greatest of the Little—A Most Important Route

Some of the most important railroad lines in the United States never carry a passenger, and indeed many of the shippers who benefit by the services of these roads may not even be aware of their existence.

Yet without these so-called "overhead carriers," freight movement would be slower and more expensive, and major city freight yards would be constantly taxed beyond their utmost capacity. These are the lines that, running over relatively short rights of way, nevertheless provide vital links between railroads serving the big cities of the nation, and that make it possible to shuttle freight cars from one road to another by means of a series of strategically located interchange points.

Such a railroad is the Lehigh & Hudson River Railway. Its main line totals only 73.77 miles, but this trackage makes it possible for shipments to take place between such communities as Boston and Chicago, or between St. Louis and New Haven, while completely avoiding the congestion of the busy Port of New York area.

The road's main line runs from Maybrook, New York (just west of the Hudson River and about sixty miles above New York City) to Belvidere, New Jersey (on the Delaware River, the boundary between New Jersey and Pennsylvania). The L&H holds trackage rights over the Pennsylvania's Belvidere division from that point to Phillipsburg, New Jersey, at which its own main line runs .7 miles on the bridge over the Delaware to

63

Easton, Pennsylvania. Trackage rights are also maintained over Lackawanna lines between Andover Junction and Port Morris, New Jersey, and there is a small branch line of .83 miles between Hudson Junction, New York and Greycourt, New York, to provide a connection with the Erie Railroad at the latter point.

All in all, counting its main and branch lines as well as the above trackage rights, the Lehigh & Hudson operates over a total right of way of some 96.6 miles. Yet its trackage is so located that it is able to operate ten vital interchange points with seven different railroads, thus providing an important link in the transportation of the nation's freight.

The Lehigh & Hudson's symbol freights make connections with the New York, New Haven & Hartford at Maybrook; with the Erie at Greycourt; with the New York, Susquehanna & Western at both Sparta Junction, New York, and Franklin, New Jersey; with the Lackawanna at two points, Andover and Port Morris, New Jersey; with the New Jersey Central at both Easton and Allentown, Pennsylvania; with the Lehigh Valley at Phillipsburg; and with the Pennsylvania at Belvidere.

Through the Lehigh & Hudson's strategic linkage, a freight shipment leaving Springfield, Massachusetts, for example, on a Tuesday evening, can be in Detroit early Thursday morning, or in Chicago Thursday night, or in St. Louis by dawn on Friday. Here is how such a shipment might run, with its connecting railroads and the interchange points at which freight cars would be transferred from one line to the next:

Moving via New York, New Haven & Hartford, the Springfield cars would reach the Maybrook interchange at 9:15 A.M. Wednesday. They might be in the same consist with cars moved out of Boston, Worcester, Providence, New Haven, and Bridgeport at various hours between Tuesday noon and 1:10 A.M. Wednesday. Here they would be picked up by the Lehigh & Hudson's No. 31, which will make the run to Port Morris, in northern New Jersey, in two hours and ten minutes; here the westward-bound cars are transferred to the Lackawanna, which brings them into Buffalo at 10:15 that same evening. Further interchange at this upper New York State lake port carries the freight cars to Cleveland or Chicago via Nickel Plate, to Detroit via Chesapeake & Ohio, or on to St. Louis via Wabash.

Similar connections facilitate the same movement eastward, with the Lehigh & Hudson's No. 30 making the daily run from Port Morris to Maybrook between 1:00 A.M. and 5:00 A.M.

Eight daily trains and one that runs daily except Monday are maintained on a regular schedule by the Lehigh & Hudson. Five make the run between Port Morris and Maybrook, and the remaining four move vital freight loads from Maybrook on to Allentown or back. Ten crews are assigned to handle these trains, as follows:

WESTBOUND SYMBOL TRAIN SCHEDULES

VIA L&HR—DL&W AND CONNECTIONS

| L&HR No. 31 | Leave | Maybrook, N.Y. . . . | 9:15 A.M. |
| | Arrive | Port Morris, N.J. . . . | 11:25 A.M. |

| L&HR No. 35 | Leave | Maybrook, N.Y. . . . | 10:30 P.M. |
| | Arrive | Port Morris, N.J. . . . | 12:15 A.M. |

VIA L&HR—LV AND CONNECTIONS

| L&HR OA-1 | Leave | Maybrook, N.Y. . . . | 1:00 P.M. |
| | Arrive | Easton, Pa. . . . . . | 5:40 P.M. |

VIA L&HR—CNJ—RDG—WM—N&W

| L&HR OA-3 | Leave | Maybrook, N.Y. . . . | 4:00 P.M. |
| | Arrive | Allentown, Pa. . . . | 9:00 P.M. |

VIA L&HR—CNJ—RDG—WM—B&O

| L&HR OA-1 | Leave | Maybrook, N.Y. . . . | 1:00 P.M. |
| | Arrive | Allentown, Pa. . . . . | 6:30 P.M. |

EASTBOUND SYMBOL TRAIN SCHEDULES

CONNECTIONS VIA B&O–WM–RDG–CNJ–L&HR (CSD)

L&HR HO-6	Leave	Allentown, Pa. . . .	5:35 P.M.
	Arrive	Maybrook, N.Y. . . .	9:30 A.M.

CONNECTIONS VIA N&W–WM–RDG–CNJ–L&HR (*Blue Ridge Dispatch*)

L&HR AO-4	Leave	Allentown, Pa. . . .	9:45 A.M.
	Arrive	Maybrook, N.Y. . . .	3:00 P.M.

CONNECTIONS VIA LV–L&HR AND PRR–L&HR (*Traders Dispatch*)

L&HR EO-2	Leave	Easton, Pa. (LV) . .	11:00 A.M.
	Leave	Belvidere, N.J. (PRR) .	12:00 NOON
	Arrive	Maybrook, N.Y. . . .	3:00 P.M.

CONNECTIONS VIA DL&W–L&HR (*Lackawanna dispatch*)

L&HR No. 30	Leave	Port Morris, N.J. . . .	1:00 A.M.
	Arrive	Maybrook, N.Y. . . .	3:10 A.M.
L&HR No. 32	Leave	Port Morris, N.J. . . .	7:30 A.M.
	Arrive	Maybrook, N.Y. . . .	9:45 A.M.

EASTWARD VIA CONNECTIONS WITH DL&W–L&HR–NYNH&H

			Daily	
			Time	Day
Lv. St. Louis, Mo.	(WAB)	. . . .	10:30 A.M.	Mon.
Lv. Chicago, Ill.	(NKP)	. . . .	8:30 A.M.	Tues.
Lv. Detroit, Mich.	(C&O)	. . . .	1:30 P.M.	Tues.
Lv. Cleveland, Ohio	(NKP)	. . . .	12:30 P.M.	Tues.
Lv. Buffalo, N.Y.	(DL&W)	. . . .	8:15 A.M.	Wed.
Lv. Port Morris, N.J.	(L&HR #30)	. . . . . .	1:00 A.M.	Thurs.
Arr. Maybrook, N.Y.	(L&HR #30)	. . . . . .	3:10 A.M.	Thurs.
Arr. Hartford, Conn.	(NYNH&H)	. . . . . .	3:50 A.M.	Fri.
Arr. Bridgeport, Conn.	(NYNH&H)	. . . . . .	2:25 A.M.	Fri.
Arr. New Haven, Conn.	(NYNH&H)	. . . . . .	12:30 P.M.	Thurs.
Arr. Boston, Mass.	(NYNH&H)	. . . . . .	8:35 P.M.	Thurs.
Arr. Providence, R.I.	(NYNH&H)	. . . . . .	11:15 P.M.	Thurs.
Arr. Springfield, Mass.	(NYNH&H)	. . . . . .	10:10 P.M.	Thurs.
Arr. Worcester, Mass.	(NYNH&H)	. . . . . .	10:40 P.M.	Thurs.

			Daily except Fri., Sat., Sun.		Fri. Sat., Sun.	
			Time	Day	Time	Day
Lv.	Boston, Mass.	(NYNH&H)	12:55 P.M.	Mon.	12:55 P.M.	Fri.
Lv.	Providence, R.I.	(NYNH&H)	2:30 P.M.	Mon.	2:30 P.M.	Fri.
Lv.	New Haven, Conn.	(NYNH&H)	5:40 P.M.	Mon.	5:40 P.M.	Fri.
Lv.	Maybrook, N.Y.	(L&HR #35)	10:30 P.M.	Mon.	10:30 P.M.	Fri.
Arr.	Port Morris, N.J.	(L&HR #35)	12:15 A.M.	Tues.	2:00 A.M.	Sat.
Arr.	Scranton, Pa.	(DL&W)	3:20 A.M.	Tues.	6:00 A.M.	Sat.
Arr.	Elmira, N.Y.	(DL&W)	5:50 A.M.	Tues.	11:30 A.M.	Sat.
Arr.	Buffalo, N.Y.	(DL&W)	9:35 A.M.	Tues.	6:00 P.M.	Sat.
Arr.	Detroit, Mich.	(C&O)	7:45 A.M.	Wed.	6:45 P.M.	Sun.
Arr.	Chicago, Ill.	(NKP)	2:00 A.M.	Wed.	11:00 P.M.	Sun.
Arr.	St. Louis, Mo.	(WAB)	9:30 A.M.	Wed.	5:05 A.M.	Mon.

WESTWARD VIA NYNH&H–L&HR–DL&W AND CONNECTIONS

			Daily	
			Time	Day
Lv.	Worcester, Mass.	(NYNH&H)	11:30 A.M.	Tues.
Lv.	Springfield, Mass.	(NYNH&H)	5:40 P.M.	Tues.
Lv.	Boston, Mass.	(NYNH&H)	7:25 P.M.	Tues
Lv.	Providence, R.I.	(NYNH&H)	9:15 P.M.	Tues.
Lv.	New Haven, Conn.	(NYNH&H)	1:10 A.M.	Wed.
Lv.	Bridgeport, Conn.	(NYNH&H)	11:45 P.M.	Tues.
Lv.	Hartford, Conn.	(NYNH&H)	7:45 P.M.	Tues.
Lv.	Maybrook, N.Y.	(L&HR #31)	9:15 A.M.	Wed.
Arr.	Port Morris, N.J.	(L&HR #31)	11:25 A.M.	Wed.
Arr.	Buffalo, N.Y.	(DL&W)	10:15 P.M.	Wed.
Arr.	Cleveland, Ohio	(NKP)	6:20 A.M.	Thurs.
Arr.	Detroit, Mich.	(C&O)	6:15 A.M.	Thurs.
Arr.	Chicago, Ill.	(NKP)	11:00 P.M.	Thurs.
Arr.	St. Louis, Mo.	(WAB)	5:05 A.M.	Fri.

Because it is an overhead carrier, primarily concerned with transferring freight cars from one road to another over a vital section of track linkage, the Lehigh & Hudson owns comparatively little equipment. The railroad owns only 123 cars; 103 of these are closed-top ore cars which handle the limestone and zinc ore that constitute the bulk of the road's originating freight from their source at Franklin, New Jersey, along the railroad's main line. There are 15 cabooses and 5 work equipment cars. Motive power of the L&H is furnished by 13 diesels, all of them 1600-horsepower Alco road switchers. Of these 2 are fully owned, while the balance of 11 are operating under conditional sales agreements that mature November 1, 1958. The railroad is in an exceptionally healthy financial state, the agreements on the 11 diesels representing the only long-term indebtedness of the line.

There is no such thing as completely local business carried on the Lehigh & Hudson; that is, no freight is carried solely between any two points on the line's right of way. Because of its primary function as a bridge carrier between the lines of other roads, it carries carload traffic almost exclusively, its l.c.l. loads being restricted to less than 5 per cent of total annual revenue. Here, for example, is a breakdown, by total dollar revenue, of the percentages of different commodities carried by the Lehigh & Hudson River Railway in a recent typical year:

Agricultural products, 4.1 per cent; animals and animal products, 6.2 per cent; anthracite coal, 9 per cent; bituminous coal, 9.5 per cent; limestone, 2 per cent; zinc ore, 7 per cent; other mine products, 1.7 per cent; forest products, 1.8 per cent; various manufactured and miscellaneous products, 47.8 per cent; and carload forwarded traffic, 6.8 per cent. This shows a total of 95.9 per cent of revenue from carload hauls, with only 4.1 per cent resulting from l.c.l. shipments.

The Lehigh & Hudson River Railway Company assumed its present name and corporate structure on April 2, 1912, following the earlier road's acquisition of the South Easton & Phillipsburg railroad and the Mine Hill railroad. Five years earlier it had bought up the Orange County railroad, and the completed combination now made it possible for the Lehigh & Hudson to offer the efficient, time-saving, less costly interchange and bridge service on which it has since built its solid operational foundations.

Prior steps in its history had set the stage for this move. In 1889 construction was begun on the bridge across the Delaware River between Easton and Phillipsburg to establish connection with both the Lehigh Valley and the Central Railroad of New Jersey on the Pennsylvania side of the river. A year later agreement was reached with the Orange County line to permit the Lehigh & Hudson to operate between Hudson Junction, New York and Maybrook, New York. Seventeen years after this agreement the Orange County road was absorbed by the L&H, as noted above.

The year 1891 was also one of great meaning for the future of the Lehigh & Hudson River. In that year zinc ore was discovered at Franklin. Today fifteen to twenty cars of zinc ore are picked up daily and run to Allentown, where the cars are handled by the New Jersey Central to the smelting plant of the New Jersey Zinc Company at Palmerton, Pennsylvania. Together with limestone that also originates near Franklin, the zinc ore represents the bulk of the freight originating today along the right of way of the Lehigh & Hudson.

In 1891, too, construction work was started on a railway line over the Hudson River near Poughkeepsie. By providing relief for shipments to and from the New England states that had heretofore been confined to trackage on the east side of the river, the new line, in the language of the times, promised to be one that, "when completed, will no doubt so facilitate the traffic as will greatly relieve the frequent blockades that occur between Greycourt and Fishkill-on-the-Hudson."

Fourteen years later this new line of track over the Poughkeepsie bridge proved its value to the Lehigh & Hudson, for in 1906 agreement was reached between the Lackawanna and the New York, New Haven & Hartford railroads to interchange their freight traffic via that mid-Hudson span instead of over the Harlem River at New York City. This brought the strategic location of the Lehigh & Hudson's trackage into full play.

During the First World War the operation of the railroad was taken over by the United States Railroad Administration, which continued to run the line until the termination of Federal control on March 1, 1920. Much vital war material and a great many troop trains passed over L&H trackage during the period. Preparations were made during World War II also for use of the road by the military authorities as an inland route to and from

New England, in case there were an enemy attack on the Port of New York.

For a time during its history the Lehigh & Hudson handled passenger traffic, but this service has been discontinued since July 9, 1939. Since the line traversed what was, and still is, essentially an agricultural area and touched upon no large communities, passenger revenue even during peak years accounted for only a small portion of its total revenue. From 1912 to 1916 this traffic was at its highest.

In October, 1912, the Pennsylvania and the New Haven railroads, which jointly ran the famous Federal Express between Boston and Washington, decided to substitute the Poughkeepsie bridge as a route in place of the earlier—and often risky—method of transferring the train by float across New York's rivers.

This was undertaken as a temporary arrangement, since the Hell Gate bridge was under construction and was completed in January, 1916. With this span, which operates to this day for the transferral of trains between New England points and stations on the Pennsylvania Railroad, New York, New Haven & Hartford trains branch off the road's main line as they enter New York City, pass over the Hell Gate Bridge to a switch point in Queen's County, and there join the tracks of the Long Island Rail Road. From here they move underground into New York's great Pennsylvania Terminal, from which point they run under the Hudson River and out along the Pennsylvania's main line in New Jersey, bound for Washington or other points.

But the three-year use of its trackage for Boston-to-Washington passengers was not without its benefits to the Lehigh & Hudson. This arrangement hastened the laying of the main line with 100-pound rail and expedited the installation of automatic block signals along the entire L&H line, a task that was completed during 1913.

However, with the building of improved highways and the constant increase in the use of privately owned automobiles as well as of bus transportation, passenger earnings declined from a high of $116,000 in 1914 to only $1,380 in 1938. All passenger service was therefore discontinued the following year.

In addition to the fluctuation in passenger traffic, a number of other interesting changes have taken place in the character of the traffic carried by the Lehigh & Hudson over the years. In 1880, for example, milk accounted for about 50 per cent of the gross revenue of the old Warwick Valley line, predecessor to the L&H. In fact the Lehigh & Hudson pioneered in transporting fluid milk to New York City, and it was the first railroad anywhere to have specially designed refrigerator milk cars built for the express purpose of handling that basic dairy product. But today not a drop of milk is handled by the L&H, and all agricultural products, as pointed out earlier, amount to less than 5 per cent of the road's annual revenue.

Coal, too, is another product whose changing value in our economy has been reflected in the operations of the Lehigh & Hudson. In the early days of the company's history both anthracite and bituminous coal, coming from the nearby mining areas of Pennsylvania, were important sources of revenue. Prior to 1938 this traffic consistently amounted to some 45 per cent of total annual revenue. But the gradual replacement of coal by other types of fuel brought this percentage down to about 21.5 per cent in 1953, and it continues to decline. In consequence the Lehigh & Hudson has begun an aggressive campaign to solicit other types of freight and has opened traffic offices in Boston, New Haven, New York, Pittsburgh, Detroit, and Chicago, where traffic representatives urge local shippers to consider the savings of time and money resulting from use of L&H bridge services.

The steady improvement of American railroad equipment, resulting in the need for heavier rails to sustain speedier schedules for more substantial locomotives and cars, is reflected in the rail-laying history of the Lehigh & Hudson. From 1905 to 1909 the road was completely relaid with 80-pound rail, then considered heavy enough to do the required job. Four years later, as a result of the handling of the Federal Express over its trackage, the Lehigh & Hudson completed the job of reconverting its main line to 100-pound rail. Today over half of the line's track is of the 131-pound variety, and the task of relaying the balance of the road with this weight of rail is constantly going forward.

71

For many years the railroad has had a policy of applying only ties that have been treated, and as replacement of old ties is a continuing process, some 98.6 per cent of all ties in place today have been treated prior to application. Within a very short time, as other old ties are succeeded by the newer varieties, all trackage, whether on main or branch lines or sidings, will be mounted on treated ties.

Over the years, as new equipment has succeeded old, sidings have been lengthened, yards enlarged, bridges strengthened, and new shops constructed. From the 4–4–0 Cooke locomotives that were placed in operation in 1892, through the Baldwin 2–8–0 prime movers that went into service in 1906, until the present-day diesels, the Lehigh & Hudson has constantly improved the level of its service, keeping at all times abreast of latest mechanical and technical developments.

In 1906, for example, it purchased and installed semaphore signals along its entire right of way. Automatic block signals succeeded these between Maybrook and Belvidere in 1914, and it is believed that the L&H was the first railroad in the country to install the absolute permissive block signal system. Electric accounting and tabulating equipment for the rapid and accurate calculation of freight-handling statistics and charges was first put into operation in the road's offices in 1940 and has been continually added to and expanded in the ensuing years. All radio equipment complete over all road was installed in 1957.

Working with its connecting carrier lines, the Lehigh & Hudson forms a vital part of several well-known and widely used through freight routes, such as the Central States Dispatch, the Blue Ridge Dispatch, and the Lackawanna Line. These operations, which run regularly between the Southern and Western states and the New England area, publish day and hour schedules between their various points of origin and destinations, and the traffic they carry is handled in scheduled trains over each one of the cooperating railroads whose facilities are used to make up these through routes that are of such importance to the shipper.

The nine regularly scheduled freight trains of the Lehigh & Hudson, therefore, are an integral part of the daily freight operations of a highly populated section of the United States. Without this well-run, carefully regulated 96.6 miles of track, much time would be lost in the transportation of the country's products between many of its largest industrial cities. The unsung L&H plays its important role, day in and day out, in keeping America's goods on the move.

In Bob Huyler, its president, the L&H boasts of a completely rounded railroad man, who has one of the industry's leading financial heads. Its vice president and general auditor, Harold Quinlan, is an able authority on his work. R. G. Winchester, general freight traffic manager, is one of the best posted freight traffic men I know. And P. W. Early, Superintendent, is a fine operator who was made on the Reading. This line-up completes the big four who keep the wheels rolling on this amazing little property.

CHAPTER XII

THE CHESAPEAKE & OHIO

It Gets Better and Better—Fast Freights, Car Ferries, Coal, and Perishables

The story of American industry during the postwar years has been that of a trend toward diversification. Successful business organizations have found that it is profitable to manufacture and distribute more than one kind of product. Such a policy tends to protect a huge producer against the effects of a possible sales slump in any one field, and it leads to economies of production and management all along the line.

That is why today a company formerly known for its chemical products only is manufacturing and selling perfumes, firearms, bicycles, and other diverse items as well, and why the nation's leading producer of razor blades now manufactures automatic pencils too.

The benefits of diversification as a sound business policy have also been brought to the attention of the nation's railroad executives. In the recent history of the Chesapeake & Ohio railroad there can be seen a primary example of how a major railway has taken advantage of this new trend to increase its volume of operations.

C&O retains its long-time position as the nation's leading carrier of coal. Yet its more than $150,000,000 total annual freight revenue in non-coal haulage represents about 49 per cent of its total income from all freight. Just prior to World War II the percentage of non-coal freight hauled by C&O was only about 33 per cent. The broader base has resulted from a deliberate campaign on the part of the road's management to improve serv-

74

ice and to attract new industries to its rails during the past ten years.

The biggest single factor in the change, as has been the case with so many other industrial companies, was a merger. In 1947 the C&O acquired the Pere Marquette, thus bringing into its organization an extensive, already developed merchandise traffic. The merging of the two roads, each with its separate traffic characteristics, immediately resulted in a more stable, more efficient railroad operation.

The newly merged lines have benefited greatly from the industrial development that has taken place along the lines of the two districts. Modern sales promotion techniques, combined with the addition of needed freight services, served to develop the potential that lay in the establishment of new industries and the enlargement of older ones along the right of way.

To add to its previous concentration on coal haulage, the C&O freights now move chemicals and petroleum products, cement from both Michigan and Virginia, glass from Charleston, West Virginia, and automobiles and parts from the Detroit area. A modern C&O terminal at Newport News handles an ever increasing volume of export and import goods, including such diverse products as iron, manganese, chrome and barite, Turkish tobacco, Swedish wood pulp, meat, flour, and cigarettes. Scheduled freights move this wide variety of cargo, and well-thought-out manifest train schedules have played an important part in achieving the road's increased freight volume.

Two of these scheduled freights are No. 91, the Speedwest, and No. 90, the Expediter, its eastbound counterpart, which run the main line between Newport News and Louisville, Chicago, Columbus, Toledo, Buffalo, and the western shore of Lake Michigan. The Speedwest, for example, makes the 940 miles between Newport News and Chicago in a matter of about forty-three hours, stopping en route at only a very few junction points. Yet its stops are used to feed branch-line trains that make it possible for the C&O to serve many other communities rapidly and efficiently.

At Potomac Yard cars are made up to be delivered at Strath-

75

more, Virginia, where they are picked up by the Speedwest. Russell, Kentucky, serves as a transfer point where Speedwest cars are detached and routed to such points as Detroit, Grand Rapids, Ludington, and Buffalo, with another branch operation out of Russell picking up cars bound for Louisville.

Eight additional scheduled freights, four westbound and an equal number eastbound, operate over all or part of the same route. One of them—No. 97—picks up Florida perishables from the Clinchfield at Elkhorn City, Kentucky, a type of cargo that the C&O has expanded greatly during the last few years. Other perishables are picked up daily at Richmond, and much of this type of freight moves to the Cincinnati gateway area via interchange with the Southern Railway System.

Most railroad lines have to stop operations when their tracks reach large bodies of water, but the C&O has used the vast expanse of Lake Michigan to develop an extensive ferry service that has expanded its operations in such cities as Kewaunee, Manitowoc, and Milwaukee. Although this train ferry operation, carrying freight cars, automobiles, and passengers, has been a successful part of the road's functions for many years, millions of dollars have recently been invested to improve its services to an even greater extent.

The *Badger* and the *Spartan*—two new ships costing $10,000,-000 each—were launched in 1952. Each ferry is 410 feet long. Operating between Ludington, Michigan, and the three Wisconsin communities named above, each ship can carry 32 freight cars or 150 automobiles, plus several hundred passengers, at a speed of 18 miles per hour. Three other C&O ferryboats in this cross-lake service have been augmented by the addition of two ships acquired in the Pere Marquette merger, which were remodeled, repowered, and lengthened by 40 feet each. Thus the road runs a vital fleet of seven ferries that connect east and west across one of the country's greatest bodies of inland water.

Yards at both Ludington and Port Huron, across the state of Michigan, have been improved and enlarged, and a complete centralized traffic control system is in operation on the line that connects those two cities. At the latter community the C&O runs other ferries across the Saint Clair River into Sarnia, Ontario, from which point, on C&O rails, freight rolls through Canada and back into United States territory at Buffalo. All of the road's ferry lines—both river and lake—operate 365 days of the year, regardless of weather conditions.

At Newport News and at Presque Isle, Ohio, a port on Lake Erie, the road has constructed new heavy coal and ore docks where train-to-ship transfer is effected by means of mechanized machinery and equipment.

On the C&O northern region, two of the most important freight manifests daily are No. 42 and No. 40, both out of Chicago. No. 42 carries perishables to Detroit, where they must arrive in time for the daily morning auction. Anywhere from forty to one hundred carloads make the trip each day, spurred on by full dieselization and CTC. The cars are moved onto their interchange tracks prior to 3:00 A.M. daily, and a few hours later, empties are routed back to their point of origin for use the following day. In Detroit the produce terminal is shared by the C&O, the Wabash, and the Pennsylvania roads, and Wabash crews spot the reefers whose cargo is destined for the daily auction.

No. 40 is the fast meat train out of Chicago to the East. Some of its reefers are turned over to the Canadian Pacific, while the balance move over C&O rails to Buffalo.

The establishment of new industries along its right of way, which has had its effect on C&O volume, was not merely an accidental development of which the railroad took advantage. An important factor in this growth has been the railroad's expanded Industrial Development Department, with headquarters in Cleveland and offices at Huntington, West Virginia, and Detroit. An Industrial Research Department undertakes detailed studies of sites and prepares reports for industrial companies that express interest. Maps are always included with such reports, and the C&O has made extensive use of aerial photographs in the preparation of such maps.

The research unit is also responsible for the training of personnel in the various bureaus of the Industrial Department.

Training of personnel in modern sales and sales promotion techniques has also proved an effective factor in the C&O's new diversification policy. Formerly, like other railroads, the C&O employed young men as stenographers and then moved them up into sales positions as vacancies occurred; but this procedure can no longer be followed, since few young men today plan to enter stenographic careers. Accordingly, it has become increasingly difficult to find adequate numbers of traffic salesmen.

Today the railroad is aiming its fire at college graduates—particularly those with traffic degrees—whom it puts through an intensive training course lasting for a period of two full years. After screening them and giving them aptitude tests, the road places the successful candidates in its fifty-six traffic offices, where they learn the business under the eyes of C&O salesmen who have shown particular talent for instructional posts.

A special business car, equipped and organized for its specific purposes, is in constant use, always carrying a group of trainees on a twelve-day tour of the railroad. The student salesmen ride both freight and passenger trains, examining yards and terminal facilities under the supervision of an experienced operating man. A typical tour might run from Chicago to Detroit, Columbus, Buffalo, Russell, and Newport News.

To support its efforts at developing diversification of freight cargos, the C&O has been running a concentrated advertising campaign aimed at the industrial traffic manager. The ads, running in news, business, and traffic magazines, are addressed to men on the top management level, and point out the importance of the traffic manager.

Thus extensive use of all the key tools of modern industry is enabling the Chesapeake & Ohio to diversify its freight operations and to add profitable merchandise cargos to the coal haulage in which it leads the nation's railroads.

(Read Down)

CENTRAL-EASTERN REGIONS

95	193	393	403	93	391	891	91		Station		C.T.	90	190	92	192	292	392	492	692a	94
		400A	700P	230P	330P		700A	LV	Indiana Harbor	AR	C.T.									945P
								LV	Chicago (Rockwell)	AR	C.T.									800P
130P							1230A	LV	Norfolk (C&O Terminal)	AR		†1030A								†1030A
530P							430A	LV	Norfolk (Sewells Point)	AR										845A
830P							700A	AR	Newport News	AR		630P								345A
								LV	Richmond (Fulton)	LV		400P								1245A
1000P						530A	830A	LV	Richmond (Fulton)	AR		915A								530P
1035P						830A	915A	LV	Richmond (2nd St. Yd.)	AR		845A								500P
						1015A		LV	Potomac Yard	LV										
								AR	Lindsay	AR										
								AR	Strathmore	AR										
1030A		1030A					1030A	LV	Strathmore	LV										
		300P						AR	Charlottesville	AR										
		530P	1220P					LV	Charlottesville	LV								745A		
		930P	145P					AR	Waynesboro (U. S.)	AR								540A		
			210P					AR	Staunton	LV		545A						510A		150P
400A							100P	LV	Gladstone	AR		445A								1145A
457A							145P	LV	Lynchburg	LV		230A								930A
840A			605P				445P	AR	Clifton Forge	AR								215A		
1045A	145P			900P	215A		545P	LV	Clifton Forge	LV		115A	415P	1159P						730A
430P				130A	540A		900P	LV	Hinton	AR		1030P		800P						430A
835P				455A	845A			AR	Charleston (Elk)	AR				111P						1215A
1050P				730A	1215P			AR	Huntington	AR				1115A						1100P
1120P				830A				LV	Ashland	LV				1015A						1000P
							135A	AR	Elkhorn City	AR						400P				
1230A				900A				LV	Russell	LV		515P		950A		930A				930P
430A	915P		200P				400A	LV	Russell	AR		415P		745A	605A		435A			
	130A							AR	Lexington	C.T.							1045P			
	415A							AR	Lexington	C.T.							945P			
							700A	AR	Louisville	C.T.		130P			100A		650P			
								AR	Columbus (Parsons)	C.T.			130P							
								LV	Athens	AR									530A	
	915P							AR	Columbus (Parsons)	LV			1245P		1030P				100A	
	130A							LV	Columbus (Parsons)	AR			905A		455P					
	415A							AR	Fostoria	LV			800A		400P					
								LV	Toledo (Walbridge)	LV										
840A			630P	200P				AR	Cincinnati (Stevens)	AR		130P		400A						
310P			145A	145A			100P	LV	Cincinnati (Cheviot)	C.T.		800A		800P						615A
645P			420A	420A			430P	AR	Muncie	C.T.		445A		430P						315A
850P			700A	700A			530P	LV	Peru	C.T.		315A		300P						145A
1130P			815A	815A			700P	AR	Peru	C.T.		215A		130P						1230A
				945A				AR	La Crosse	C.T.										
330A			100P	100P				LV	Burnham	AR				1100A						1000P
500A			430P	430P			1130P	AR	Chicago (Rockwell)	C.T.		1000P		915A						830P

79

CHAPTER XIII

THE SOUTHERN PACIFIC

Its Track Is One of the Best—Here's How It Maintains It

When a railroad maintains and operates a total of 18,799 miles of track in desert country, over snow-capped mountains, and through vast plains areas, the problem of keeping such an extensive network in top operating condition requires the use of well-organized, highly extensive work forces, machinery, equipment, and supplies.

This is the problem faced by the Southern Pacific Railroad as its lines cross about three-eighths of the continental United States, through the great Southwest and up the Pacific coast to Portland. The railroad averages 1.5 miles per day of track laid somewhere along its extensive line of rails.

Main tracks that carry high-speed passenger and important freight consists now are being laid only with 132-, 115-, and 113-pound rail, with the older standard of 110- and 90-pound rail almost all removed by now from main line and relaid on sidings. As 112- and 113-pound rail is currently removed from main track, it is being assigned to duty and relaid on branch lines where traffic is not as heavy as on the main right of way. During 1955 SP installed 287 miles of track (132- and 113-pound) on its Pacific lines and another 81 miles of 113-, 115-, and 132-pound rail on its lines in Texas and Louisiana; during the ten years immediately following World War II, the railroad laid a total of 3,026 miles of track on its various main lines in different sections of the country.

With this upgrading of trackage weight, the Southern Pacific

Southern RR #3, fine new streamliner Royal Palm, running around the crack automobile special "Sparkplug" north of Somerset, Ky. showing the advantage of reverse running in CTC territory on the CNO & TP Div.

Southern Pacific Extra 6232 east running along the Humboldt River in beautiful Palisade Canyon on the Winnemucca Subdiv. of the Salt Lake Div.

Lackawanna #20, crack overnight freight train from Buffalo, heading in Hoboken, New Jersey freight yards with plenty of piggyback on the head-end.

Santa Fe new high-level El Capitan crossing Apache Creek climbing Glorieta Pass in Apache Canyon east of Lamy, N.M. junction point for Santa Fe and Indian Detour territory. Third Dist., N.M. Div.

Interior of Santa Fe's high-level sky lounge in service on the El Capitan. Steps from the lower level which also contains an attractive cafe-bar are in the center of the car.

Outside view of Santa Fe El Capitan high-level sky lounge designed and built by the Budd Co. These cars give a very quiet and smooth ride and like the other high-level cars provide the best way to view the excellent scenery along the Santa Fe.

Interior of new Santa Fe high-level coach in service on El Capitans. Note roominess between the seats making the passengers far more comfortable than they would be in deluxe sleeperettes, the best accommodation found on some airlines.

Santa Fe new high-level coach of the El Capitan built by Budd. Toilet facilities and extra space for hand baggage is on the lower deck and the low step on boarding or leaving the car is especially advantageous for older people.

Spacious dining room on Santa Fe's high-level El Capitan is largest on any railroad with facilities to serve 80 persons at one sitting. Food is sent up to the dining room on the top deck by means of two electric subveyors from the kitchen on lower level. Built by Budd.

Waiter taking tray of one of the two electric subveyors on which food is sent up to the high-level dining room on the El Capitan.

Southern Pacific Extra 6368 passing Port-rero Tower leaving Bayshore with San Francisco in the background. These S.P. truck trailers will make passenger train speed all the way to Los Angeles. This is the San Francisco Subdiv. of the Coast Div.

"Piggyback" paraphernalia occupies these eight tracks in the Los Angeles yards on a typical day. Trailers are ready for travel on the flat cars at left. Empty flat cars to right show sheet-metal "bridges" which span openings between cars when lowered so that trailers, once aboard one car, can be moved easily across the tops of several. Other fixtures atop flat cars are securing devices for parked trailers. Flat cars can be loaded from six ramps simultaneously in the Los Angeles yard. Ventura Subdiv. of the Los Angeles Div.

naturally has recorded a steady increase in the average weight of main track throughout the system, amounting to about 0.8 pounds per year. In 1953 main rail averaged 119.8 pounds. In 1946 SP boasted some 578.6 miles of 132-pound rail, a mileage figure which, by 1955, had grown to 2,179.4 miles! Trackage of 113-pound rose from 1,062.1 miles to 2,011.97—almost double— during the same period.

The road's Texas and Louisiana lines alone placed some 691.79 miles of new rail and relaid 421.69 miles of used trackage during that same postwar era. The newer, heavier rail installed in this area—113-, 115-, and 132-pound—was laid in the road's main-line operation between New Orleans and El Paso; it was also placed in the high-speed passenger and freight run that connects Dallas and Houston and in a high-speed freight line between two important Texas cargo points, Hearne and Flatonia.

Modern methods of checking wear and tear on its trackage are constantly employed by the Southern Pacific. In addition to the standard devices used by all railroads, SP uses a template-making machine that makes an actual drawing of a cross section of rail while it is still in track service. When this drawing is held up against a standard rail section drawing, the amount and location of seriously worn spots can be instantly checked and a field examination is called for. Then it can be decided whether or not the worn rail needs replacing.

Age alone, of course, cannot be the only factor used in determining whether a section of rail needs replacement. The amount of traffic and the speed of trains regularly running over a specific section will prove of importance in the condition of any piece of rail over longer or shorter periods of time. Knowledge of these factors, augmented by the template drawing checkup described above, helps SP track supervisors and maintenance engineers make their decisions. This method has proved particularly valuable in keeping curved sections of track in proper service condition, where there is a constant tendency toward flattening on the low side. H. M. Williamson, SP's assistant engineer for maintenance of way and structures, has said that this two-step system insures for the road a uniform standard for renewing curve rail all through the Southern Pacific system.

On a railroad line that must stand up under so many different kinds of extreme weather and such great variations in temperature, a replacement program must be worked out taking those factors into consideration. For example, even though a particular section of curve track may show up in its various tests to be serviceable for several months to come, it may be that railroad officials will decide to replace it at the time of testing rather than risk waiting for the balance of its indicated life. For by then it may be necessary to replace it by working in an area covered with snowdrifts some fifteen feet high.

Mechanization has affected not only SP's methods of track checking but the organization and complexion of rail gangs as well. Medium-sized extra gangs, averaging forty to fifty men each, working on individual divisions of the road, do its rail-laying. Extensive use of trucks and of rail-side roads is made to transport not only the work gangs but machines and materials too.

Since 1952 system gangs have been responsible for laying about 80 per cent of all new rail, except on the Pacific lines, where system steel gangs are not employed.

Each gang of some fifty men has been found to be able to average about a half-mile of new track per working day, and the over-all system gains about 1.5 miles of new rail each twenty-four hours. By careful planning and by shifting its work gangs to strategic points, SP is able to take advantage of the wide geographic area it covers to make it possible to do some track-laying work somewhere along its extensive system at all times of the year, regardless of extreme weather conditions in other areas that the line serves.

But Southern Pacific engineers and executives know that track-laying operations are only one part of the program of maintaining an effective steel highway for the transportation of people and things across a nation. Track maintenance must always be given close attention if the newly laid rail is to prove of maximum benefit to the railroad's performance.

Large jobs, such as out-of-face surfacing, out-of-face ballasting, rail relays, tie renewals, street or road crossing renewals, scaling of bluffs, grouting roadbed, and the like, are handled by special or by extra gangs. This plan presents a twofold advantage: the men engaged in this type of work soon become specialists in it, while the section gangs can be used solely to concentrate on the lighter tasks connected with ordinary track maintenance.

Modern machines, constantly under experimentation for possible improvements, are used by SP. In rock ballast territory, gangs are always equipped with small compressors capable of operating two to four tamping guns, with clay spade, digging forks, and other power equipment of that type. As work requirements make necessary, machines like cross grinders, joint-oilers, tie-pushers, and bolters are shifted from section to section. Gangs on the Texas and Louisiana lines are equipped with 150 air-powered spot tampers and 128 electric tampers. The use of this type of machinery has resulted in a diminution of the "personal factors" often found in manual labor, where the amount of work performed by various individuals will greatly differ, and has tended to more nearly equalize the output per individual man. Over-all costs of track maintenance have been reduced through the use of this kind of equipment, and more uniform track work throughout the entire system has also resulted, as well as a speeding up of production. Two power ballasters added to the Texas and Louisiana lines gangs' equipment during the past few years, plus such tools as a power cribber, lining and surfacing scopes, a Jack-all, and ballast regulators have also been found to add to the general level of efficient operation.

The Pacific lines in a five-year period surfaced 1,512 miles under new rail and 800 miles under second-hand rail, while 810 miles were surfaced in Texas and Louisiana during that same time. Adding to this another 700 miles of surfacing on other sections of the vast SP lines, a total is indicated of some 3,822 miles that have been out-of-face surfaced by the Southern Pacific Railroad during this period, with more under way at the present time.

Multiple tampers are being used extensively to speed up this surfacing task and to improve its quality. Large off-track air compressors, capable of operating from twelve to sixteen tamping guns, aid in this work, and in some cases it has been found practicable to perform out-of-face surfacing by doubling up the smaller compressor units.

The variety of climatic conditions through which SP track runs also affects the surfacing program. On some stretches of track it has been found that, with section gangs keeping it in good condition, ten years or more may safely elapse between surfacing jobs. Other sections may require a regular out-of-face surfacing project every five years because of extreme temperatures or moisture content. Road officials estimate eight years as a good average over-all figure for the entire SP system.

Although work programing is used extensively by the road, local peculiarities in many sections make it necessary to permit some deviations at the discretion of the section supervisor, who is held responsible for watching the development of conditions limited to his specific area of operation and for adjusting his gangs' work schedules accordingly.

The Southern Pacific equipment shop at Oakland, California, is constantly experimenting with and developing new equipment to be used by the railroad in its track maintenance program. A tunnel-cleaner, which has drastically cut the cost of removing fouled ballast from tunnels, is one of its products, as is a new multiple tamper, two of which have been built and are constantly in use somewhere along the system's lines.

Near the road's general shops at Sacramento another such shop is maintained, which specializes in equipment needed for reclamation and rebuilding of frogs and switches. The road has a 16½-foot and a heavy duty 24-foot switch and a frog planer and a twelve-spindle inclined drill press for frogs, which makes quick work of drilling bolt holes. Two twelve-spindle vertical drill presses are also being built. With acetylene welding used to build up worn manganese frogs, this shop fabricates and flame-hardens some thousand switch stock rails a year.

Ballasting, as performed on Southern Pacific's main lines, is essentially a refresher project undertaken in connection with ballasting operations. In a recent five-year period this amounted to a total of 3,822 miles, followed by a twelve-month period in which 29 miles of cinder ballast was replaced with crush rock and about 645 miles of reballasting in connection with surfacing was scheduled.

The SP was a pioneer in the use of scientific rail-testing equipment. The road owns and operates two detector cars with which it tests some 5,000 miles of track each year, about 90 per cent of which is main-line rail. The use of these two cars enables the SP to test each foot of its Pacific main line and important sidings three times every year. Another car, leased by the road, is used for track-testing purposes on the Texas and Louisiana lines, and checks some 4,000 miles there each year.

This rail-testing program is augmented by the use of nine portable Audigage units, which are employed generally to check wing rails of frogs and heels on main-line switch points. It is possible with these nine units to cover the entire SP system once a month.

Tie replacement also plays an important part in Southern Pacific's track maintenance program. In the period from January 1, 1946, through June 30, 1955, the railroad's Pacific lines alone installed a grand total of 8,355,935 new ties! That figure includes 6,195,576 on main lines, 1,266,404 on branch lines, and 893,955 on sidings. By the end of 1955 the Pacific lines had planned to install an additional 860,000 ties.

During the same time the Texas and Louisiana lines placed 5,504,029 ties and had scheduled a tie-laying program totaling some 500,000 for 1955.

Second-hand ties are also used, when in reasonably good condition, on less important trackage sections, because it has been found that ties removed from main track as a result of mechanical wear will last for many years if reinstalled in tracks that are scheduled to carry only light traffic.

Three SP plants are employed to treat the ties used on the road's Pacific lines. Douglas fir, plus a few pine and hemlock ties, brought from the northwest section of the country, are treated at Eugene, Oregon, and at West Oakland, California, while a

85

plant at Alamogordo, New Mexico, treats mostly gum, plus some representation of oak and pine. The two western plants use 25 per cent creosote by weight and 75 per cent petroleum, with impregnation done by the Bolton & Rueping pressure system.

Track-laying and track maintenance have gone a long way in the hundred years since the laying of the first rail of what is now part of the Southern Pacific railroad in the Sacramento valley. But constant improvements in rolling stock, faster and heavier trains, and increased demands for both passenger and freight service have brought scientific methods into track-laying and track maintenance work. The Southern Pacific, ever mindful that change never comes to a halt and that progress is a continuing thing, devotes its time, finances, and energies to an unceasing search for new and improved methods.

CHAPTER XIV

PIGGYBACK ON THE LACKAWANNA

This Road Was One of the Leaders in This Important Development

When the trucking industry first began to compete with the nation's railroads as haulers of cargo, little did its leaders imagine that a technique borrowed from a favorite game of every child would provide the means by which the railroads are now rapidly regaining much of their lost traffic.

"Pickaback" is a word that Webster's dictionary defines as "on the back or shoulders," and there is barely a person anywhere whose daddy did not supply him with this universal means of transportation as a youngster. But "pickaback" is not an easy word for little shavers to say, and so it has come down through the years as "piggyback."

Today many of the nation's railroads, notable among them the Lackawanna, are using this device to serve shippers more efficiently, more rapidly, and at lower cost than has been possible before. As applied to cargo haulage, piggyback is actually a "trailer on a flatcar" service, in which freight is loaded into a motor vehicle semitrailer, moved from the shipper's place of business right through city streets to a rail terminal, loaded onto a railroad flatcar, and hauled to its distant destination, where the reverse process takes place.

This type of movement provides for only one loading and one unloading operation, since the freight remains in the trailer throughout the entire door-to-door shipment. With this method, no longer is it necessary to load cargo onto a truck, drive it to a rail terminal, unload and reload into a freight car, and then go through the same duplicating process at the other end.

The Lackawanna's most recent and boldest drive for business has a background that goes back a century and more. Today, together with sixteen connecting roads, it provides piggyback service reaching more than six hundred points, including thirty major city areas, throughout the country.

Historical records reveal that as early as 1843 the principle was applied of carrying freight loaded aboard one medium of transportation by hauling the entire carrier on another medium of transportation. From that year until 1857, sectionalized canal boats carrying cargo were transported on flatcars between Philadelphia and Columbia, and between Hollidaysburg and Johnstown, as part of a Philadelphia-to-Pittsburgh combined rail-and-water service.

Farmers' trains carrying four loaded produce wagons per flatcar were introduced by the Long Island Rail Road in 1885, while the carrying of railroad freight cars on barges is a sight common in many of the nation's great harbors. But the first application of the idea of placing a loaded motor vehicle trailer on a flatcar is believed to have taken place in the Chicago-Milwaukee area in 1926, and similar services were instituted in other parts of the country during the 1930's.

Development of this type of service was not rapid, however, and began to assume major proportions only about 1952. The most recently established services of this kind, including the Lackawanna's, differ from earlier ones by virtue of being entirely operated by the railroads themselves. In previous years, while the concept was being developed and expanded, it was usual for the shipper to make his arrangements with the motor carrier operator, who in turn made his contract with the railroad for the shipment of the loaded trailer from rail terminal to rail terminal.

Now the shipper deals directly with the railroad, and the freight moves over its entire journey—door to door—on a railroad bill of lading at rates established by the railroad and published in regular rail tariff form. Pickup and delivery in the rail terminal area is performed by truckers having their own contractual relationship with the railroad, but the shipper has no concern with such arrangements.

The trailers themselves are owned outright or leased by the Lackawanna, in exactly the same manner that the railroad owns or leases its freight cars.

On July 30, 1954, the Interstate Commerce Commission issued a series of important decisions growing out of new legal questions that had arisen as a result of this change in relationship among shipper, motor carrier, and railroad. For one thing, the ICC decided that no motor carrier certificate would be required for trailers riding flatcars; it found also that collection and delivery of trailers at rail terminal points would be regulated by the rail section of the Interstate Commerce Act, not by the motor section.

These conclusions are important, since, covering the basic issues that have arisen, they now offer assurance as to fundamental legal principles with which both shippers and carriers are concerned. The Lackawanna, as well as the other interested railroads, is now enabled to proceed with plans for extending and broadening these services, secure in the knowledge of the correctness of its legal position.

Much interesting and unique special equipment has been developed and procured by the Lackawanna for this piggyback service. Of course the facilities generally used by railroads—locomotives, signals, rails, roadbeds, yards—are essential, but in addition much extra equipment is needed.

Ramps or depressed-well track arrangements have been constructed at terminal points, so that trailers can be backed into position by their prime mover motor cabs, and then backed on or hauled off the flatcars. The cars themselves have been fitted with jacks, tie-down chains, and blocks, as well as with guide rails at the sides of each car floor, and end ramps that enable the trailer to be moved on and off the car by a tractor or motor cab.

Anchor chain brackets, usually four or more, have been attached to the trailers themselves, where they remain permanently since they do not in any way interfere with the normal operation of the trailers when they are being hauled along highways or city streets. It is a relatively simple task, however, to remove the jacks and the other extra equipment from the flatcars when it is desired to use them in ordinary service for other than piggyback operations.

The Lackawanna's flatcars are 40 feet long and have been equipped with all the special tie-down equipment and guide rails in the road's own Keyser Valley shops. Trailers acquired by the railroad vary in length from 26 or 28 feet to 30 and 32 feet. The smaller trailers are used primarily for l.c.l. operations, providing an additional service for shippers whose freight does not reach carload proportions. Many of the larger trailers are tandem axle models, permitting handling of heavier loads within legal highway regulatory limits.

There are some open-top trailers too in the Lackawanna service; these are principally employed when loading or unloading at the shipper's or consignee's place of business is done by crane.

Once the trailer has been backed onto the flatcar, it is a simple matter for the Lackawanna's capable and experienced hands to tie down side hangers and to securely fix the trailer for its journey between rail terminal points.

Trailers on the Lackawanna piggyback service move on the railroad's fast freights. Currently, overnight service is provided between the New York–Newark area and Buffalo, with second-morning delivery at Chicago, Cleveland, Detroit, and St. Louis.

On the western move the trailers depart the Lackawanna's eastern terminal point, Hoboken, New Jersey, at 9:30 P.M., on train HB-3, arriving at Buffalo the following morning. Here connections are established with NKP train NCS-5 for Chicago, St. Louis, and Cleveland, and with train Advance 91 of the Wabash road for Chicago, Detroit, and St. Louis.

A new train, No. 20, established by the Lackawanna primarily for this trailer service, makes the eastern move, leaving East Buffalo every day at 5:30 P.M., following connections with NKP train CSN-2 from Chicago, St. Louis, and Cleveland and with Wabash 82 from Chicago, St. Louis, and Detroit. It arrives at 5:30 the next morning at Secaucus, New Jersey, where the trailers are unloaded from the flatcars and hauled by prime mover to their destinations in the great metropolitan area of New York City and nearby New Jersey.

Shippers are particularly pleased with the development of l.c.l. piggyback service, which is a feature of the Lackawanna's trailer operations. This represents a great improvement in service for smaller shippers, particularly in the metropolitan district areas of Newark and Passaic, New Jersey, where intermediate transfers have been completely eliminated, and the Lackawanna is planning extension of l.c.l. service to several other points along its lines.

The piggyback techniques need not be restricted to trailer loads of manufactured commodities. Experiments are already in progress with the hauling of milk in tank trucks loaded on flatcars.

In both rates and service the Lackawanna piggyback operation provides a technique that is truly competitive with motor carriers. Shippers making use of the trailer operation find that the railroad gives them a fast, dependable, delivery schedule, not nearly so subject to weather delays as is long-distance truck shipping.

The high-speed freight trains that the Lackawanna uses in its piggyback service have convincingly proved their reliability and dependability and have operated generally well in accordance with announced schedules.

Shippers also find that less damage is likely to occur to cargo, since two handling operations are completely eliminated when piggyback shipping is used. The possibility of damaged or broken crates that may occur in loading freight cars from trucks and then reversing the process at the other terminal does not exist with piggyback, since these two transshipping operations are no longer necessary. And, with roadbeds normally in better condition than many highways, the cargo gets much smoother riding when the trailer makes its long jump on the back of a flatcar.

Piggyback, as pioneered and developed by the Lackawanna, is giving shippers an opportunity to move merchandise in a smooth, fast-riding, reliable, door-to-door operation at rates they can readily consult in publicly available tariff tables.

James L. Barngrove, Jr., able general traffic manager of the Lackawanna, is one of the big piggyback minds in this country, and with Traffic Vice-President Harry Schmidt, another most able all-around traffic and rate expert, making up the other member of the head end crew, it is little wonder that this program has proved so successful.

CHAPTER XV

THE SOUTHERN'S FINE PASSENGER SERVICE

It Gives the People of Dixieland New Trains, New Facilities, New Cars

The Southern Railway System, which includes the Southern Railway, the CNO&TP, the AGS, the NO&NE, and the GS&F railroads, is well aware that transporting passengers by rail is big business in Dixieland. Its annual passenger revenues are well over $25,000,000—an important part of Southern's over-all operations, amounting to more than 10 per cent of total income.

To develop this business to its fullest extent, the Southern Railway System has invested about $15,000,000 since the end of World War II in a gigantic modernization program; it has initiated several crack streamliners, re-equipped important trains with some 150 or more new passenger cars, improved services, impressed employees with the advantages of courteous dealings with travelers, increased the comfort factor, and even modernized its famous yellow and black timetable folder.

Today it is the South's biggest mover of people. Its fleet of about 1,100 passenger-train car units includes some 150 streamlined types, added in an effort to hold the business of thousands who as GI's or civilians switched to rail traffic when wartime restrictions prevailed on bus, private car, and plane transportation. The railroad estimates that about half of those it carried during the war years had never before been on a railroad train; thus their introduction to rail transportation came at a time when trains were badly overcrowded, and when, through no fault of the Southern, rail service was slow and relatively poor. These conditions served to prejudice many against railroad travel, and a large part of Southern's efforts since the end of the war has been directed at overcoming these earlier impressions.

The program has met with outstanding success, and today four of the road's streamliners are consistent money-makers. The Southerner, running from New York to New Orleans; the New Royal Palm, carrying passengers from the Great Lakes area and Cincinnati to Florida; the Tennessean, plying the rails between New York and Memphis; the Crescent, which also runs between New York and New Orleans—each of these shows a high rate of steady profit for the Southern.

Supplementing its new streamlined coaches, the railroad continually employs the facilities of its shop at Hayne, South Carolina, to modernize older rolling stock. New reclining seats, modernized lounge and wash rooms, and air-conditioning feature the upgraded cars that come rolling off the reconditioning lines at Hayne.

Part of Southern's campaign to increase travelers' acceptance of railroading as a primary method of transportation is wisely aimed at Dixie's younger people. Small children in the South's elementary schools enjoy the thrill of riding trains on prearranged station-to-station trips. The youngsters purchase their own tickets (at special reduced rates), ride on an up-to-date streamliner, experience the sensation of rail travel, and are furnished with specially prepared kits of printed matter that tell them many fascinating facts about the operations of a major railroad.

High school students are also encouraged to ride the Southern. Senior class annual pilgrimages to Washington receive the benefits of a special excursion rate, while low-cost round-trip fares are also offered for group journeys involving twenty-five or more people, of whatever age or occupation. Special trains are run to important football games, to state fairs, to industrial and agricultural exhibits, etc. Encouraging people to use rail travel through special inducements of this type means more business for the Southern in the future.

That this program is paying off is indicated by the fact that the average passenger on the Southern Railway System's lines traveled 300 miles in 1957—about two-and-one-half times the average established just prior to the war. Passenger traffic on the Southern today remains fairly steady all year round; there is some increase noted during the winter months, when vacationers seek out the warm climate of Florida's resorts, but this peak is leveling with the development of Florida as a year-round vacation area.

The longer average passenger run that Southern has noted in recent years has been accompanied, of course, by adverse effects on short-run local trains, where competition from private automobiles and local bus runs daily becomes more intense. To guard against undue losses in this area of its operations, the system keeps close watch on the financial record of every passenger train, and it takes steps to discontinue those that become unprofitable, although this often proves to be a difficult and time-consuming process. In 1951 alone, however, Southern saved about $200,000 by eliminating local trains that were no longer showing a profit. In the period 1947 to 1953, about 5,500 miles of operation were discontinued for this reason, with an accompanying saving of over $1,000,000 each year.

But even this unfortunate series of service discontinuations has proved beneficial to the railroad's passengers. For the sums saved by eliminating local runs have been applied to improvements on long-run operations. Even main-line trains of secondary importance today are better equipped and offer better service than ever before; prior to the war, for example, virtually every Southern coach was of the conventional 69-foot, 88-passenger type, whereas now many of the coaches are the more comfortable, more luxurious 85-foot length, seating only 52 travelers. And today every Southern Railway System passenger train is drawn by powerful, fast, smooth-running diesel units.

The diesel program, in fact, has proved to be the most important single factor in the Southern's ability to improve its passenger service. From the time six 750-horsepower motor cars were purchased for local haulage, back in 1939, through the purchase in 1941 of road-type diesels to move the Tennessean and the Southerner, diesels have enabled the railroad to operate

95

longer trains (carrying greater numbers of passengers and consequently bringing the road increased revenue) with no discomfort to its travelers, with increased ratio of on-time performance, and with less dirt and grime.

But new locomotives and new cars alone will not guarantee increased passenger use of railroad transportation, and the Southern has supplemented its improved equipment program with other modernized factors. Since it is not a high-speed road, the Southern system concentrates on giving its passengers comfort and convenience. Continual surveys are in progress, and schedules are changed whenever a considerable proportion of the traveling public indicates that such a shift in time would be more convenient.

To guarantee maximum comfort to the Crescent's passengers, railroad officers rode this train's new equipment between Atlanta and Washington for five complete round trips. Connected by telephone with personnel stationed in various parts of the train, an observer located in the diesel cab called off the mileposts and the train speed at the beginning of each curve; the observers in the coaches, the sleepers, and the dining cars then recorded their reactions. As a result, timetable changes were made to insure smoother, more pleasant riding, by trimming speed on some curves and stepping it up elsewhere, at points where passenger comfort would not be sacrificed for such added speed.

Improved service in dining cars is also offered by the Southern, with special consideration being given to preparation and serving of food in line with the road's philosophy that a meal in the diner can be the high spot of a trip for the traveler. The road refuses to yield to the modern trend toward speeding up dining car turnover by eliminating side dishes, and follows a policy of serving a full, unhurried meal at all times.

The road has built modern, comfortable, pleasant depots and local stations in many areas. It has increased its efforts to provide adequate service for those desiring to make reservations or just to obtain information. Some two dozen off-line ticket offices, many of which have direct telephone service to the on-line agencies, have been set up in large cities throughout the country.

Through modern machinery, ticket-selling operations have been speeded up, and even the road's timetables have been redesigned and printed in type that is easier to read than formerly.

Southern officials realize that passenger operations can be highly profitable to their road, and they are therefore concentrating their efforts to give better service to more people, thus encouraging more widespread use of the rails as a means of pleasant, comfortable, reliable travel.

New Passenger Cars

A combined program of purchase of 141 passenger cars of the newest type, plus extensive renovations of older cars, has resulted in postwar upgrading of the Southern Railway System's passenger equipment to a point at which the road's facilities for its travelers now rank with the best in the country.

Southern took stock of its passenger car status with the close of armed hostilities in 1945. Recognition of the need for acquiring much new equipment was tempered by a realization that the road's entire fleet of 1,100 passenger cars could not be replaced entirely by newly purchased equipment, because funds were also needed for many other types of equipment and service improvements.

Solution to the problem was arrived at through placing of orders for 141 new streamlined cars—of which 101 were delivered to Southern, at a total investment of $11,500,000—including 43 coaches, 72 sleepers, 14 dining cars and 12 head-end units. The 40 remaining cars were paid for by other railroads over which the through streamliners of the Southern operate.

The system's top trains—the Southerner, the Tennessean, the Royal Palm, and the Crescent—were equipped with the new streamlined units, making it possible to release their older streamlined cars for use with other trains. However, postwar demand, plus materials shortages and strikes in key industries, resulted in a delay of about four years before the last cars in the huge order were actually delivered.

During this period of waiting for the new equipment, Southern's car shops at Hayne, near Spartanburg, South Carolina, and at Citico, near Chattanooga, were kept fully occupied with the considerable task of modernizing a great many of the railroad's older coaches and diners, and with the conversion of about a hundred obsolete cars into head-end units. So efficient was the work of these two yards that passengers even today often find it hard to tell whether they are riding in brand-new streamliners or in older coaches that have been redesigned and rebuilt.

For example, one group of fifteen coaches was completely stripped down to underframe and shell and then rebuilt from these bases at Hayne. As reconstructed, these coaches feature Dreamliner-type reclining seats, fluorescent overhead lights, individually controlled reading lights, blue night lights, illuminated seat numbers, and double-pane breather-type windows that screen out 25 per cent of the heat rays and 40 per cent of the glare on a hot, sunny day.

In addition, to accommodate modern trends in personal luggage, aluminum baggage racks that are 24 inches wide have been installed. In both the main passenger section and the lounge areas, side and end walls have been faced with attractive, long-wearing Formica, while color schemes throughout the new cars are blended of restful pastels.

Steam-jet air-conditioning, as well as zone heating with fin-type radiators, make the new cars all-weather comfortable. New welded sides and turtleback roofs present an exterior appearance of contemporary lines, enhanced by the use of flush-set windows. Pneumatic automatic openers have been installed in end doors, and composition flooring has been laid over new steel flooring and cross-bearers, surmounted by a rubber tile surface.

Hayne supplemented this type of output by converting seventy-two old tourist sleepers into 80-foot baggage cars, and by making 50-foot box express cars out of twenty-five older all-steel box cars. The tourist cars were converted in a six-stage operation, where wooden clerestory roofs were replaced with welded steel turtlebacks, side sheets were applied over earlier window openings, new side and door posts were placed, large baggage doors were cut in, new wooden flooring was installed, and steel antislip plates were set in opposite the newly placed doors.

The cars were then moved on to the sand blast house, the paint shop, and, in a final step, the coach shop, where new interior fittings were installed. While these processes were being carried out, the trucks were separately being overhauled in another area of the Hayne shops, where they were rebuilt and reinforced to increase their capacity to 100,000 pounds from the previous 80,000-pound limit.

This program carries out and extends a modernization plan initiated by Southern as early as 1937, when the road began to install air-conditioning in its cars. As of today, a total of 483 cars are thus equipped, while some 157 units have roller bearings. Mechanical refrigeration systems are standard equipment on many of the system's new dining cars and on some of the older, rebuilt dining units.

Strict attention to sanitation and cleanliness is a keynote of Southern's passenger car operations. At each terminal, every car gets a thorough going over with chemical cleaners, while crews work on both the roof and the sides of every passenger car; an alkali is applied during this step to counteract any affects on the stainless steel that may have arisen from the application of the first acid cleaning coating.

Stainless steel girder sheets have been used exclusively in these new cars, in place of the more usual low-alloy sheets, to minimize possible corrosion from the cleaning compounds.

CHAPTER XVI

SANTA FE'S NEW EL CAPITAN

High Level, Luxury Coach Train Built by Budd

The Santa Fe system's popular El Capitan, famous all-chair-car transcontinental streamliner, has gone "Hi-Level."

Following two years of experimentation, during which two of the new cars were operated as part of the conventional train, the road is now running complete hi-level units, each consisting of seven chair cars, a hi-level dome lounge car, and a hi-level diner.

The new El Capitan equipment, built by the Budd Company, is 15½ feet in height, or two feet higher than conventional equipment. Passengers, seated in comfortable reclining seats eight feet above the rails, are treated to a panoramic view of the countryside from a vantage point a full four feet higher than in the regular chair car. The extra elevation also provides the rider with smoother and more enjoyable transportation, because there is less noise and vibration than in the conventional car.

The double-level arrangement of the ultramodern cars eliminates vestibules and provides for twenty-eight more seats in each car than were formerly carried on the older El Capitan coaches. The new train thus has a capacity of 496 passengers in its seven hi-level coaches, compared with the earlier capacity of 350 persons in eight cars.

Doors are located on both sides of each car directly in the center of the coach, and are built at platform level. As passengers enter these easily accessible center doors, they climb a short stairway to the coach compartment, which extends the full length of the car on the upper level.

Space on the lower level, on each side of the center stairway, is utilized for luggage, which is handed to the porter as the passengers enter. A special locking device makes it possible for the attendant to keep all baggage securely under lock and key until it is called for. The luggage is unloaded at stations from the outside, through a separate opening in the side of the car. In this way the vestibule is kept clear for rapid and easy loading and discharge of passengers.

In addition to space for baggage, the lower level has ample room for all service equipment, auxiliary power units, air-conditioning equipment, generators, batteries, etc. By designing a special central corridor running the length of the car on its lower level, Santa Fe has made it possible for all this equipment to be serviced, if required, from the inside of the coach while the train is in motion.

The upper level of each new coach is the last word in modern design and riding comfort. Each car has sixty-seven rotating and reclining seats upholstered in foam rubber and covered in a handsome blue needlepoint. To give passengers adequate headroom while passing from one coach to another the center aisle is depressed. Carpeting is of a special cactus design, and colors of the Indian Southwest prevail in the new cars.

Each modern hi-level car is fully equipped with a public address system carrying recorded music, radio programs, and train announcements.

One of the pet peeves of the experienced railroad traveler has been completely eliminated by the design of El Capitan's new hi-level dining car. With all kitchen work confined to the lower level (occupying the same relative area as that used for baggage and service equipment in the coaches) waiting in line in the traditional narrow corridor next to a steamy kitchen is no longer necessary. With all dining service on the upper level, provision has been made for seating eighty diners at a time.

All food is transported from the kitchen to the dining area by means of two elevators, and the separation of the two phases of preparation and serving has resulted in quieter, more comfortable dining rooms combined with more efficient, faster service.

The dome-type hi-level lounge cars each seat a total of eighty-six passengers on two decks. On the upper level dome windows run the entire length of the car, providing unusual visual opportunities for the sixty passengers on the upper deck. Lower deck space, where twenty-six additional riders enjoy the scenery through 56-inch picture windows, is utilized by a refreshment bar, a newsstand, rest rooms for the convenience of passengers, and the service equipment that is also found on the lower level of the coaches and diner.

For a period of two years Santa Fe regularly attached two of its new hi-level coaches to the regular El Capitan streamlined cars in order to test passenger reaction. The two cars were joined together at the ends having upper-level doors, while stairways led down to join the cars of conventional level at the other end of each coach.

Passenger representatives rode the hi-level cars, checking performance and discussing the new coaches with the passengers. Today the railroad has a huge file of reports proving that the overwhelming majority of riders were highly enthusiastic about the new cars.

One man said, "This is the most comfortable chair car I've ever ridden," while another wrote to Santa Fe to tell the railroad that his trip in a hi-level coach was "the smoothest and most comfortable ride I've ever had."

During each trip for that two-year period a survey was conducted among its passengers. Features that the riders said they liked included less track noise, smoother riding quality, the advantage of a view from a higher-than-normal point, lower-level baggage storage, and the larger rest rooms that the new cars' design makes possible.

On a typical run late in 1954, for example, seventy-three out of the seventy-nine passengers reported that they approved of the new cars. But the surveys and interviews also helped Santa Fe to make improvements, all of which have been incorporated into the thirty-five hi-level coaches, the six hi-level sky lounge cars, and the six hi-level diners that have been delivered to make up the consist of the 39½-hour Chicago–Los Angeles El Capitans.

Some passengers, for instance, suggested that small racks be placed near the seats on the upper levels for hats and small hand luggage that they wanted to keep with them during the run. Another problem involved the inconvenience experienced by elderly or infirm persons who preferred not to be required to go upstairs and downstairs to make use of the washrooms on the lower level. Both of these objections have been met and overcome by the road, and in the new El Capitan hi-level coaches there are small package racks near the seats as well as two washrooms at one end of the upper level of the lounge car.

The new hi-level streamliners provide Santa Fe with great opportunities for economy of operation and maintenance. With greater seating capacity, fewer cars will handle a great number of passengers. Increased diner capacity also means greater economy of operation, while at peak periods additional passengers can be accommodated with snack-type meals served in the lower level of the lounge car.

While the hi-level coaches are heavy cars, their additional capacity gives them a considerable edge when figured on a weight-per-passenger basis. Each coach weighs about 2,300 pounds, but divided among its eighty passengers, it averages some 250 pounds less than the conventional equipment that it has replaced.

To introduce its ultramodern concept in railroad travel to the American public, the Santa Fe staged a public exhibition of the new hi-level El Capitan from mid-June through early July, 1956, just prior to putting the new cars into service. The train was enthusiastically hailed by long lines of viewers in the dozen cities from coast to coast where it was on display during that period. Communities whose citizens had an opportunity to see the new train on exhibit included Washington, Pittsburgh, Youngstown, Cleveland, Detroit, Chicago, Kansas City, Los Angeles, Pasadena, San Bernardino, San Diego, and Long Beach.

The new train was officially inaugurated on Sunday, July 8, when the initial eastbound and westbound El Capitans met at Albuquerque, New Mexico, during the two hundred and fiftieth anniversary celebration of that city. Regular daily service was put into effect gradually thereafter, as sufficient equipment arrived from the Budd Company factory.

Structural design features of the new equipment make it possible to include a depressed floor section between the trucks, which accounts for the ability of the cars to hold all the extra equipment, as described above, on their lower levels. Each car has its own diesel-generating equipment, and the extra load required for the kitchen is furnished by two 60-kilowatt Caterpillar D318 units, which supply the volume of 220-volt three-phase alternating current that the electric kitchen needs.

Under-floor fuel tanks in the diner supplement the main fuel tanks that are built into the end underframe assemblies of each of the new hi-level cars. These and underframe units are constructed of fabricated, arc-welded, low-alloy, high-tensile steel, while the remainder of the car structure and sheathing is made of stainless steel. Another variety of this universally applicable metal—carbon steel—is used in the interior lining of equipment spaces and on some of the lower-level partitions.

Aluminum backed with felt sound-deadening material has been employed for the linings of the side and end walls of each of the cars, as well as for upper-level ceilings. Stairwell walls and wainscoting make use of Westinghouse laminated Micarta, while Formica has been employed for pier panels. Ceilings on the lower levels, partitions, and interior doors have been fabricated of plywood, which has been faced on each side with zinc-coated steel. Stainless steel lines the entrance areas of each car.

Specially designed Pyle-National multivent ceiling panels, combined with side slots, provide for the necessary air distribution to the upper levels of each new car. Lower levels obtain their ventilation through a bulkhead system that employs Triflex grills.

Dining cars and lounge cars also have an additional four-ton evaporator-blower that meets their special needs, providing the kitchen and the lower lounge each with 1,200 cubic feet per minute air delivery.

Two electrically driven ten-ton Trane compressors are the source for refrigeration in each of the hi-level cars of the new El

Capitan, the coaches and lounge car having two separate dry-type condensers, while the diner has a single split-type condenser. The equipment section of each diner contains as well three additional small compressors for food refrigeration equipment, while the needs of the lounge cars in this respect are met by two such units.

Steam heating is provided for in all cars, using a modified Vapor unizone system, which includes fin-type radiation on both levels of each car. To provide maximum protection under adverse temperature conditions for water tanks and diesel engines, automatically controlled equipment has been installed to heat the lower-level areas. This is supplemented by separate manually controlled units, which can be thrown into operation whenever necessary.

No window curtains are provided for upper-level windows in the hi-level lounge cars, but Adlake curved double-glazed sash units are set in the roof, to create an effect much like that obtained in the dome cars of recent vintage.

All the cars were built in accordance with Budd Company's standards, featuring stainless flat, fluted, and corrugated outer sheeting over stainless frames. Design of the end underframe units has made it possible to affix a welded attachment to a 20-inch-square vertical structure column, in such a manner as to distribute the longitudinal load to the upper floor structure and to the depressed center sill. Some parts of the load are taken up by side sills through the use of body bolsters and through those structural partitions that stand at the inner sides of each of the two vertical structural columns. Actually, the entire car structure has been designed as a modified girder, in which the roof and the floor are the chord members and the sides the shear-carrying members.

Ultralite thermal insulation, three inches thick, has been employed throughout most of the body of each hi-level car. Acoustic insulation has been provided for by spraying with Insulmat.

The self-regulated diesels used for the generating equipment have been ingeniously devised so that they can be rolled out of the cars on track extensions with comparative ease, and their flexible fuel, water, steam, and electric lines can be rapidly disconnected when inspection or repair work proves necessary. In the event of the failure of any one engine on the coaches, diner, or lounge, the train's electrical system automatically cuts loads in half. Emergency lighting, diesel-starting, and control apparatus of various kinds receive their current from Exide storage batteries that are housed in two battery boxes under one end of each car; a 25-ampere selenium rectifier produces the necessary voltage for charging these batteries.

Two 220-volt, three-phase Pyle National receptacles are installed on each side of every car for stand-by electrical service. Westinghouse has provided motorized circuit-breakers, which furnish a simple control arrangement that is interlocked to prevent more than one source of power from being used at any one time.

The regular consist of the ultramodern, hi-level El Capitan is made up of thirteen units, with storage mail car, baggage car, and dormitory baggage car immediately following the locomotive. Then come a 68-passenger hi-level coach, two 72-passenger hi-level coaches, the hi-level diner, the hi-level sky lounge, three more 72-passenger hi-level coaches, and finally another 68-passenger hi-level coach.

The 68-passenger coaches differ from those of slightly larger capacity in that they have a stairway at one end leading to standard platform level. This arrangement makes it possible to use the new cars in composition with standard level coaches when desirable.

El Capitan passengers these days are really riding high. As Santa Fe's president Ernest Marsh put it, the new train is the road's "latest bid for the American traveler, and with the safety implicit in rail travel will offer the most comfortable way to make a journey.

"With family fares available and with a system in effect for renting an automobile at a nominal cost at destination, the traveler will find it difficult to equal the new El Capitan no matter which other form of transportation he considers using."

CHAPTER XVII

SOUTHERN PACIFIC'S FREIGHT MOVES

Fast and Diversified—Piggyback Lumber and Perishables

The huge amounts of perishable fruits and vegetables that originate in California, Arizona, and Oregon, combined with great lumber harvests in the Northwest, pose a special problem for the Southern Pacific Railroad.

The road is predominantly an originating carrier, moving its greatest freight volumes eastward, an operation that involves a heavy movement of empties. The empty-car movement in the case of perishables will normally run between 75 per cent and 83 per cent of loaded mileage, while two cars out of every three used to load lumber in Oregon must be moved in empty from other points, because of a smaller volume of loaded deliveries to the forest areas.

Yet, despite this abnormal burden, SP traffic officials have worked out their schedules so that the road's over-all ratio of empty to total freight mileage stands up well in comparison with that scored by all the nation's Class I roads, most of which do not have this problem to cope with, at least not to the extent resulting from SP's 13,459 miles of line. During 1954, for example, Southern Pacific's proportion was 37.3 per cent against the total Class I ratio of 36.9 per cent.

By 1954, Southern Pacific's gross-ton-miles per train hour had risen to 57,590, reflecting a 59 per cent boost since 1945. It came about as a direct result of expansive spending during the postwar years, particularly on new diesel power, but on new tools for the road's employees as well. Rapidly mushrooming industrial expansion in the area served by the Southern Pacific made it mandatory that the road's officials concentrate on the development of a program that would result not only in bigger tonnages but in faster speeds for the movement of trains.

The efficiency record that SP has evolved is all the more remarkable in that its routes cross six of the nation's major mountain summits in the western states: the Cascade, Siskiyou, Sierra Nevada, Santa Margarita, Tehachapi, and Beaumont. Naturally, train speeds in such areas are slower; in one range, for example, there is a 7,000-foot rise within less than a hundred miles.

There are four principal entry gates to the road's Pacific lines, located at Portland, Oregon; Ogden, Utah; El Paso, Texas; and Tucumcari, New Mexico. There are likewise four main gateways through which traffic flows on the Texas and Louisiana lines of SP: New Orleans and Shreveport, Louisiana, and El Paso and Corsicana, Texas.

Changes in the nature of the freight load carried by the lines are constantly studied for the purpose of determining what the railroad will need in the way of equipment and rolling stock in the years ahead. Perishables were for many years the largest single commodity handled by Southern Pacific, but since 1949 the road's Pacific lines have carried more lumber than any other single item. During the last year of the dominance of the perishables, 236,229 cars of them were carried, compared with 223,530 cars of lumber. In 1954 the totals were reversed, lumber having jumped to 281,106 cars as against 237,569 of perishable commodities.

The railroad has made many changes to take care of its heavily increased freight volume, and is planning many more.

And here are just a few more of the marked improvements that SP has installed all along its lines during the past few years, to make freight service faster and more efficient for its shippers:

Centralized traffic control now exists on the Shasta route between Eugene, Oregon, and Redding, California, and on the Los Angeles division between Alhambra and Yuma.

There are push-button-controlled classification yards at Los Angeles, Roseville, Eugene, and Houston.

A new joint yard is in operation at Ogden, Utah.

Additional trackage has been constructed at the El Paso yard.

Around busy Los Angeles a bypass line now operates between Puente and Los Nietos, where there is a junction point with Pacific Electric, and then on to Studebaker on the Santa Ana branch.

A modern electronically controlled classification yard is in operation at Houston, Texas, described elsewhere in this book.

These new push-button yards now make it possible for SP to get freights through other terminals, via a detailed blocking operation, in fifteen to thirty minutes, where two to four hours formerly was required.

Increased over-the-road speeds, combined with more efficient terminal operations, have resulted in substantial reductions of over-all road times. For instance the North Coast Perishable, which used to make the Los Angeles to Portland run in 78 hours as recently as 1949, now connects the two points in an elapsed time of only 58.5 hours.

The completion of the modern yards at Los Angeles and Roseville and the installation of additional trackage at El Paso have resulted in an expansion of blocking operations to the point that in many cases no switching need be performed on trains between origin and destination. The "LNSW" operates all the way from El Paso to Los Nietos (near Los Angeles) normally with no switching except for caboose changes, while trains running from the San Francisco–Oakland area and from Los Angeles to the Pacific Northwest are so blocked at Roseville as to permit a through operation to Portland. Cars for various connections at that point and for local delivery are segregated to expedite their handling through terminals and for advance delivery at connecting points.

Through cooperative measures taken with connecting railroads, delivery schedules of transcontinental perishable and manifest freight have been cut as much as twenty-four hours during recent years. Each of the roads joining to make up a

109

cross-country route has absorbed its proper proportion of the time-saving schedule.

To handle its tremendous volume of freight shipments, the Southern Pacific operates a big fleet of both time and symbol freights, some of which run at passenger speeds. There are sixty-five symbol freights run by Pacific lines and forty-four time freights operated by SP's Texas-Louisiana routes. Included in the Pacific lines fleet are ten merchandise-trailer-flatcar freights used for merchandise and for piggyback traffic.

By the end of 1954 Southern Pacific operated 16,489 route miles of truck service for shippers as part of its coordinated rail-truck operation, a figure that represents 23 per cent more mileage than SP's total trackage plus that of its solely controlled affiliates. The trucking subsidiaries that year handled 931,406 tons of freight for SP in intercity service and an additional 917,-880 tons in pickup and delivery. For special railroad purposes, such as relieving trains of head-end traffic, they hauled another 146,040 tons, and they carried 307,102 tons for public purposes under their own billing. In that same year they also moved 287,388 tons of new General Motors cars to various points in California and handled an additional 17,464 tons of Railway Express shipments.

Although there has been a gradual decline in l.c.l. business throughout recent years, SP has partially offset this trend both by fast overnight merchandise trains and by means of pickup and delivery service. A rapidly expanding piggyback service is also expected to have its effect on checking l.c.l. losses.

SP's merchandise train service has been augmented for the purpose of piggybacking l.c.l. in truck trailers on the road's flat-cars. When shipments are handled in that manner, in trailers directly from the door of consignor to the door of the consignee, the railroad estimates that it saves from three to four dollars a ton in handling charges.

The railroad's Pacific lines have 178 flatcars equipped with necessary tie-down devices, and its trucking subsidiary operates 425 trailers. Each of the flatcars can handle one 35-foot trailer or two vans of 22- or 24-foot length. There are 75 flatcars and 294 subsidiary-owned trailers doing piggyback duty on SP's Texas-Louisiana lines, which have been carrying up to 18 per cent of their total tonnage this way.

Fifty-eight cities are now equipped to handle piggyback operations along SP's Pacific and Texas-Louisiana lines, of which twenty-seven had piggyback ramps according to a recent count. At Los Angeles the ramp feeds from a spacious paved area onto flatcars standing on six adjacent parallel tracks.

Here are the communities where SP offers its piggyback service, some of which offer connecting service to Union Pacific, Northern Pacific, and Great Northern:

On the Pacific lines, these terminals have unloading ramps—in Oregon: Portland, Eugene, Klamath Falls; in California: Roseville, Stockton, San Francisco, Oakland, San José, Salinas, Los Angeles; in Arizona: Yuma, Phoenix, Tucson; in Nevada: Reno.

On the Pacific lines, these terminals have piggyback service available—in Oregon: Tillamook, Salem, Springfield, Coos Bay, Roseburg, Grants Pass, Medford, Ashland; in California: Dunsmuir, Ukish, Healdsburg, Santa Rosa, Petaluma, Sausalito, Calistoga, Napa, San Luis Obispo, Santa Barbara, Los Angeles Harbor, Santa Ana, San Bernardino.

On the Texas and Louisiana lines, these terminals have unloading ramps—in Texas: San Antonio, Skidmore, Edinburg, Brownsville, Victoria, Houston, Fort Worth, Lancaster (serving Dallas), Ennis, Waco, Beaumont; in Louisiana: Lake Charles, Shreveport, Lafayette, New Orleans.

On the Texas and Louisiana lines, these terminals have piggyback service available—in Texas: Austin, Jacksonville, Lufkin, Port Arthur, Galveston, Corpus Christi, Harlingen; in Louisiana: Alexandria.

All along SP's widespread rail network, seasonal variations are an important factor affecting train loadings. In the season when perishables are at their height—during June and July—the railroad loads to the maximum in order to get the greatest use of its motive power and to keep the total number of cars on the lines to a minimum, so as to reduce traffic density all along the line.

During this season additional local and perishable hauler trains are made up as required, and they are pressed into the service of moving perishables from origin point to terminals, where traffic is concentrated and then made up in blocks for forwarding to concentration points.

The Pacific Fruit Express Company, owned jointly by Southern Pacific and Union Pacific, has complete charge of the distribution of empty reefer cars. It issues the orders to SP operating divisions for car movements of empties from PFE shops and cleaning tracks to originating areas. En route, PFE takes care of icing and heating chores while the cars are carrying their perishable cargoes, and the company informs all interested representatives of the nature and whereabouts of loads on the line.

Fast freights have always been a Southern Pacific aim. When a train began its run on June 24, 1886, it was called SP's "first special fast fruit train." This is a goal that the railroad has always kept in mind, and it has consistently employed the most up-to-date means that scientific railroading has made available to keep it always in position to offer its shippers a fast, efficient, dependable freight movement.

C & O 3-unit diesel with eastbound coal train climbing the .56 grade at White Sulphur Springs, West Va. on Allegheny Subdiv. of the Clifton Forge Div. The tonnage is 11,000 and the pusher is out of sight on the rear end.

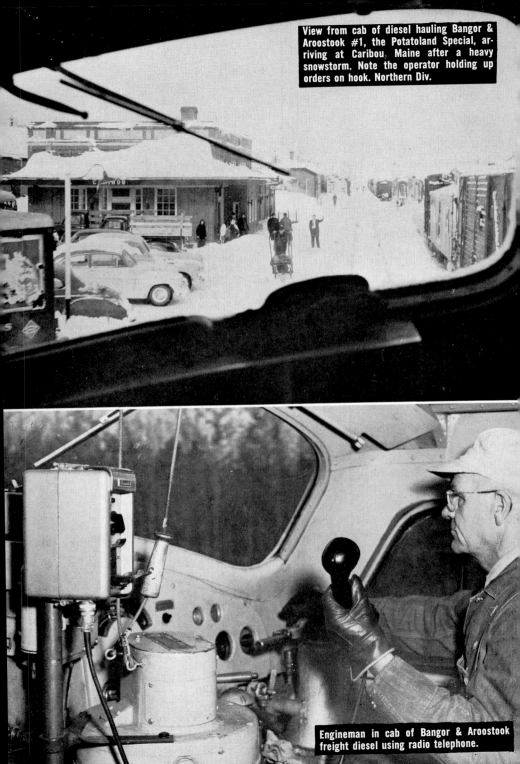

View from cab of diesel hauling Bangor & Aroostook #1, the Potatoland Special, arriving at Caribou, Maine after a heavy snowstorm. Note the operator holding up orders on hook. Northern Div.

Engineman in cab of Bangor & Aroostook freight diesel using radio telephone.

New Freuhauf truck trailers in service on the Lackawanna showing the portable ramp as used by that road at Hoboken, Scranton and Binghamton. The road has 100 of these trailers in service.

New Lackawanna 1200 h.p. diesel tugboat, one of 3 recently built for service in New York Harbor.

Mechanical refrigerator car as seen from the Crest office as it rolls down the incline towards master retarder of the Northern Pacific new classification yards at Pasco, Wash. Retarder tower in yard in the background.

Northern Pacific motor trailers mounted on specially equipped flatcars which move in regular freight trains handle less than carloads and full trailer loads in piggyback operation being switched by 1200 h.p. EMD diesel St. Paul Terminal.

Astra-dome looking towards rear and stairs in Union Pacific new lounge cars.

Comfortable lounging facilities in new Union Pacific dome lounge cars looking forward towards steps to dome.

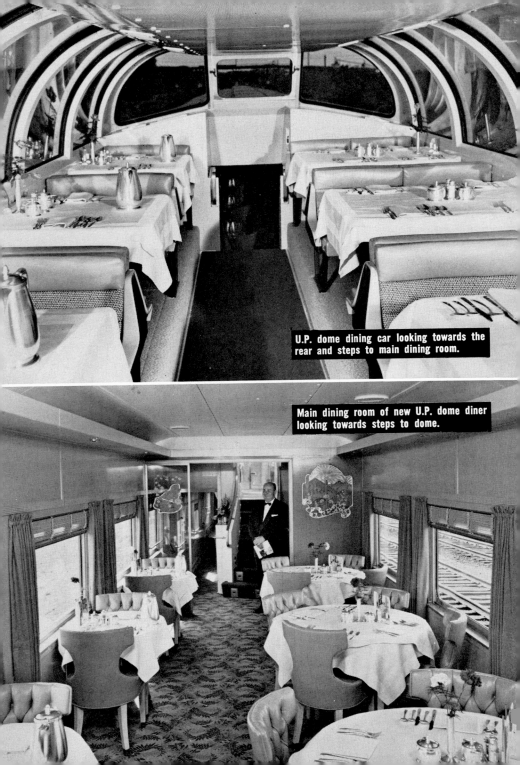

U.P. dome dining car looking towards the rear and steps to main dining room.

Main dining room of new U.P. dome diner looking towards steps to dome.

Attractive enclosed cafe and bar of U.P. lounge cars showing mural of new U.P. gas turbine freight locomotive.

Private dining room of the U.P.'s beautiful new astra-dome diner.

Rear end of U.P.'s redwood lounge car astra-dome dining car and dome-lounge car in #103, the City of Los Angeles, near Granite, Wyo. on the Second Sub-div. of the Wyoming Div.

New U.P. redwood lounge cars in service on several trains. Bar not shown at other end.

CHAPTER XVIII

RADIO ON THE BANGOR AND AROOSTOOK

Maine's Leading Carrier Up to Date for Its Shippers and Customers

Entering the yard at Oakfield, Maine, a freight train of the Bangor and Aroostook railroad broke a knuckle. The conductor walked forward until he came upon the break, inspected it, noted the size of the knuckle that needed replacement; with his five-mile-range walkie-talkie radio he talked to the yardmaster, reporting the incident.

A few minutes later a yard engine arrived exactly opposite the damaged car and delivered a new knuckle. It was put in place, and the long freight moved into the yard.

This is just one of the incidents, both regular and emergency, that have helped prove to Bangor & Aroostook executives, engineers, conductors, and all crew members that the railroad's investment of slightly over $100,000 to install complete radio communications along the entire line is more than paying off.

Bangor & Aroostook personnel can now talk to one another— enginemen in their diesels to train crews in cabooses or alongside, to enginemen of passing trains, to dispatchers, operators, and yardmasters at twelve fixed points along the 342-mile right of way from Searsport on the south to Van Buren on the north. In addition to these two terminal points, radio sending and receiving installations are in operation at Northern Maine Junction, South La Grange, West Seboois, Millinocket, Sherman, Oakfield, Houlton, Squa Pan, Presque Isle, Caribou, Stockholm, Madawaska, and Fort Kent.

Economy of operation and extensive, time-saving service improvements have been the chief advantages derived from the over-all system-wide radio network. It is difficult, according to Curtis M. Hutchins, chairman of the board, to assign an actual dollar value to the benefits that radio has brought to the railroad, because other changes such as replacement of steam engines by diesel locomotives, rescheduling, and traffic fluctuations have also taken place during the period of years in which the radio installation was completed.

But from the president right on down the line, all are agreed that radio has made railroading safer, faster, and more efficient. In the words of Lawrence Ward, veteran passenger train engineer, "Train radio is the best thing that ever happened on this railroad."

Experiments with short-wave radio were started by the Bangor & Aroostook as early as 1949, when a test period of three months of operation indicated that at least one hour's delay per train per day could be eliminated. So during the following year seven Southern Division stations, fourteen locomotives, and eight cabooses were fitted with sending and receiving equipment.

Today, with the entire system radio-equipped, every train on any run is at all times able to keep in touch with at least one fixed station. Now a total of forty-seven locomotives are equipped with units that can make contact up to a radius of thirty-five miles. Originally, eight of the cabooses were fitted with diesel motor generators for power supply, but important installation savings have been effected by the subsequent use of walkie-talkie sets in all remaining cabooses, and these portable installations provide a flexible means of communication that would not be available with fixed equipment.

Many of the cabooses, too, are used only seasonally, such as during the important potato move months, and railroad officials realized that installing radio sets of a permanent nature, along with generating equipment, was hardly justified in those cases.

Two full-time radio maintenance men have been added to the railroad's staff. Each works in a new radio service shop to provide constant checking and servicing of the equipment; one is at Northern Maine Junction, the other at Oakfield.

Great operational advantages have accrued to the Bangor & Aroostook since the completion of over-all radio installations. Quicker movements of freight trains along the entire right of way, as well as in and out of yards, have resulted. As a train approaches any one of the road's freight yards, the engine crew is able to contact the yardmaster and to give him completely accurate, up-to-the-minute positioning of the train. With this information the yardmaster is in position to line up his crew, provide track space, and verbally inform the engineer of his movements. "Move into track No. 4," he might say, "with your whole train. Your caboose will be taken care of by the yard crew."

With this kind of direct, instant word-of-mouth communication, there is no longer any need to halt the train out on the main line or to resort to flagged instructions to the head brakeman. At the same time the yardmaster is able to talk to his own crews, and can move them about as needed, based on the verbal information he receives directly from incoming trains.

When the train is ready to leave the yard the same advantages apply; the yardmaster can advise the train crew when the yard work has been concluded, and the rear-end crew can tell their engineer directly when added locomotive power is hooked up to the caboose.

Safe, speedy meeting of trains headed in opposite directions is also assured with the use of Bangor & Aroostook radio installations. When approaching meeting points, crews of all trains—whether passenger or freight—can talk directly to one another to mutually advise on location, train lengths, speed, or other pertinent information. It is possible for one crew to inform the other that its train is in the clear and let the other engineer know the position and setting of switches. And when a train leaves a passing track to return to the main line, the rear-end crew can tell the engineer just how many cars behind him are still short of the main track, when all have cleared, when the switch has been returned to normal position, and when the flagman is back on board. There is no longer any guesswork or estimating involved, and the entire operation is thus that much speedier and safer.

In addition, crews of passing trains have had the experience of noting hotboxes or lowered brake rigging on trains going by them, and have been able to notify the engineer of the defect. Employees stationed at wayside points have also contributed this valuable kind of service as they have spotted trouble in trains passing by their locations.

When a caboose crew notes a defect on its own train, it no longer runs the risk of possible cargo damage from the rough stop that usually follows use of the conductor's valve; a radioed word to the diesel ahead brings about a normal application of service brakes. On the Bangor & Aroostook, where a high proportion of freight traffic consists of rolls of easily bruised newsprint paper, this improved situation is of outstanding importance.

The railroad has already experienced demonstrations of radio's great value in emergency situations. Several panels of ties were completely cut up and destroyed in a derailment at a remote point along the right of way that was not easily reached from any highway. Immediate radio contact with the railroad's headquarters resulted in a hasty check of current schedules, and it was quickly revealed that a local freight was just about ready to leave Millinocket. Another radio message to that point, from headquarters, caused the attachment of a carload of ties to the departing freight, which was quickly moved to the derailment scene. The track was restored to service in several hours' less time than would have been possible without this instantaneous communication, and the movement of a special train bearing the new ties was completely avoided.

On another occasion a ninety-car freight train developed trouble with its third diesel unit. When the train was brought to a stop, it was not necessary for the conductor to walk forward this entire distance to ascertain the reason for the halt; he had been notified by radio from the engineer and was prepared for the stop. The unit was cut out at the crest of a grade, the flag was whistled in, and the next division point was notified of the trouble, again through the medium of the engineer's transmission

116

unit. When the train arrived at that next point a new diesel unit was standing by, prepared to move into its proper location in the long line of cars. Without radio, such a situation might have caused major delays, not only for the train concerned but for several following it.

Federal-Farnsworth radio telephone communication equipment, furnished by the Federal Telephone & Radio Corporation, is the equipment that the Bangor & Aroostook has used for its permanent installations in engines and in those cabooses originally fitted with fixed-position transmission and receiving sets. The walkie-talkie units are the product of the Hallicrafters Company.

"In bad weather," says Curtis Hutchins, Chairman of the Board of the Bangor & Aroostook, "radio is all but indispensable. It takes a lot of guesswork out of yard operations, and it expedites movement over the road, reducing crew overtime and fuel consumption. At the same time it improves our service to shippers.

"Now that we have radio," Mr. Hutchins adds, "we don't know how we ever did without it."

CHAPTER XIX

KING COAL ON THE C&O

The Road Overlooks Nothing in Its Desire to Serve This Important Industry

The future role of coal in American industry is a subject of constant study and tremendous importance to the Chesapeake & Ohio Railroad, for this road alone each year transports close to one-sixth of the nation's total production of bituminous coal.

In 1953, for example, C&O cars carried 56,000,000 tons of coal loaded directly at mines served by the railroad, and a total of 70,000,000 tons when overhead tonnage and the amount received from connections with other roads are added in.

The coal industry, however, has been in something of a slump in recent years. Development of oil and gas for heating purposes in both industrial and residential areas, increased use of water power for generation of electricity, even the potential use of the atom, have all left their mark on the level of activity in the nation's mines. These are concentrated in West Virginia and eastern Kentucky, an area served by C&O, and the future of these workings is of vital importance to the road's operational plans.

Through diversification of its freight cargoes, already discussed in an earlier chapter, C&O has built its tonnage and revenues in other areas of operation. But coal still constitutes 51 per cent of its freight dollar income and an even higher percentage of its freight tonnage. So the railroad is constantly active in its efforts to promote the use of coal on all levels of the nation's activity.

But the Chesapeake & Ohio is primarily interested in transportation; its major efforts, therefore, are devoted to modernizing and improving its own facilities for handling coal, in order that it may reach its end users quickly, efficiently, dependably, and at low cost—all factors that will encourage companies and people to continue to use coal instead of other sources of heat or power.

One of the problems involved in this effort lies in the nature of coal-mining operations themselves. Throughout the coal fields, as mines are worked bare and new fields discovered, there is a constant closing of old mines and a continuous opening of new ones. For C&O, this means a never ending picking up of old rail and a continual laying of new branch lines and spurs. In the period between 1946 and 1953, for example, C&O, either by itself or jointly with other roads, built twenty-three new branch line extensions or spurs in order to provide convenient loading facilities at new mining properties. These operations totaled 110.69 miles of new trackage, which cost the road some $32,-000,000.

Modern coal terminals—at Newport News, Virginia, and Toledo, Ohio—are the basic units in the road's system of coal transportation. Piers 14 and 15 at the Virginia port are considered to be among the most efficient along the entire Atlantic coast from Maine to Florida. Pier 14 is 1,078 feet in length and is equipped with tandem rotary dumpers, making it possible to dump the contents of two coupled cars simultaneously into two separate hoppers. There are four huge loading hoppers on Pier 14, each of which can handle 1,500 tons per hour. In 1953 those four towers alone dumped just about half of all the coal exported from the United States—a total of 6,300,000 tons from this one C&O pier!

The Presque Isle coal terminal, on Lake Erie near Toledo, is equally vital to the road's coal-haulage operations. About one-third of all the coal riding Great Lakes barges or used on Great Lakes ships goes through this terminal each year. The Ohio facility handled more than 14,000,000 tons of coal in 1953; it proved its amazing capacities in 1950, when it handled and dumped a peak total of nearly 17,000,000 tons. During one day in that record year, Presque Isle serviced 2,029 cars carrying a total of 119,675 tons.

Despite the fall-off that has affected coal-mining operations, C&O officials, taking the long-range view, are optimistic. For one thing, they point out that two of the major users of coal are the steel and electric utility industries, and both of these are continually expanding their capacities. Indications for the future, with a burgeoning economy and a growing population, are that these two industrial fields alone will provide a tremendous market for coal. In steel, for example, a ton of coal must be used for every ton of the metal that is produced in the nation's big mills, so about 20 per cent of C&O's coal tonnage is delivered to steel plants. Utilities consume another 18 per cent, some 14 per cent goes into export, and another 14 per cent is used by the retail market for home heating.

With C&O's main lines connecting the coal fields with the area mainly occupied by great steel mills and then running on to the lake ports, the future of this industry is closely watched by the railroad. Tests have shown that reserves of high-grade coal still to be mined are more than adequate to meet the needs of the next period of many years. So-called "proved" reserves, buried underneath the ground in areas served by C&O, will last, at current production rates, for the next sixty-five years, and actual reserves are in effect many times that figure.

In the heart of the nation's coal fields, at Huntington, West Virginia, is the headquarters of the railroad's Coal Development Bureau, whose job it is to keep track of the coal reserves in properties on or near the railroad's right of way. Together with its predecessor, this department of the C&O has been in continual survey operations since 1900.

The Coal Development Bureau has to know as much about mines as do their operators and owners. When a new mine is opened and the road is asked to construct a spur or branch to serve it, the C&O must know exactly how profitable it will be, and how practical it is, to comply with the request. The road's management officials must be convinced that the mine can be operated successfully and that it can be made to produce for an amount of time that will make worth while the investment tied up in the construction of new trackage. Furthermore, when a mine becomes depleted, the C&O finds it advantageous to be able to point out to its owners a spot where a new and profitable mining operation may be developed.

Statistics will show how valuable this bureau's services have been to the road's over-all operations. Between 1946 and 1953 the C&O began serving eighty-two new coal mines; of that number, thirty-five had ceased operations by 1953, but the remaining forty-seven produced a total of 9,000,000 tons of coal, which represented 17 per cent of the C&O's total coal haulage during that year!

The railroad and its subsidiary companies own thousands of acres of coal-bearing land, but the C&O does not operate any of them. Much of this property is leased to companies that do the actual mining, under the close supervision of the railroad's Coal Development Bureau. Periodic inspections are performed by the railroad over its leased properties, and checks are made of the mining practices and techniques being used by the operating lessees. The C&O also performs drilling operations to ascertain the whereabouts of both coal and gas reserves.

Great advances have been made in the past few years in the application of mechanized operations that have resulted in greater productivity in coal-mining operations at lowered costs. Here too the Coal Development Bureau of the C&O has taken active leadership in experimentation and in constantly encouraging mineowners to install the machines that will make more coal available to American industry more quickly and more reasonably.

Just as concentrated advertising campaigns have been playing their important part in the development of merchandise freight for the C&O's program of diversification, so have they been effectively used to find new markets for coal and to regain lost ones for that fuel. Within the past three years the railroad's Coal Traffic and Development Department has undertaken the promotion of coal as a desirable source of heat and power through a series of national advertisements appearing in general news magazines, nationally distributed business publications, and periodicals that circulate among industrial engineers.

The advertisements are aimed at demonstrating the important part that coal plays in producing electrical energy, at showing that coal is a dependable and economical fuel for the heating of schools and private homes, and in reassuring the population that adequate reserves of coal exist for many years in the future.

The C&O management has cause to be extremely pleased with the results of the advertising campaign. They cite the example of a large industrial company in Norfolk that was just about to convert its plant to oil as a basic fuel. After reading one of the C&O's ads, the company contacted the road and consulted with one of the railroad's combustion engineers, who resold them on the superiority of coal for their purposes. Result: another coal freight customer retained on the C&O's books.

With its long-range surveys of coal deposits, its understanding of the growing and future needs of American industry, its advertising campaigns designed to bring this information to industry and private consumer—with all these and its constant improvement of coal-handling facilities, such as its 13,050-car Newport News coal yards, the C&O faces future coal freight operations with confidence, knowing that its lines are so strategically located that increased use of coal almost anywhere in the United States means increased coal tonnage for the Chesapeake & Ohio Railroad.

CHAPTER XX

NORTHERN PACIFIC'S NEW PASCO YARD

A new standard of freight service has been set with the completion of the newly rebuilt Pasco yard of the Northern Pacific Railway at the extreme southeastern corner of the state of Washington.

This new yard was constructed at an investment of $5,500,000; the result is said to be one of the most technically advanced classification yards to be found anywhere in the world.

Pasco represents a natural hub of a wheel, the spokes of which are the diverging lines of the Northern Pacific—west to Seattle and Tacoma, south to Portland, east to Spokane and to Lewiston, Idaho, and to the states of the Great Plains. Pasco thus represents to the NP the logical location at which to classify the stream of freight that constantly flows in both directions.

All-electric retarders, automatic electronic retarder control, push-button automatic switching, a modern yard layout, and an up-to-date communications system have all been combined here to provide new levels of speed, efficiency, and safety in picking up inbound freight cars and regrouping them with others headed toward the same destination.

For that is the basic function of the freight classification yard. Most cars carrying goods from one city to another will travel not only over several divisions of a given railroad, but over the lines of several different roads. To keep the nation's goods moving, a full car destined for a particular community is not kept waiting at its point of origin until enough cars are accumulated there to make up a full train bound for the same city. Instead, the original car is made up into a train of cars all of which are headed in the same general direction. At various freight classification yards throughout the country, the trains are broken up, and each car is regrouped with other cars—which have come in from different points of origin as parts of other trains—to make up a new train headed for the ultimate destination.

But yard classification work is even more complex; it requires that the freight cars that are made into a train be placed in an order making it possible for each one to be dropped off as its destination is reached with a minimum of disruption to the balance of the train. In some cases, then, an outbound train leaving a yard is not a train made of a new combination of cars, but is the same group of cars that had arrived some time earlier, merely rearranged in proper delivery order.

To accomplish all this with the many trains and the many hundreds of cars that run through a yard each day clearly requires not only skilled and trained personnel, but also the very latest in accurate, rapid, and automatic scientific equipment.

Every classification yard in the country is built around the focal point of its "hump," which is the top of a small, artificially constructed hill. From this gentle height the tracks of the classification yard spread out through a maze of switches and controls. Each car in an incoming train is pushed to the top of this little hill, uncoupled from the next car, and permitted to roll down the hill, under force of gravity, to be switched onto a classification track along with other cars, from its own and from other trains, that in a few hours will make up a new train.

The fully automated yard assures that each car will move onto its properly scheduled track. Furthermore, when a car reaches the end of its run from the hump, it is stopped only by the fact that it runs into another car already standing there; if this contact is made at too great a rolling speed, damage can result to both cars as well as to their lading. The automatic yard, with its electronic controls, sets the proper speed for each car, taking into account such factors as its weight, the distance it must travel, wind and weather conditions, track and switch resistance, etc.

At Pasco the process starts in an eight-track receiving yard, where clerks equipped with walkie-talkies radio identification of each arriving car to the yard's modern office. To assign these cars to their correct outbound trains, switching lists are made up at the yard office from this radioed information and sent by pneumatic tube to the yardmaster's office, to the retarder operator's office, and to the hump office, which is located at the side of the track directly at the crest of the little hill.

In this hump office an operator presides over a panel board containing forty-seven buttons, each one controlling the switching series that must be set up to guide a car from the hump to the classification track designated by the equivalent button number. As each car passes over the hill the operator consults his copy of the switching list and presses the appropriate button. Thus, as the pin that uncouples the car from its train is pulled, the car is carried to its correct destination without further need for individual switch-setting along the way.

As the car, gathering momentum on its downhill journey, proceeds along lengths of track, it passes through a series of automatically controlled electric car-retarders. These are sets of rail brakes that squeeze against the car's wheels and slow it to a proper speed. Connected with the retarders are radar units, which record the speed of each car and transmit that information to a centralized electronic brain. Weather—no matter how severe—cannot interfere with the accurate operation of this equipment.

The central computer receives the retarder's speed data, information from the track push-button machine in the hump office, and car weights sent by detecting units in the track. It remembers and it computes; taking all this data into account, it instantaneously sets retarders along the route and throws the correct switches so that every freight car, in proper order, is guided at the correct speed to a gentle, rolling halt as it couples with the car already waiting on the proper classification track.

Despite the operations of all these modern electronic marvels, the human element is not completely eliminated. In addition to the operator who pushes the track classification buttons in the hump office, a retarder operator monitors the system. Located in an air-conditioned office high above the yard, he checks the course of each car and is provided with control levers that make it possible for him to effect changes whenever, in his judgment, flexibility is needed in the operation.

The yardmaster, too, occupies an office at the very top of Pasco's modern glass-enclosed tower. Here, through simple monitor switchboard connections, he keeps in constant touch with all personnel who are involved in getting traffic into and out of the great yard. Intercom systems, multiple-channel radio, telephone, teletype, pneumatic tube, and telegraph—all play their part in keeping the human members of the team constantly in touch with each other.

Loud-speakers are set up on poles throughout the 260-acre yard, enabling the yardmaster to talk to any group or individual on his staff. Connected with them are microphones, enabling anyone, anywhere in the yard, to converse with the yardmaster too.

All this apparatus, of course, requires tremendous amounts of electricity to keep it in operation, so Northern Pacific has prudently guaranteed against interruption to or failure of regular sources of electric power. A huge bank of powerful storage batteries is always kept fully charged and in perfect condition to supply the power that would be needed to keep Pasco's electronic servants in operation for many hours.

Thus the hub of the great Northern Pacific Railway, its Pasco freight classification yard, makes daily use of the latest developments of today's scientific achievements to expedite its task of speeding the Northwest's freighted goods on to their destinations.

Robert S. MacFarlane, President of the Northern Pacific, frequently rides his railroad to see that it is always a "Railroad of the Hour" as does C. H. Burgess, Operating Vice President and a great all around railroader.

CHAPTER XXI

BEAUTIFUL NEW DOME COACHES, LOUNGES, AND DOME DINERS ON THE UNION PACIFIC

A brand-new dimension in pleasurable railroad travel has been added to the Union Pacific's famous transcontinental streamliners. It is now possible to enjoy one of the UP's fine meals while viewing the dramatic Western scenery from the dome of a new three-level diner.

Actually, the ten new cars that have been placed in service on the City of Portland and the City of Los Angeles contain three separate dining rooms each. There is a main dining room, on the conventional level, seating eighteen passengers; above it is the unique, breath-taking dome dining area, also seating eighteen; while a few short steps down from the main room each car has a unique private dining room where ten persons may be served.

The new dining cars are part of a $10,000,000 new-car program initiated by Union Pacific, involving the addition of some thirty-five dome cars in all. Dome coaches have been added to the City of Portland and to the Challengers, and dome-lounge cars to the City of Portland, the City of Los Angeles, and the City of St. Louis.

A unique feature of the new dome diners is found in the arrangement of tables in the entrance-level main dining area. Instead of the usual severe line-up of small rectangular tables coming one behind the other, the new dome diner main room seats its eighteen passengers at three round tables for two diners each and three round tables seating four each. This arrangement creates an air of informality and hospitality that many passengers have found delightfully "homelike." All tables and chairs in both the main area and the dome dining section are secured to the car floors, and all of the seats are upholstered in leather.

The new diners assigned to the City of Portland are decorated in a manner to pay tribute to Oregon's major community, the City of Roses. Partitions and side finish in the special private dining room are of white Formica over which is a pattern of roses in a red silk-screen print. At the passageway the famous Columbia hybrid tea rose is carved into the separating glass partition.

In the main dining area the color scheme used is one of ivory, green, charcoal, and gray, while the flowers and trees of the Pacific Northwest are the bases used for polychrome gesso designs worked into the Formica and glass panels. The same color motifs have been carried up to the dome dining level.

Appropriately enough, a Hollywood design scheme features the décor of those dome dining cars running with the City of Los Angeles. In the reserved dining area on these cars there is an all-over white pattern on green, including representations of movie cameras, the Los Angeles sky line, Grauman's Chinese Theater, and a typical Hollywood première. Green, sand, and terra cotta mark the color scheme in the main rooms and dining domes of the City of Los Angeles diners. Landscapes and floral patterns typical of the Southwest are emblazoned in the gesso designs on the bulkheads and the partitions.

In both groups of diners the unique color combinations that mark the private dining rooms are enhanced by the use of Dirilyte golden tableware and furnishings.

There are a well-equipped pantry and a complete kitchen beyond the private dining room in each of the ten new dome dining cars. A quiet, pneumatically operated elevator, located at one end of the kitchen and toward the center of the car, efficiently carries orders to the dome dining section and serves to expedite removal of used glassware, dishes, silverware, and linens. Like the refrigerators, sinks, range, and lockers that outfit the kitchen and pantry, this dumb-waiter is finished in stainless steel.

The dome lounge cars represent the first of their kind to combine aluminum and steel construction. The sturdy underframe is of low-alloy high-tensile riveted and welded assembly; except for the dome ends, the superstructure is made almost completely of aluminum alloy.

The lower level of each dome lounge car houses a private game room at the front end, a cocktail lounge in the center, and a rear observation lounge that seats twenty-one passengers. The lounge section is outfitted with contemporary-style furniture that the individual can move about informally to create conditions of maximum visibility or personal comfort. There are a comfortable settee at the front end of the lounge, a magazine locker, a table, and a convenient writing desk.

Moving forward from the lounge area, the passenger may either step down into a passageway that leads to the cocktail lounge or take the short stairway up to the high-visibility dome area. In the bar all the equipment is finished in stainless steel. Here the passenger may relax over his choice of soft drinks, beer, or cocktails; here, too, is a centrally located annunciator panel, which registers any call made by a passenger from the rear lounge section, the private card room, or the dome area, to summon an attendant.

Up front, the game room is designed especially for the benefit of private parties. There is a circular table large enough to seat six comfortably around its rim.

Up in the dome area twenty-four passengers may enjoy the rapidly passing vista while relaxing comfortably on sofa-type seats that are slightly angled so that each person faces somewhat to the side for maximum visibility. The huge windows, which curve back overhead till they meet the narrow roof section, provide a sweeping view of scenery and sky even for those seated next to the center aisle. This is no doubt one of the most beautiful railway cars ever built.

Then there are the new Astra-dome coaches, thirty-five of which are in service. The lower level of each of these modern de luxe coaches seats thirty-six persons in "Sleepy Hollow" type foam rubber seats that have adjustable head rests and full-length leg rests. In the dome area divan-type seats accommodating twenty-four passengers are mounted at an angle just like those in the upper level of the dome lounge cars, to provide maximum visibility with comfort.

The Astra-dome coaches feature four communications channels, providing one for pickup of radio broadcasts, two for recorded music, and another for public address messages. The system installed is the latest high-level type made by RCA.

The decorative schemes of all three types of dome cars— diners, lounges, and coaches—are based upon three fundamental designs, variations of which are employed in floor coverings, drapes, and chair upholstery. They are the Gold Quartz, the Snowflake, and the Palm Frond motifs.

In the back bar mural that graces the cocktail lounge of the new dome lounge cars, there is a scene showing the famous Gold Spike ceremony at Promontory Point, Utah, the rite that joined the rails of the first transcontinental railroad line ever to span the United States. From this scene decorators developed the over-all pattern that is used in varying designs and color harmonies in the coaches and the dome lounge cars of the Challengers.

Employed in two tones of green and gold on a beige background, the Gold Quartz theme is used throughout these trains, and is also used in the drapery material found in the Challengers' dome coaches. The same design is found in the facing material for the partitions and bulkheads of the coach sections and is repeated on the Formica wall coverings in the Challenger cocktail lounges.

All Challenger dome coaches carry carpets bearing the Palm Frond theme, while the Snowflake motif enhances the dome observation cars on the City of Portland. This design unit is based on a section of a Sun Valley mural in which winter sports form the basic theme material. It appears in rose and beige in the carpeting on the City of Portland's dome observation cars and is repeated in the Formica bulkheads and partitions of that train's dome coaches. Here, too, the motif is further developed by using a pattern of ski trails in the carpeting design and again in the lounge cars' draperies.

The new dome coaches feature a center depressed section housing two large lounges for men and women. Each contains two Crane lavatories and a dental basin that is foot-operated. In addition, the women's lounge has a Formica-covered dressing table, a vanity mirror, and a chair. The cars are so arranged that the thirty-six-seat lower level is divided by this rest-room section, with sixteen passengers accommodated forward of it and twenty to the rear.

The dome coaches also feature unique carved mirrors, each with antique finish, which are mounted on the forward bulkheads of the lower level. Each mirror bears a carved representation of a bird indigenous to the Southwest. Mirrors in cars built for the Challengers have backgrounds in green and gold, while those on the City of Portland are of blue and copper.

But the comfort that has been built into these new dome cars is not attributable exclusively to their eye-pleasing, harmonizing interior design. Structural engineering qualities and the use of the latest types of heating, lighting, and ventilating devices make a journey in these new units an experience that delights all passengers.

Magnificent riding qualities can be credited to the use of General Steel Castings Corporation's all-coil spring, four-wheel, outside swing-hanger, single equalizer trucks. They are arranged for Budd disc brakes, Houdaille friction shock absorbers, and Westinghouse A-P decelostats, and have been equipped with Hyatt roller bearings and journal boxes. The trucks are insulated with Fabreeka pads, and the journal boxes have heat indicators of the stench-bomb type.

All the new dome cars are heated by the Unizone system of the Vapor Heating Corporation. There are two mercury-contact thermostats in each car, one located in the passageway on the lower level, the other near the top of the stairway leading to the dome. They control the steam regulators that feed the steam to the car radiator system.

A unique Vapor Solar Disc is mounted in the roof of each

131

car, in front of the center dome window. This sensitive device automatically controls the settings of the two thermostats in accordance with outside temperatures and thus helps vary the functioning of the heating and air-conditioning operations within each car.

There is also a sixteen-ton electromechanical system in each car that assures an adequate amount of properly conditioned air within each car at all times. A product of the Safety Car Heating and Lighting Company, it contains two 8-ton compressors as well as a 16-ton split-capacity evaporative condenser, the latter with two 8-ton-capacity coils, a motor-driven fan and pump, and two receivers. The condenser is equipped with a Farr dynamic grille so arranged as to provide for intake from both sides of each car. All this air-conditioning equipment is mounted under the new dome cars.

Separate lockers on each side of the cars, at their vestibule ends, hold ACBX-8 air-conditioning units, with divided evaporators and expansion valves. One of these units supplies conditioned air to the lower level of its car, while the other takes care of the dome level. Each unit contains a heating coil of 98,000 B.T.U. per hour capacity as well as a fan of 2,400 cubic feet per minute; the evaporator and the heating coils may be removed as separate units for inspection and repair.

Fresh air is brought into the cars by means of two Farr intake hoods, which are set in the roof on each side. After mixing with the return air in the chamber surrounding the air-conditioning unit, it is distributed throughout the car. Two 16 x 20 x 4-inch Farr filters are attached to the units, and the combined fresh and recirculated air is passed through them before entering the passenger areas of the cars.

Luminator Inc. designed and supplied the lighting fixtures for the new cars. In the dome coaches all the lighting is of the incandescent type. In the dome observation-lounges and in the new dome diners there are both incandescent and fluorescent lighting facilities. The rear of the roof of each new observation unit carries a Mars combination warning and back-up light, while mounted on the rear of these dome units is an illuminated stainless steel sign, with a safety glass front, carrying the name of the train.

The cars have 32-volt electrical systems, which are powered by a Waukesha Diesel Enginator, consisting of a six-cylinder 60-horsepower liquid-cooled engine connected to a fully enclosed ball-bearing generator. The entire generating unit is mounted on a cushioned roll-out base. Fuel is supplied from two tanks, each of 100 gallons capacity, and there is a roof exhaust.

In the observation cars, AC power is supplied by a 2,000-watt motor alternator, converting current that comes from a 32-volt Exide starting battery into 115-volt, 60-cycle alternating current. Made by Safety Car Heating & Lighting Company, this unit supplies the power required for operation of the radio and the public address system. There are separately powered 115-volt receptacles in the dome coaches, used for razor and curling iron outlets, as well as 32-volt outlets for vacuum cleaners and water-coolers; these receive their power from a Cornell-Dubilier vi-brator-convertor.

All wiring is carried in ducts and in sherardized steel conduit of standard weight. Four electric trainline circuits are employed in the new dome units, used respectively for air-brake control, telephones, emergency lighting, and the radio and public address systems.

But these bright, comfortable, pleasant modern cars represent just a portion of Union Pacific's new rolling stock. UP has also had built and delivered, for use in connection with the three types of dome cars, twenty improved sleeping cars. Of these fourteen are the conventional open-section type, while the remaining six have five bedrooms, two compartments, and two drawing rooms each. In addition, the sleek "dome liners" now speed cross-country adding to the comfort and ease of their passengers with new lunch-counter diners that accommodate twenty-one people at a long snack bar and sixteen more at four tables in an adjoining room.

UP's new equipment means more enjoyable and more luxurious travel through the nation's scenic West.

133

CHAPTER XXII

TIMKEN ROLLER BEARINGS FOR
FREIGHT CARS

More Are Being Installed, and All Railroads Must Go Roller Freight

Over the years American railroads have taken gigantic steps to improve their operations and services. Mainly these great developments have been experienced in three major categories—power, tracks, and safety.

Power was tremendously improved with the shift from wood-burning to coal-burning locomotives and, more recently, to diesel. The standardization of a single, universal, interchangeable gauge, replacing the previous twenty-three different track widths, marked another great forward step, while the introduction of standardized air brakes and couplings, automatic signal devices, etc., meant a great upgrading in the level of operational safety.

Now some authorities believe that the roads are on the brink of a fourth great improvement, the elimination of the pesky hotbox problem through the use of tapered roller bearings on freight cars.

Advantages of roller bearings over the conventional friction bearings are said to be great. For one thing, inspection time is reduced merely to the interval necessary for a track worker to feel the housing and check for temperature, as opposed to a series of nine inspections required for friction bearings. This saving alone, it is claimed, reduces terminal inspection time some 90 per cent, while lubrication costs are cut as much as 95 per cent. The manufacturers of the new Timken heavy-duty type AP bearing assembly say that it can run for three years without requiring any added lubricant.

The principal of the Timken roller bearing is that it rolls the load instead of sliding it, thus eliminating metal-to-metal sliding friction, the cause of the hotbox troubles that, during 1957, averaged a set-out every 189,000 car miles.

Roller bearings have been successfully used on passenger cars; in fact, without them, present-day streamliners could not run at their sustained high speeds. The benefits to railroaders were proved so great in this type of usage that progressive railroad men began to think about their next natural extension—to use them on the nation's freight cars.

Cost, however, has been a major factor in retarding application of roller bearings to all of the nation's 2,000,000 freight cars. Roller bearings, up till now, not only cost considerably more than conventional friction bearings, but they have proved more difficult to install. But, say the manufacturers, tremendous progress has been made on both of these fronts. Improved designs and better production methods have led both to greatly reduced initial cost and to greater ease of installation.

The cost factor, therefore, is proving less and less of a deterring influence when noted against maintenance savings, improvements in service, reduction of out-of-service time, and greater adherence to transportation schedules.

One prime example of a railroad that has adopted the roller bearing wholeheartedly is the Atlantic Coast Line. Back in 1949 this road tried out roller bearings on twenty-one of its freight cars. Four year later the total of ACL freight cars running on Timken bearings had reached well over six thousand.

Now every freight car with friction bearings going into an Atlantic Coast Line shop for major repairs is automatically switched to roller bearings, so that today ACL new cars plus conversions total nearly seven thousand cars on Timken bearings —some 21 per cent of the road's entire fleet.

It has been estimated by the manufacturer, following a survey of American railroad operations, that when every freight car in the country operates on roller bearings, there will be a saving of $288,000,000 per year in operating and maintenance costs. This will lead to improved earnings and consequently to more business and greater profits.

Meanwhile, of course, speedier shipping and elimination of traditional hotbox delays will mean that the freight-shipper will be able to count on faster, more reliable delivery service, a great advantage both to himself and to the customers he serves.

Here are listed some of the ways in which the manufacturer believes railroads can effect savings through the use of roller bearings:

Lower hotbox rate; lower bearing failure rate; lower maintenance costs; increased car availability and therefore reduced car ownership; quick wheel change with pedestal-type side frames; saving in locomotive hours; better safety record because of less accidents and fewer fires; reduced switching costs; reduced locomotive fuel costs; elimination of tonnage reductions in cold weather; less loss and damage to lading; reduced coupler and gear maintenance; centralized wheel and axle shops; better relations with shippers; fewer schedule delays; higher-speed operation and reduced scheduled terminal layovers; decreased dead weight; reduced wheel slip.

Based on the 1955 figure of 16,200 miles of use per average freight car, it has been calculated that annual savings per car through the use of roller bearings would come to $144 per year.

The survey noted, too, that there are specific advantages to the use of roller bearings in certain specialized types of operation, even where high mileage figures are not racked up. Low maintenance requirements, for example, are of benefit to operations of industrial-type cars carrying such material as hot metal, slag, and cinders. Again, cars used in the pulpwood and phosphate service normally travel over inaccessible single tracks, where bearing failures bring service to a halt because of the difficulty of bringing maintenance or repair crews to them.

The major point made by the Timken survey is that railroads can achieve a substantial return on the additional investment required to equip all their freight cars with roller bearings. The company notes that the upward movement of labor and material costs that has taken place since July 1, 1955, would have cost American railroads some $48,000,000 per year less than it actually did had all cars been running during that period on roller bearings.

CHAPTER XXIII

SANTA FE'S SAN FRANCISCO CHIEF

Fine New Train Has Proved So Popular—Ultrasonic Car

One of the real thrills awaiting any traveler is to make his journey on a famous Santa Fe Chief.

Today more people can accomplish this travel miracle than ever before, because the road has added a new luxury streamliner to join its Super Chief, Chief, Texas Chief, and Kansas City Chief. The newcomer, the San Francisco Chief, has brought a new conception of modern railroad service all along its route from Chicago through Topeka, Amarillo, Clovis, and the lush San Joaquin valley to the City of the Golden Gate.

Making the eastbound run in 47 hours 20 minutes and the Chicago–San Francisco trip in just 10 minutes more, the new lightweight Pullman-coach train features radio, recorded music, courier nurse service, comfortable chair cars with reclining seats, and the very latest in full-length dome cars. Its schedule is so arranged as to give passengers maximum opportunity to observe the great scenic beauties of the West during daylight hours.

Westbound, it leaves Chicago daily at 3:15 P.M., arriving in San Francisco at 2:45 P.M. on the second day. Thundering eastward, the San Francisco Chief departs its coast terminus at 11:00 A.M. each day and brings its passengers into Chicago at 2:00 P.M. the second afternoon.

To maintain this schedule on a daily basis, Santa Fe officials provided six fully equipped trains when the new Chief began its runs in June, 1954. It was the first new "name" train to be introduced to the Western territory in five years.

The glamorous new train furnished first-class east-west service for the first time to residents of the San Joaquin valley, one of California's most productive agricultural sections and a source of a great deal of the traffic in perishable farm products carried by the Santa Fe road. In addition, the San Francisco Chief makes it possible for passengers to obtain the fastest available service to and from Houston and New Orleans and the West Coast, with Clovis, New Mexico, serving as a cutoff point where cars are dropped from the eastward run or picked up to join the west-bound journey.

Routed through Amarillo and Clovis, the San Francisco Chief provides service to communities in west Texas previously not available to them.

The very name—the Chief—brings to mind romantic associations with the big scenic attractions through which these Santa Fe trains pass. And the road has spared nothing to make a journey on any one of these famous name trains an experience to be treasured and long remembered.

The all-stainless-steel dome cars that seem to bring the old West right into the train itself ride so smoothly; they weigh 207,000 pounds each and are equipped with six-wheel, outside swing-hanger trucks and ASF combination disc-tread brakes.

Budd brakes are installed on the luxury coaches, the result of Santa Fe officials' conviction that they add much to riding comfort while at the same time maintaining topnotch safety standards and keeping maintenance costs at a reasonable level.

Extensive tests, in which the Santa Fe constantly indulges, resulted in equipping the coaches of the San Francisco Chief with the very latest General Steel Castings four-wheel, outside swing-hanger trucks with a 9-foot wheelbase.

In the bustling Santa Fe car shops at Topeka, Kansas, San Bernardino, California, and Cleburne, Texas, remodeling and modernization of car equipment is a continuous process. Imaginative engineers and first-class workmen here combine their talents to incorporate in many of the Santa Fe's other trains some of the features that passengers have welcomed so enthusiastically on the San Francisco Chief.

Coach seats with adjustable leg rests, adjustable backs, and adjustable head rests are constantly being installed. Snack bars have been added to chair cars, conversions have been made to lunch-counter diners, improved lighting fixtures have been installed, and both radio and wire-recorded music installations have been made. All in all, more than two hundred passenger cars have been refurnished within the past few years.

At the San Francisco Chief's Chicago terminal, the road has installed the latest type of car-exterior washing machines, which can wash down the entire train, including roof and trucks, in one single operation. Powerful air vacuum ducts provide the car interiors with a thorough cleaning at each end of the run.

The Chiefs have gained a loyal following among America's travelers because of their comfortable, luxurious accommodations, their rapid service, and the high standards of maintenance upon which Santa Fe constantly insists.

The road links the densely populated eastern half of our country with the rapidly growing Southwest and West Coast, a condition that brings in its wake an unusually large proportion of passengers using its services for long trips. Its average income per passenger is more than seven times as great as that of America's Class I railroads in general; average ride on the Santa Fe is 565.41 miles, compared with 72.46 for all railroads. Consequently, Santa Fe's concentration on comfortable, fast, luxurious streamliners is something that is highly valued by passengers, who make such journeys as the 2,224 miles from Chicago to Los Angeles or the 2,081 miles between Houston and San Francisco via the new San Francisco Chief.

A Chicago-to-San Francisco journey on the new train takes one through the pages of American history in less than forty-eight hours. The Great Plains areas, the nation's "breadbasket," the fabulous Indian country of the colorful Southwest, the lush agricultural valleys of California, and finally the great, bustling city of San Francisco—all of which have played their important roles in the development of our nation—can be observed in luxurious comfort as the streamlined beauty glides smoothly, quietly, and rapidly, eating up mile after mile.

And this great American panorama can be seen now to even fuller advantage than ever before in the history of railroading, for the shining new San Francisco Chief, in its full-length dome, provides a new kind of angled sofa seat. No longer is it necessary to sit hour after hour with one's head turned to view the glorious sun-baked country of the Southwest, for on the upper deck of the dome lounge the cozy double seats have been installed at an angle that permits every passenger to enjoy the benefits of a full-dimension view without craning his neck.

Here are seats for fifty-seven passengers, while at the rear of the same upper level eighteen more can find comfortable accommodations at tables in the car's refreshment lounge. At night, riding along under the stars, an appealing charm is imparted to the smooth, silken journey with the most modern of indirect lighting installations.

On the lower deck San Francisco Chief patrons find the intimate atmosphere of a colorful cocktail lounge a delightful experience. It is a complete contrast to the open-air feeling that pervades the full-length dome above. Indian designs, typical of the country through which this magnificent train speeds, are etched in glass and hammered on metal plaques that decorate the walls. Mesa red, Zuñi turquoise, and Pueblo beige are the highly appropriate colors in which this charming lower-level cocktail lounge has been accented. Budd has done their usual fine job.

Then, of course, there are the relaxing "stretch-out" seats that add comfort to the roomy chair cars, with their radio and taped music that contribute so much to the restful atmosphere. A choice of the most modern sleeping accommodations, from wonderfully efficient roomettes to spacious suites, is offered the traveler, while famous Fred Harvey meals make every trip to the smooth-riding diner a rare treat.

Convenient connections are available for a short jaunt off the main route of the San Francisco Chief to the most famous of America's scenic wonderlands—Yosemite National Park, where the 2,425-foot-high Yosemite Falls has been thrilling visitors since its discovery. Daily sightseeing trips are conducted for those

141

eager to see such natural wonders as abound in Yosemite Valley, the Mariposa Grove or Glacier Point. Hiking and saddle trips can be arranged into camps in the High Sierras.

And then back onto the smooth-riding, glistening San Francisco Chief for the all-too-quick journey to the romantic City of the Golden Gate, once described as "the most exciting city known to man." The Orient, glimpses of old Europe, ships from all the seven seas, exotic foods—all these the traveler will find awaiting him in San Francisco, terminal of Santa Fe's San Francisco Chief, a wonderful new train to bring the traveler to a wonderful old city.

Comfortable, safe journeys on the San Francisco Chief and on all the other famous Santa Fe streamliners are assured not only by the splendid equipment with which the trains themselves are outfitted but also by an ultramodern method used by the railroad to uncover any weaknesses or faults in its many thousands of miles of trackage.

Electronic equipment, mounted in a Fairmount combined road and rail unit truck, automatically reveals such faults as bolt hole breaks or head and web separations while the car travels over Santa Fe track at speeds up to sixteen miles per hour.

As the car-truck combination moves along the rails it emits a combination of ultrasonic electric frequencies. As this energy is reflected back from the steel rails, it reflects what it has picked up by means of a pen mark on a continuous strip of chronograph tape within the road-rail unit. An operator continuously inspects the line on the tape, watching for defections from the straight, even line that indicates the existence of sound rail.

Although the sensitive electronic tape mechanism shows every normal rail end, every expected bolt hole, with a slight variation of the penned line, the experienced technician is trained to watch for the major deviations that reveal actual serious faults. When a sharp deflection of the line indicates such a condition, the Fairmont unit is brought to a halt and a hand test is run over the rail section with portable hand equipment brought from the road-rail truck. The defective rail is marked, a report is made of its location, and the car continues on its tour of inspection.

The unit is equipped with regular flanged guide wheels for use on the Santa Fe lines, but when these are raised, the road-rail car runs on regular truck tires and can leave the right of way at the first convenient motor road. This unique flexibility makes it possible to keep lines clear for regular railroad traffic.

The Santa Fe Railroad has found the new ultrasonic car to be highly efficient as well as economical in operation. It has proved especially valuable in detecting tiny flaws in close quarters, such as between bolt holes, where more traditional methods of inspection might often have failed to reveal faults.

Only minor modifications were found to be necessary in the Fairmont truck body to house the ultrasonic equipment, which was assembled by the railroad's engineers from standard units, in accordance with specifications worked out by two of Santa Fe's assistant detector car operators, I. L. Joy and R. B. Ball.

CHAPTER XXIV

THE LACKAWANNA

A Modern Railroad Must Have Buildings, Shops, and Facilities—New Service Roads

The language of a country changes with its history and its development, because many of the words with which everyone is familiar at one particular era lose their meaning as conditions change.

Every American during the past seventy-five years or so has been acquainted with the use of the term "tank town" to describe a very small community, but probably by the next generation this will be a dead phrase. A tank town got its name because the giant water tank, silhouetted against the country sky, was usually the most prominent structure in the entire hamlet. The tank was there because the railroad that passed through the town needed its water to refill the boilers of the old steam locomotives.

Today, along the route of the Lackawanna, as along the route of many other railroads, the water tanks and coal docks, the roundhouse and the erecting shops, are disappearing. Progress is replacing the steam locomotive with the newer, faster, more powerful, more efficient diesel. No longer is it necessary to slow down a schedule in order to take on water. So the tank is disappearing from the American landscape, and at the same time other significant changes are taking place along the Lackawanna's thousand-mile right of way.

For a railroad like the Lackawanna is more than trains and schedules. It is even more than just stations and freight houses and the similar kinds of structures that people associate with

144

Motor Special on the Pine Bluff-Texarkana Subdivision near Gertrude, Arkansas.

Santa Fe's #2, the San Francisco Chief, with diesel #308 meets #1, the west-bound San Francisco Chief, at Rheem, Cal. on Third Dist. of Valley Div. Note the magnificent new full length Budd built dome lounge cars in service on these and other Santa Fe trains.

Lackawanna HB-9 west of Blairstown, N. J. on the Scranton Buffalo Div. showing third track taken up to install a track service road. Note the excellent roadbed.

Lackawanna's 60-ton gantry crane, largest in port of New York, used tandem or single in Hoboken Terminal.

Chicago Great Western #41 crack fast freight gets a clear order board at Fairbanks, Iowa on Des Moines Dist., Eastern Div. Note the piggyback on the head-end.

Santa Fe #22, the new high-level El Capitan with diesel 24 climbing the 3.2 grade at Lynn, N.M. just before reaching the top of Raton Pass. Historic Fisher's Peak in the left background.

"Ribbonrail" on way to Santa Fe's Okla. Div. for main line service rounding curve in the famous Flint Hills grazing and fattening country on CTC territory near Matfield Green, Kan. on the Second Dist. of the Middle Div.

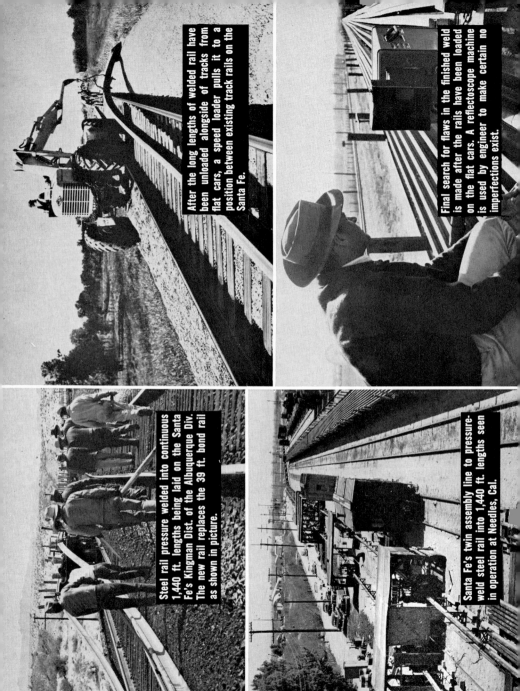

After the long lengths of welded rail have been unloaded alongside of tracks from flat cars, a speed loader pulls it to a position between existing track rails on the Santa Fe.

Final search for flaws in the finished weld is made after the rails have been loaded on the flat cars. A reflectoscope machine is used by engineer to make certain no imperfections exist.

Steel rail pressure welded into continuous 1,440 ft. lengths being laid on the Santa Fe's Kingman Dist. of the Albuquerque Div. The new rail replaces the 39 ft. bond rail as shown in picture.

Santa Fe's twin assembly line to pressure-weld steel rail into 1,440 ft. lengths seen in operation at Needles, Cal.

Excellent night view of the Southern's new Norris Yard at Birmingham, Ala. showing cars going down the hump.

New Citico Yard of the Southern Railway at Chattanooga, Tenn. Hump retarders in yard tower in the foreground. It cost $14,000,000 and shows what the U.S. railroads will do in spending money to speed freight.

New General Office Building of the Cotton Belt Railroad at Tyler, Texas, as it looked a few days before it was formally opened on March 22, 1955.

View of Accounting Department's machine room equipped with IBM key punch machines and comptometers.

Picking the marvelous Maine potatoes in Aroostook County.

Unloading Bangor & Aroostook mechanical reefers. State of Maine potatoes are given every care in hauling and handling by this railroad.

View from one of Northern Pacific North Coast Limited's four Vista-Domes of the Rocky Mts. Absaroka Range just east of spectacular Bozeman Pass, First Subdiv. Rocky Mt. Div.

Interior of Budd light-weight Pioneer III coach showing seats for 88 made of fiberglass with plastic snap-on seat covers. Seats are surprisingly comfortable. Interior of car is also entirely plastic, including the washroom which is made in a one-piece mold.

Budd's light-weight Pioneer III coach with radically different truck completed over 100,000 miles of satisfactory tests under all operating conditions. 6 are now in operation on the PRR for commuter service in electrified territory out of Philadelphia. This car, designed and built by the Budd Co., is the only light-weight car which is of standard length and standard height and should have a great future.

C & O time freight #32 with connections easily made for Buffalo and east crossing Suspension Bridge, Niagara Falls, N. Y. hauled by 2 EMD GP 9's.

C & O recently acquired Budd RDC rail diesel cars which are successfully operating as the Chessie Liner between Newport News, Va. and Charlottesville, Va. and have received many compliments.

On the Santa Fe piggyback is known as T-O-F-C (trailer on flat car) and it has an outstanding damage-free record for handling of freight, almost 100%.

Interior of trailer showing portable cooler units used by the Santa Fe to protect perishable shipments in hot weather. Heaters are used in winter months.

Northern Pacific's new self-propelled rail diesel car, the Budd RDC-2, which operates between Spokane, Wash. and Lewiston, over the Lewiston Branch. The air-conditioned car seats 70 passengers, has a baggage compartment and is powered by twin 300-h.p. engines. Superstructure on roof houses engine, radiators, fans, stacks and bell.

NP Extra 5410 east with 85 loads of perishables on the Third Subdiv. of the Rocky Mt. Div. at Bonner, Mont. hauled by 5400 h.p. EMD diesel. Note excellent track.

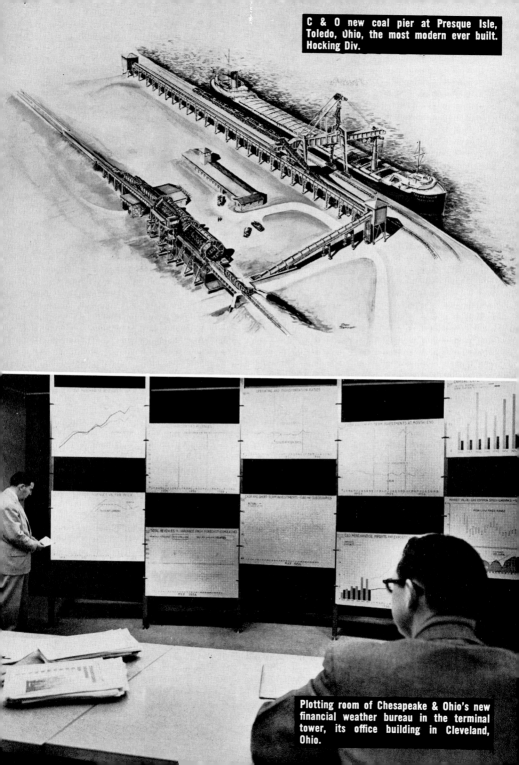

C & O new coal pier at Presque Isle, Toledo, Ohio, the most modern ever built. Hocking Div.

Plotting room of Chesapeake & Ohio's new financial weather bureau in the terminal tower, its office building in Cleveland, Ohio.

The "African Rainbow" unloading C & O Railway's Pier 9 on the pier's first full day of operation in 1957 at Newport News.

Aerial view of the Chesapeake & Ohio Railway's ice-free port of Newport News, Va. which links the C & O to the world's shipping lanes.

railroading. The Lackawanna owns a total of 1,074 buildings, enough to dignify a good-sized community, and every one of these structures plays a vital part in operating the railroad, guaranteeing prompt delivery of freight and speedy, comfortable travel for passengers.

At the Lackawanna's eastern terminus, for example, there are many buildings that are designed for specific purposes needed there at Hoboken, New Jersey, which are not duplicated anywhere else along the railroad's main or branch lines. At that point, just across the river from New York City, problems of transferring freight loads and flatcars across the Hudson are met with special covered and open freight-handling piers, facilities for moving cars on and off car floats, traveling cranes, and coal-dumping apparatus.

The lines run westward through Scranton, Pennsylvania, to Binghamton, New York, and on up to Buffalo, another port city, on Lake Erie. A branch runs north from Binghamton through Syracuse to Oswego, with a finger off to Cincinnatus. Another branch from Binghamton goes to Utica, with a finger off to Richfield Springs. Kingston, Bloomsburg, and Northumberland are all served by a branch running southwest from Scranton, and in New Jersey a complex web of lines exists to serve the many communities between Hoboken and the Delaware Water Gap.

All these lines and the trains continuously running on them require a multitude of buildings to keep them properly in operation, from a tiny watchman's shanty at a crossing to tremendous freight-storage houses and office buildings. Some of these structures are of a kind that are designed for specific use only by a railroad, while others could be used equally well by almost any industry in any community.

A complete list of the varying structures owned and operated by the Lackawanna would tax a reader's endurance, but here are just a few of the many different kinds of buildings maintained by the railroad:

Stations, signal towers, freight houses, shop buildings, ferry houses, air-brake shops, upholstering shops, power plants, car-wheel truing shops, fuel-oil pump houses, bunk houses, garages, compressor houses, foamite houses, scale houses, yard offices, crossing cabins, firehouses, tool houses, coach and freight-car repair shops, stores buildings, interlocking towers, section houses, and switchmen's shanties.

Also a livestock yard, a coal-thawing shed, a snow-melter garage, a boat-repair yard, a truck-repair shop, a milk house, a relay house, a grain office, an ice house, a coal-dust control house, a transformer house, and waste-reclaiming building.

In addition, there is a Pullman maintenance and supply shop, a diesel locomotive repair shop, a special building devoted only to maintaining the electric MU cars used in New Jersey commuter service, and a control house for car-washing; and there are power substations, storage buildings, and pier houses for motors and hoists.

While these various structures are required to maintain the railroad at maximum operating efficiency, they themselves must be properly maintained and kept in tiptop condition. The Lackawanna maintains a well-staffed department—Maintenance of Way and Structures—whose job it is to watch over the well-being of all these structures and to keep them in good repair.

This department operates hundreds of pieces of modern equipment, many of which were designed by Lackawanna men. Laying track, removing it, and keeping the lines in best operating shape are important parts of the responsibility of this department, which has contributed much to the development of technological progress in this field.

Track maintenance, in the early days of railroading, was a back-breaking job done by gangs of brawny men with picks and shovels, spike mauls, crowbars, sledge hammers, and other such hand tools. But thanks to the ingenuity of such men as B. Geier, Lackawanna's engineer of equipment and design, scores of efficient machines exist today to do the job more quickly, more efficiently, and with less effort on the part of the men who run them.

Under the direction of G. A. Phillips, chief engineer of the Lackawanna, a high degree of mechanized maintenance has been achieved. On the Lackawanna, for example, such machines were developed as the tie-puller and inserter, the hydraulic track-aligner, the ballast-conveyor and the ballast-regulator and scarifier.

A maintenance-of-way shop is operated by the railroad at Scranton, under the supervision of Mr. Geier. During late fall and winter all of the many mechanical tools used by the department are inspected, overhauled, and given a fresh coat of protective paint. A crew of twenty-six men work at this task, of whom fifteen man the shop on a year-round basis. During the spring and summer, when weather permits actual track operations, the other eleven men work as operators of the equipment.

The shop has been called one of the most modern in the country. Opened in 1953, it was designed by J. P. Hiltz, Jr., who at that time was engineer of maintenance of way and structures for the Lackawanna, and by Mr. Geier.

The current engineer of maintenance of way, R. F. Bush, supervises the annual program of track maintenance and improvement. Between spring thaws and the frosts of October, when outdoor work ceases, the Lackawanna spends more than $5,000,-000 each year to provide strong, reliable, smooth-riding, safe trackage for its passengers and for its freight loads.

A constant replacement schedule has been undertaken during recent years, in which heavier rail is being installed on main lines to provide for the operation of heavier trains at the higher speeds of today, and there is the continuous battle to be fought against the ravages of moisture, vegetation, weather, and insects, as well as normal track wear. Track maintenance is a never ending job.

In an average year of spring and summer operation, the Lackawanna will install perhaps fifty miles of new rail. Most of this will be of the 132-pound variety, while 105-pound rail will be used for suburban runs in the Hoboken-Newark area in New Jersey.

About one person in every five on the Lackawanna's payroll is connected with the job of maintaining track to provide safe and efficient transportation. In a typical year they may find themselves occupied also with raising 125 or so miles of track by three inches and another 275 miles of track by an inch and a half.

Thanks to the ingenuity of Lackawanna engineers, some 80 per cent of the railroad's total trackage is easily accessible for maintenance and repair work through a series of service highways that run parallel to the lines. This system, now used by many railroads, was pioneered by the Lackawanna in 1941.

This service-road system developed out of a program of widening cuts to ease snow conditions and to obtain improved drainage of the right of way. The soil that was removed from these cuts was deposited along the fills, often in sufficient width to provide a road for the fleet of highway vehicles owned and operated by the railroad.

Existence of these new service roads has brought in its wake a whole new concept of the transportation of maintenance personnel. Railroads had always carried work gangs on small motor cars that ran over the same tracks as were used by freight and passenger trains, causing inconvenience and delays in getting the crews to and from their job sites. But now motor trucks, carrying not only men and their tools but equipment as well, have added a new note of flexibility to the entire operation as they run along service highways without interfering with or being delayed by the regular schedule of trains.

Lackawanna service roads were planned with public highway systems in mind, and entrances and exits have been located to take full advantage of parallel public highways throughout the railroad's operating territory. Today a fleet of 187 motor trucks has access to points along the right of way wherever service is needed, whether on a regularly scheduled basis or in case of emergency.

Of this total, 169 trucks are assigned to maintenance and engineering forces and the remaining 18 to the mechanical, transportation, and police departments of the railroad.

In some cases, Lackawanna service roads were constructed along a line where a third main-line track or a passing track had been removed because of obsolescence. But more typical of the operation is the service road link completed between Kearny and Jersey City in 1953. Although it is only three miles long, it enabled the road to remove a troublesome fire hazard that had developed alongside this three-track electrified main line, which handles not only Lackawanna's through trains but the heavy New York City commuter traffic as well.

This is an area of swampy meadows, where the thick grass often grows to a height of seven to eight feet. Standing directly up to the shoulder of the roadbed, the swamp grass surrounded the poles supporting the electric transmission lines, so that, when the grass caught fire, as it not infrequently did, it created a real danger for the power lines. Now the new service road at the side of the tracks, completely cleared of the grass, operates as a fire-break, eliminating the likelihood of fire damage and of subsequent interruption of power feed.

This road across the meadows is 25 feet wide, with a varying elevation of two to three feet above the ground line. To construct it the Lackawanna hauled earth from its freight yard at nearby Secaucus, New Jersey, where an improvement program, going on at the time, resulted in ample availability of excavated soil.

Drop-end gondolas of 70-cubic-yard capacity were used to haul the fill. They were loaded at Secaucus with a truck-mounted crane and a crawler crane, each of which was equipped with clamshell buckets.

At the construction end a swing conveyor deposited the material, while a bulldozer spread it the width of the planned new road. At intervals the area was widened to permit trucks to make a turn-around.

Yes, a railroad like the Lackawanna is a good deal more than trains, stations, switches, and signals. It is a huge operation, requiring hundreds of structures, many pieces of specialized equipment, and the men and women who plan and carry out the thousands of unseen, unsung tasks that make passenger travel smooth, speedy, and safe and that get freight shipments to their proper destinations on time.

149

CHAPTER XXV

CHICAGO GREAT WESTERN'S OELWEIN CENTRALIZATION

Manifest Freight Trains

The great car-icing plant and installation of the Chicago Great Western is merely one important facet in a complete, modern, forward-looking centralized operation program put into effect by the railroad at its Oelwein hub. A new communications setup, streamlined car record systems, revised schedules based on a changing concept of shipments in CGW territory, dieselization, rebuilt shops and offices—all these mark the establishment of one of the most progressive headquarters operations carried on by any American railroad.

Many railroads have their headquarters at a major city that marks the terminus of a long, cross-country line, but Chicago Great Western has been concentrating all of its executive, operating, engineering, and mechanical facilities to take maximum advantage of the unique geographic layout of the railroad's right of way. At Oelwein, Iowa, the four spokes that are the road's main lines come together from Chicago, St. Paul–Minneapolis, Omaha, and Kansas City.

From the central headquarters at Oelwein, engineers and maintenance men can quickly and easily move out along any of the radiating lines to reach any point on the railroad. The CGW has none of the problems normally connected with a vast expanse of rail lines stretching out for 1,000 miles or more from some terminal point. The run from Oelwein headquarters to Saint Paul, for example, is only 179 miles, while Chicago is only 245.8 miles away from the centralized operation at the

Iowa hub community. This gives CGW a flexibility in utilizing its locomotives not enjoyed by very many other railroads.

Every step in the development of the Oelwein operation has been closely tied in with the railroad's program for full dieselization. In 1950 this stage was achieved with the acquisition of 7 passenger diesels, 85 freight locomotives, 40 switch engines and 2 gasoline units. Two years later these totals had been increased to 102 road locomotives and 39 switchers, for a total of 143 diesel units, including the 2 gas engines.

Shop facilities are of major importance in the servicing of such an extensive diesel fleet, and CGW went about creating shops for both heavy and running repairs at Oelwein. What had been the steam back shop was converted, by the addition of a separating fire wall, into the two necessary diesel repair shops with pedestal-type servicing facilities. Steel grate, nonslip flooring was installed at the upper or car-body level to reduce the possibility of workmen slipping on excess oil or grease. In the running repair half of the shop, each of the two tracks will accommodate a four-unit diesel for simultaneous work.

A renewed and rebuilt classification yard was put into service at Oelwein in 1952, increasing the trackage available for handling the longer trains that CGW is now running, resulting from dieselization and increased traffic. It has thirty-six tracks, the longest of which can hold 173 cars, and has a total capacity of some 3,000 cars. The outbound main track, with its 197-car capacity, is also the running track and must therefore be kept clear; the inbound main receiving track can hold 192 cars. The yard's first four tracks are also used for incoming traffic and have capacities of from 156 to 173 cars.

Special attention was given to a replanning job done on the miscellaneous yard services, in order to insure the proper and efficient functioning of the Oelwein operation. To bring to a minimum special movements of stock cars, which constitute a large portion of CGW freight traffic, stock facilities were placed at the west end of the yard, where they are adjacent to the independent lead near the west yard office. The icing facility, described earlier, is located at the opposite end of the yard.

A new, compact car-repair shop, handling repairs to about a dozen cars weekly, now stands at the yard's west end. It has sheet-metal walls and a concrete floor and is conveniently located right next to the rip track where running repairs are handled. A smaller building, similar in appearance, stands nearby; it is used for reclamation and for equipment repair work. Equipped with up-to-the-minute welding and forging facilities, it is used for building up working track surfaces, for repair on roadway tools, and for all general reconstruction and repair work.

A rebuilt passenger station at Oelwein houses the CGW private branch exchange telephone switchboard, while the station building serves also as a reception room for business callers, who are then directed to the appropriate building. Dispatchers and the road's car service bureau are located in a two-story building right next to the station, which is also occupied by a yard office, a telegraph office, and the CGW communications center.

A 52-foot steel tower supports the yardmaster's office, whose wide glass windows command a complete view of all operations. There are seventy talk-back speakers, through which the yardmaster can talk to virtually any man in and about the yard or any of its facilities, which he controls from a panel at the front part of his desk. There is also at his disposal a twenty-station intercommunications system giving him direct access to the road's principal executive desks. Radio and telephone networks make it easy for him to maintain complete control over yard operations at all times, while a pneumatic tube system, through which he can send or receive written messages, links him directly with the yard office, the telegraph office, and the depot office.

The conversion to complete dieselization of the Chicago Great Western railroad led as well to other changes at Oelwein. Elimination of steam power resulted in the railroad being faced with having facilities on its hands for which it no longer had any use. The roundhouse, for example, was revamped, many of its windows were bricked up, and it was rented to a local warehouse storage organization, which finds the existing trackage that leads to the building a great benefit to its own operations.

At the same time this arrangement provides added revenue for the railroad.

A back shop located at Oelwein soon proved to be much larger than was any longer needed for repair or servicing of the railroad's diesel fleet. A row of offices was constructed along the front of the old back shop, and currently CGW's motive power department, communications offices, and communications laboratories are housed there. An additional unused portion of the shop was sealed off with a brick fire wall, and the space thus created is rented out for additional warehousing purposes. Since this is a lease arrangement, the railroad is in position to reclaim the rented space at any time in the future it may decide that it needs the area for expanded operations.

New car tag arrangements have been put into effect at Oelwein, simplifying the tasks of yard clerks and switchmen. Large black letters on cards 4 inches square quickly show which of the four spokes is to be used when the car leaves the yards. When the yard clerk leaves the office, he carries with him a set of cards previously prepared from the waybills, a tacker to staple them to the appropriate car boards, and a walkie-talkie to keep him in touch with the yard office. With this latter piece of equipment he is able to tell the bill clerk about any inbound cars that are scheduled to move out again on an outbound train.

Improvements in the road's communications system have kept step with physical developments at the new Oelwein hub headquarters. In addition to complete dieselization and its effect upon length of consists and upon speed of scheduled runs, the character of the road's traffic is changing in that there is less local livestock transported and an increase in the amount of manufactured products moving between the four major cities at the end of CGW's great spokes.

These conditions have led to changes in both freight and passenger schedules, with, for example, one local passenger train now being operated in each direction daily over each principal route. Train density has thus been reduced, both by fewer trains and by a smaller amount of time consumed by each train on each run.

Two scheduled freights run daily between Chicago and Saint Paul via Oelwein; one operates between Oelwein and Omaha, one between Oelwein and Kansas City, one between Saint Paul and Omaha, while there are two time freights each day between Oelwein and Kansas City. To expedite all these services, additional communication lines have been established to obtain more channels for long-distance telephones and to operate printing telegraph equipment.

Oelwein, of course, is the communications center for this vast, spreading message network. Prior to the establishment of the new circuits, CGW had telephone train dispatching on its principal routes and employed a block phone between Chicago and Oelwein, while most other communications were handled through regular key telegraph circuits. There was no long-distance telephone service between principal stations and no printing telegraph facilities at all.

Now there are sixty telephone stations between Oelwein and Chicago alone. Loud-speakers and amplifiers have been installed in all dispatchers' offices, while between Oelwein and Kansas City there are thirty-four stations on the dispatchers' circuit. Repeaters have been installed all along the major spoke lines, and it is now practicable to concentrate train-dispatching operations at the central headquarters at Oelwein. Operations in and out of the hub center have been greatly improved as a result, since all information concerning train movements is well centralized and controlled.

A series of interchangeable wire lines makes it possible to use much of this carrier for teletypewriter operations too. In addition, there is an increased amount of local and short-haul telephone equipment in operation.

Freight conductors' wheel reports are more easily and quickly classified and recorded as a result of Chicago Great Western's modernization operations, which extend to detail clerical work as well. The number of steps needed to produce tabulating punched data cards has been greatly reduced through the adoption of what is known as "marked sensing" of car data.

Before the introduction of this modern system, clerks took the conductors' wheel reports, gleaned from them the necessary information, and then punched the required card data by hand. Now this step is completely eliminated, and the new system is a miracle of present-day electronic mechanization.

Punched cards are now produced automatically from an original report form that has been marked with a special electrographic lead pencil, and only one card is used from the beginning of the car movement until the information on it is punched on a permanent record card in the accounting office.

A special IBM card is used which has twenty-two spaces for pencil markings, which, according to the location on the card, indicate such data as whether the car is loaded or empty, description of equipment, forwarding station number, tonnage, etc. Only the car initial and number need be written in by hand; all other required information is shown by means of these special sense markings.

A card is prepared by the yard clerk or agent at the point of origin for each car placed in the consist, and it is turned over to the freight conductor along with the waybills. When the car is dropped or reaches the end of its run, the conductor fills out the car card with sense markings that indicate the terminating station number, date, time, train number, class of service, etc.

The cards then go to the IBM machines in Chicago Great Western's accounting office. Here a key punch operator punches the car initial and number into the card, using an IBM alphabetic card punch. The card then goes into a mark-sensing reproducing machine, where the pencil marks are spanned by electrical contact points causing impulses that activate machinery that punches holes into another car-record card in exact accordance with the position of the pencil marks on the original sense-marked card.

Before adopting this time-saving errorproof system, CGW studied a number of methods by which recording of wheel report information could be simplified. This system was finally decided upon primarily because it requires no special equipment for either the yard office or the freight conductor except the electrographic marking pencil. Besides, almost no training is required to familiarize employees with the operation of the marked-sense operation.

The railroad did not have to purchase any new equipment to institute this system. Two different card layouts were tried, and the card finally adopted serves a dual purpose, for both recording wheel reports and interchange reports. In this way the name of the inbound and the outbound road can be shown wherever necessary, as in the case where either an intermediate short haul or a switching line is involved.

The CGW is also using punched-card operations for time-keeping among train, engine, and shop employees. A prepunched card is sent to each shop daily for each worker, and at the end of the day it is returned to the accounting department, where the IBM machine is able to translate its markings into complete payroll data.

At Oelwein a special compact soundproofed room has been set up for the punch-key and machine operators who handle all these IBM card operations. Extensive filing cabinets, in which are kept all the cards, are accessible to every employee who works in this department.

The concentration of all operational directions at Oelwein has resulted in a remarkable lowering of Chicago Great Western's operating ratio, which dropped from 75.36 per cent in 1949 to 67.7 per cent four years later. Under the direction of President William N. Deramus, III, the road's long-term debt was also reduced by several millions of dollars during that same period.

Centralization of dispatching, communications, accounting, clerical operations, engineering, and all other major railroad functions at Oelwein, together with the building of modern facilities that make these operations move smoothly and efficiently, has resulted in a consistent increase in the road's net operating income.

It was the combination of full dieselization, together with the foresight to take advantage of the CGW's unique geographic layout, that brought in its wake all the changes and improvements that today make the Oelwein hub a show place of efficient railroad management and direction.

Virtually nothing has been overlooked in creating this modern headquarters operation. Even a series of pigeonholes has been built for the filing of waybills, and they are so arranged as to be divided into four easily identified groupings—one for each spoke leading out of Oelwein to Chicago, Kansas City, Omaha, or Saint Paul–Minneapolis.

The car-repair shop has been built with an extended roof to provide for emergency working area no matter what the weather, and in the main office the working area is divided from a comfortable trainmen's reception room by a specially designed two-sided board. Names of crew members appear on both sides of plastic blocks which are slipped into glass panels that separate the two sections, so that crew assignments can be read from both sides at any given time.

With the Oelwein headquarters now functioning at a highly efficient level, the CGW has moved out along its lines to improve facilities over its entire right of way. New brick stations have been constructed at Des Moines, Fort Dodge, and Marshalltown, Iowa, and in many of the smaller cities along the road compact steel structures have replaced old frame buildings. There is a new two-story brick freight office at Kansas City, which also provides space for both a traffic office and a general office.

Yard improvements have been made at Des Moines, which now has a capacity of 1,600 cars, while at Minneapolis a large portion of the terminal yard has been rebuilt and a new combination office and freight house has been constructed. Kansas City and Council Bluffs yards have also undergone extensive face-lifting.

All in all, Chicago Great Western has embarked on a program of which the American railroad industry in general, and the CGW in particular, can be proud, as are its former president, William N. Deramus, III, and its present chief, E. T. Reidy, a fine all-around railroader, who were both there to start and complete one of this country's most amazing rehabilitation jobs.

CONDENSED SCHEDULES–MANIFEST FREIGHT TRAINS

No. 90

Lv. Council Bluffs	5:00	A.M.
" Ft. Dodge	9:10	A.M.
" Clarion	10:00	A.M.
" Oelwein	4:15	P.M.
" Dubuque	7:10	P.M.
Ar. Bellwood	1:00	A.M.
" Chicago	2:00	A.M.

No. 91

Lv. Chicago	11:00	P.M.
" Bellwood	12:45	A.M.
" Dubuque	7:01	A.M.
" Oelwein	1:30	P.M.
" Clarion	4:40	P.M.
" Ft. Dodge	5:30	P.M.
Ar. Council Bluffs	10:15	P.M.

No. 43

Lv. St. Paul	5:00	A.M.
" Randolph	8:15	A.M.
" Hayfield	11:00	A.M.

Lv. Oelwein	4:15	P.M.—No. 90
" Dubuque	7:10	P.M.
Ar. Bellwood	1:00	A.M.
" Chicago	2:00	A.M.

Lv. Oelwein	9:00	P.M.
" Waterloo	10:50	P.M.
" Marshalltown	1:40	A.M.
" Des Moines	5:00	A.M.
" St. Joseph	10:40	A.M.
Ar. Kansas City	2:00	P.M.

No. 42

Lv. Kansas City	7:00	P.M.
" St. Joseph	10:30	P.M.
" Des Moines	5:00	A.M.
" Marshalltown	8:30	A.M.
" Waterloo	11:45	A.M.
" Oelwein	2:00	P.M.
" Hayfield	6:30	P.M.
" Randolph	9:00	P.M.
Ar. St. Paul	10:30	P.M.

Lv. Oelwein	4:15	P.M.—No. 90
Ar. Chicago	2:00	A.M.

Lv. Oelwein	1:30	P.M.—No. 91
Ar. Council Bluffs	10:15	P.M.

No. 41

Lv. St. Paul	4:45	P.M.
" Randolph	7:01	P.M.
" Hayfield	8:55	P.M.
" McIntire	10:40	P.M.

Lv. Oelwein	2:00	A.M.—No. 192
" Dubuque	5:20	A.M.
Ar. Bellwood	11:00	A.M.
" Chicago	12:15	P.M.

Lv. Oelwein	11:30	A.M.
" Waterloo	1:50	P.M.
" Marshalltown	4:00	P.M.
" Des Moines	7:00	P.M.
" St. Joseph	2:00	A.M.
Ar. Kansas City	5:00	A.M.

Lv. Oelwein	1:30	P.M.—No. 91
Ar. Council Bluffs	10:15	P.M.

No. 92

Lv. Kansas City	8:30	A.M.
" St. Joseph	1:20	P.M.
" Des Moines	7:20	P.M.
" Marshalltown	9:50	P.M.
" Waterloo	12:25	A.M.
" Oelwein	4:00	A.M.
" Hayfield	9:15	A.M.
" Randolph	11:30	A.M.
Ar. St. Paul	1:00	P.M.

Lv. Oelwein	1:30	P.M.—No. 91
Ar. Council Bluffs	10:15	P.M.

No. 143

Lv. Chicago	8:30	A.M.
" Bellwood	8:55	A.M.
" Dubuque	4:10	P.M.

Lv. Oelwein	9:00	P.M.—No. 43
Ar. Kansas City	2:00	P.M.

Lv. Oelwein	4:00	A.M.—No. 92
Ar. St. Paul	1:00	P.M.

CHAPTER XXVI

UNION PACIFIC

New CTC, North Platte Yards, Electronic Yardmaster, Radio, Laramie Icing Facilities

The modern miracles of electronic controlling instruments are being put to good use by the nation's railroads to increase their efficiency, provide greater safety, reduce operating costs, speed up schedules, and improve conditions of freight-handling. The Union Pacific railroad is in the forefront of this movement to put electronics to work for the benefit of railroad, passenger, and shipper alike.

Within the past two years UP has established modern centralized traffic control over a total of 391 miles of track, installed two-way radio communications to expedite freight pickup and delivery service in a major city, adapted a device originally invented to direct guided missiles for the purpose of controlling freight car coupling speeds in a yard, and in other ways modernized and improved its services and facilities through making use of the developments of modern electronic science.

The centralized traffic control operation, or CTC as it is more commonly known, has recently been established in two separate sections of UP's vast right of way. There is a 214-mile stretch extending from Granger, Wyoming, to Pocatello, Idaho, and another 177 miles of double and single trackage that runs from Laramie to Cheyenne, Wyoming; the railroad now totals 1,770 CTC miles.

CTC presents the great advantage of completely eliminating the need for giving written orders to train crews. Through small lights that appear on a board placed in front of a dispatcher, the up-to-the-minute position of every train running over any given section of track can be seen at a glance. The board itself has on its face a simple, schematic line map of the track under control of the individual dispatcher; as he watches each train progress as shown by the changing lights on the board, he can direct and control train movements from his centralized position by flicking small switches that control signals all along the line.

Intricately designed and engineered equipment is used in setting up centralized traffic control. The 214-mile Granger-to-Pocatello stretch cost UP $9,000,000 for installation of CTC. But, as the railroad's president, Arthur E. Stoddard, has pointed out, "CTC can increase the efficiency of a line as much as 80 per cent."

In addition to the long lines of electrical connecting units and the trackside signal equipment that must be installed, the centralized control unit has to be equipped, and in many cases setting up of CTC brings in its wake redesign of line and discontinuation of some trackage as well as the laying of other new track. In the Granger-to-Pocatello project, for example, there is a concurrent 8.5-mile line change, involving grading, between Moyer Junction and Fossil, Wyoming; there is the setting up of a centralized control headquarters at Pocatello; there is the remodeling of an old roundhouse at Montpelier, Idaho, to serve as an operational base for the installation of signal equipment; and there is a retiring operation for some passing tracks in this section of the line, combined with extension of remaining passing tracks to a minimum length of 8,100 feet.

Passing tracks requiring extension operations are located at the Wyoming communities of Granger, Moxa, Nutria, Opal, Waterfall, Fossil, Orr, Leefe, Beckwith, Pixley, Cokeville, Marse, and Border; in Idaho similar extensions will be made on passing tracks located at the towns of Montepelier, Georgetown, Manson, Alexander, Bancroft, Pebble, Broxon, McCammon, and Inkom.

On the main-line track section between Cheyenne and Laramie, existing heavy-duty double track includes long grades of 1.55 per cent ascending westward over Sherman Hill. Normal traffic in this area totals some twenty-four passenger trains, fifty-two freight trains, and twenty helper engine movements daily. In connection with the establishment of CTC functions at this location, UP built a new single-track line skirting the south side of the hill, and reducing the grade to 0.82 per cent. Intended primarily for westbound freights, the new line is also used by some westbound passenger trains. As a result, the main double-track line is now employed with greater efficiency by eastbound freight trains and by passenger trains headed in either direction.

With the completion of the new line, the signal system on the main double-track line was changed to increase the use of trackage. Where it had formerly been of the automatic signaling type, for right-hand running only, it is now under control of CTC and provides for signal indication in both directions. Thus at the option of the dispatcher, who sees the entire line of trackage on the board in front of him, any track can now be used to carry a train in either direction, under fully safe conditions at all times.

Prior to the installation of the new track and of CTC, freights lost much time because of the necessity of going onto sidings in order to clear the main track for passenger trains. Now the additional single track, plus the opportunity of safely using the additional line of main track in what previously would have been considered the "wrong" direction, provides for almost complete elimination of such siding delays.

As an added safety factor, duplicate signals appear right within the cab of each locomotive, picking up and repeating the reading on the next wayside signal as the train approaches it. Varying colored light combinations show the engineman exactly what the signal ahead of him is displaying, so that, even in the most inclement weather when wayside visibility is at a minimum, the engine crew at all times has a clear indication of what lies ahead.

Set up on a four-unit block system, the cab light will show a steady green just so long as the three block sections directly ahead of it are unoccupied. When within two sections of a preceding train, the engineman will see a yellow-over-green combination on his cab unit. Moving into the block immediately behind one occupied by another train, he will see a red-over-yellow warning. And should he pass the next red wayside signal, his cab unit will continue to display its red-over-yellow combination.

The new signal system in the Cheyenne-Laramie area includes two-way indications on the original main line of 54.4 miles between those two cities; both ways on two tracks between Cheyenne and the west end of Speer, a distance of 8.8 miles, leading to a branch operation of a single line southward 12.7 miles to Carr, on the way to Denver; both ways on a single track length of 34.5 miles westward from Speer to Dale, where the single track joins the main Cheyenne-Laramie line; and 3 miles between the west end of Speer and another branch-main junction at Borie.

At Borie there formerly was a complex mechanical interlocking setup that included four switches, a crossover, and seven home signals. With the advent of CTC numerous track and signal changes were made, the old interlocking system was removed, and electric switch machines and light signals were installed. At Dale, where the new single track for westbound freights rejoins the main line, power switch machines and signals were installed, as well as at sidings built at Granite and Buford on the old main line, at Emkay, Lynch, Harriman, and Perkins on the new single-track line, and at both Warren and Carr on the southbound branch toward Denver.

This branch, prior to CTC installation, connected to the main line at a point just west of Cheyenne, in an interlocking operation known as Tower A. A second track has now been added to this line between Cheyenne and Speer, and pertinent changes have been made in the tracks and in the interlocking at Tower A. All in all, the entire CTC installation set up by the Union Pacific Railroad in the Cheyenne-Laramie operation and its branches involves seventy-three power machines, twenty-five electric locks on handthrow switches and ninety-two lever-controlled signals.

Safe operations for tracks crews are provided for as part of UP's new CTC project. At various locations along the right of way, track occupancy indicators have been established to warn employees of approaching trains. Mounted in pairs, with one indicator facing in each direction, the warning signals bear numbers indicating the milepost to which the signal refers. They are spaced on time-distance factors, automatically calculated to warn a ten-mile-per-hour motor car of the approach of a train moving at the maximum speed limit permitted in the territory in which the signal is affixed.

If a motor car encounters a signal reading "clear," its crew knows that it will have ample time to reach the next indicator before any approaching train can possibly arrive. The signals are, of course, more numerous at curved sections where line-of-sight distance is relatively short. They operate under the control of automatic track-repeater relays, and are completely independent of the signal circuits that control train operations.

The new single-track line that was constructed to handle westbound freight and passenger trains runs through deep cuts through sheer rock walls at several places. Here there is always danger of blocked trackage from rock falls, but Union Pacific has installed special equipment that reacts to such occurrences by automatically setting red signals that will warn enginemen not to enter blocked sections.

Woven wire fencing lines the track wherever such falls might occur, and the fencing is attached to a small piece of wood, so set as to be under spring tension that holds the fence taut. A circuit controller is fastened in turn to this wood block. Should falling rock strike the fence, it causes the wood block to move, and the circuit controller is then set into operation to set warning signals at each end of the affected area. The section can be signaled "clear" once again, but only after a manual resetting of the circuit controller.

General Electric switch-heaters, a valuable installation in this country of heavy snows, have been attached to the inside of the web of the UP's stock rails in this area.

The entire CTC project was planned and installed by signal personnel of the Union Pacific Railroad, and makes use of signal equipment furnished by the Union Switch & Signal Division of the Westinghouse Air Brake Company.

The application of inventions developed for the armed forces to the peaceful pursuits of commerce is strikingly dramatized by the installation and operation of the "Electronic Yardmaster" in the Union Pacific's retarder yard at North Platte, Nebraska.

Here forty-two tracks, handling up to four thousand freight cars every twenty-four hours, can be controlled so as virtually to eliminate impact damage to boxcar lading normally resulting from human errors in judgment. The "Electronic Yardmaster" is an outgrowth and development of a device originally designed to direct guided missiles; at the UP yard it not only switches, but it automatically controls the speed of freight cars as they are pushed up over the hump of the huge classification yard for coupling. Railroad officials consider it a major advancement in the science of push-button railroading.

The speed of each rolling car is regulated by a series of car retarders that are electropneumatically operated or by trackside braking devices controlled from yard towers. As each car rolls down the incline its "rolling characteristics" are electrically determined and transmitted to an electronic brain. The distance the car has to roll in order to couple with waiting cars on the classification tracks (and this may be as much as two-thirds of a mile in some cases) is computed and is fed into the electronic brain by a device very similar to that used as range-finding equipment on big guns.

A radar speed meter continuously checks the speed of the car on its journey through the yard. With all this information, the device then calculates the correct speed at which the car must be retarded and then released in order to reach its point of impact speed at a safe rate, roughly three miles per hour.

The retarder control system into which this calculation is fed then automatically releases the freight car at just the right speed to permit it to roll freely down the track until it couples with the other cars to which it has been assigned. There is even an automatic compensation operation, which shortens the range and changes the release point as the classification track becomes gradually filled with cars and lessens the distance that the car must travel to its point of coupling impact.

In the control tower there is nothing for the operator to calculate; all he is required to do is to select the tracks for which each of the cars is destined, by pushing buttons before the freight train is pushed over the hump. This information comes to him from the yardmaster, who gets it from his knowledge of the consist that is teletyped to him even before the train has entered the yard.

The machine has a memory that enables it to retain at one time routing instructions for up to 120 cars. Its superiority over human operators comes about through the superrapidity with which it makes its calculations, checks car speed, and governs braking operations. The device has also proved to be completely accurate and foolproof in its calculations and operations.

The system was developed by two Union Pacific men, Roland J. Berti, the road's assistant electrical engineer, and David O. Bettison, UP's signal engineer, in conjunction with Perry A. Seay of the Reeves Instrument Corporation. David T. Bonner, Reeves' president, has noted, "The 'Electronic Yardmaster' was developed through Union Pacific's foresight and willingness to experiment with new techniques. This fact, combined with Reeves' experience and technical know-how in automation, produced this newest of robots."

Commenting on this installation, UP President Stoddard said, "It is a great step forward in preventing damage due to human shortcomings in the yards and will aid in maintaining prompt, efficient freight service."

Union Pacific continues its progressive pioneering in other directions too.

In Omaha it has installed the first railroad application of two-way radio communication to expedite freight pickup and delivery service. All of the railroad's pickup and delivery trucks in that city and in the Council Bluffs area immediately across the Missouri River have been equipped with two-way radios, providing for constant and instant communication between every truck and the dispatcher's office.

With its transmitter located atop Omaha's Blackstone Hotel and its broadcasting equipment in the dispatcher's office in UP's Omaha freight house, the system makes it possible to assign each truck a specific route or district to which to limit its operations. When the dispatcher receives a telephoned request for a pickup from some shipper, he can immediately relay it to the truck serving that area. When the pickup has been accomplished, the truck-driver can so report to the dispatcher, and can receive further instructions directly in the cab of his truck. This has completely eliminated inconveniencing patrons by making it no longer necessary for the driver to ask the shipper's permission to tie up his telephone while the truckman reports to the dispatcher.

Faster and more convenient service has resulted, too, because crosstown travel in heavy city traffic is now almost entirely done away with. UP points out also that in the event of an emergency evacuation, the railroad's two-way truck radio network could be assigned to important tasks in the Omaha and Council Bluffs civil defense program.

Modernization and mechanization of already existing facilities are also an important part of the Union Pacific's forward-looking program.

At Laramie about 100,000 cars a year are iced to provide proper refrigerated shipping conditions for eastbound fruit and vegetable cargo. The icing plant there is owned by Pacific Fruit Express, which is a company jointly owned by the Union Pacific and the Southern Pacific railroads.

In 1955 the company spent $465,000 in a three-month period to make its icing plant more efficient by means of mechanizing its icing platform. The Laramie plant is the largest automatic installation of its kind in the United States.

With its improvements, the new platform now can handle two hundred cars at a time. Three mechanical icing machines are mounted on the platform; each can pour 11,000 pounds of ice into a refrigerator car in ninety seconds, and each can re-ice the bunkers of a refrigerator car in an average of about forty-five seconds. They are equipped with radio equipment to maintain contact with the foreman's office, and the entire platform has a two-way public address system running its complete length.

When plans for the mechanization of the platform were announced, K. V. Plummer, who was vice-president and general manager of Pacific Fruit Express, had this to say:

"We were fortunate in putting our Laramie ice-manufacturing plant into operation three years ago, as since that time the winters have been so mild it would have been impossible for us to have harvested sufficient natural ice to meet the demand."

So here too is a demonstration of the foresight and sound thinking of another of America's railroad executives. Constant analysis of problems, anticipation of future developments, and a willingness to invest in the products of American scientific research and industrial production are keeping railroads like the Union Pacific up in the forefront of our country's progress. President A. E. Stoddard and Traffic Vice-President W. T. Burns are two of the most outstanding all-around railroaders this county has produced.

CHAPTER XXVII

COTTON BELT

Trinity Industrial District at Dallas—Tyler Industrial Foundation

One of the great contributions that American railroads are making to the rapid expansion of the nation's industry lies in their cooperative activities in the development of planned industrial districts in or near many of the country's major cities.

Perhaps the outstanding example of this is the interesting history of the planning, growth, and operation of the Trinity Industrial District in Dallas, Texas. Here three railroads—the Cotton Belt, the Rock Island, and the Texas & Pacific—joined hands with a private, community-supported realty development corporation for the benefit of all.

The Trinity Industrial District embraces an area of about 1,200 acres, all carefully planned and developed, within earshot of downtown Dallas, and occupied within its first seven years of operation by more than three hundred buildings, housing many of America's leading industrial organizations. Since the end of World War II the area has grown from an often flooded wasteland of cockleburrs and weeds to a modern, efficient community of plants, warehouses, and offices.

When the first settlers in the central Texas plains founded the city of Dallas well over a hundred years ago, they heard stories from local Indian tribes that they found a little hard to believe. The quiet, meandering little trickle that the settlers named the Trinity River, they were told, had twice turned into a raging torrent during the previous twenty years. In 1866, and again in 1890, they had reason to credit the Indians' stories, for in both of those years the river did rise to cause great havoc and to impede seriously the growth and development of the new community. Then, in 1908, the river rampaged to a height of some fifty-two feet, inundating what was already the leading city of the Southwest and causing millions of dollars' worth of damage.

It was clear then that, if Dallas was ever to be able to expand industrially, steps would have to be taken to harness, control, and direct the course of the Trinity River.

In 1925, after two more serious floods had occurred, the city fathers appointed a committee to get to work on the problem and to come up with recommendations. A man named L. A. Stemmons was a member of that committee.

After some study, the committee suggested that work should be undertaken to straighten the course of the river, running it between two levees to be constructed for that purpose. Landowners in the area founded a Levee District, and in 1928 bonds were issued totaling over $20,000,000, of which amount the area's landowners themselves subscribed to $6,500,000.

With these funds a new channel was created for the river, levees and other flood control devices were constructed, and by 1932, for the first time in the city's history, some 7,200 acres of what had been bottom land had been freed for development. The entire system consists of about twenty-five miles of levees and about fifteen miles of artificially created new channels.

Under the leadership of Mr. Stemmons, who called himself a "practical visionary," many of the landowners got together to form the Industrial Properties Association. Surveys were run for proposed streets throughout the reclaimed area, trees were felled and land was cleared, and preliminary negotiations were begun with railroads and with utility companies.

Then came the depression. Because the property owners could no longer continue to pay taxes, the bonds went into default. There was no money available with which the Levee District could maintain operation of its drainage pumps, and the city of Dallas operated its own pumps only when emergency conditions demanded.

But, all through this frustrating and difficult period, Mr. Stem-

169

mons hung on doggedly to his dream of a planned, privately owned industrial district on the borders of the Trinity River, and he brought up his two sons to follow this ideal. He passed away in 1939, and thus unfortunately never saw his dream grow into reality. But today those two sons—John M. Stemmons and L. Storey Stemmons—are respectively president and vice-president of the modern, progressive, bustlingly active Industrial Properties Association.

The Trinity Industrial District, as it exists and operates today, is a splendid example of cooperation between the three railroads and the private corporation. Since inception of the actual development of the plan, which really got under way in 1946, the district has worked closely with the industrial development departments of all three roads involved. All have taken an active part in planning and construction activities and have continually placed their facilities and services at the disposal of IPA.

The Cotton Belt and the T&P serve one stretch of about three hundred acres of plant sites along the levee nearest downtown Dallas, and both railroads have shared the construction and maintenance costs on 9.6 miles of track laid to serve the area. Under the smoothly working arrangement, T&P furnishes all maintenance labor and materials, while the Cotton Belt line pays half of the costs involved. There are nine jointly used access tracks, each about 1,500 feet long, which sprout off the main track at a curvature angle of 20 degrees to serve the area's plants and warehouses.

On the opposite side of the district, the Rock Island road has constructed a 7,000-foot lead-in track as well as switching tracks that total about 6.5 miles of new line. Rock Island, as early as 1953, was able to switch some twenty to thirty inbound cars daily for the area it served, with one diesel engine. It is constructing a trestle across the now abandoned original Trinity River channel, which will enable it to reach another five hundred acres now under development.

The Cotton Belt and the T&P together switch with their own diesels on a twenty-four-hour basis in the section they serve. Many of the companies in that district have their own spur

170

tracks, and the railroads are involved in considerable switching activity. Those organizations having only occasional carload shipments have convenient access to public delivery trackage of the Cotton Belt and T&P, one of which lies directly alongside the new T&P $1,500,000 freight terminal, one of the largest buildings in the district, completed in 1952.

Carefully planned and strategically divided into zones, the Trinity Industrial District has warehousing areas, light manufacturing sections, and heavy manufacturing districts. To protect the types of industry involved, restrictions vary in the several sections, so that there is no possibility of a nuisance-type industry springing up right next to a wholesale operation, nor is a heavy industrial plant ever likely to find itself involved in litigation over the use of its property.

In warehouse and light industry areas, streets and rail easements have been depressed, so that a floor slab poured at ground level is automatically at car-door or truck-bed level; this permits of substantial savings on building construction costs. Almost every major national highway entering Dallas either skirts the district or converges here with other important roads serving the city.

There are more than nine miles of well-paved streets in the district, of 9:7:9 reinforced concrete, generally forty feet wide. Regulations prescribe that no loading dock facing a public street can be nearer than twenty-five feet to the property line or less than forty-five feet from the pavement, an arrangement that completely does away with the possibility that parked trucks will ever obstruct the free movement of traffic on the paved streets. In many cases truck wells have been designed and constructed right inside buildings.

The entire Trinity Industrial District is divided into units that are 45 feet wide, a frontage broad enough for normal rail facilities yet sufficiently small for the operations of almost any commercial organization. Depths of tracts run from 125 feet to 410 feet, and an individual company may purchase and construct on as many of the 45-foot-wide units as are necessary to meet its requirements. A utility strip has been maintained at the rear of each unit of developed property; it is 53 feet wide, of which 43 feet have been reserved for a main rail track and for two service tracks, one on either side of the main rail, to service buildings backing onto it. The remaining 10 feet of space is occupied by utility installations.

Many of the three railroads' best customers are included in the star-studded roster of names of industrial organizations occupying space in the district. The parts depot of International Harvester Company, serving all the company's dealers in the Southwest and Mexico, is the largest building in the area; other structures are occupied by Continental Trailways, B. F. Goodrich Company, Ford Motor Company, American Radiator & Standard Company, and Pittsburgh Plate Glass Company, to mention a very few. The United States Post Office has constructed and operates a modern parcel post depot and garage occupying 100,000 square feet of floor space that is surrounded by another 100,000 square feet of paved concrete parking area.

But the booming Trinity Industrial District of Dallas is not the only planned commercial area served by such railroads as the Cotton Belt. There are now some forty to fifty cities in various parts of the United States that are involved in the development of similar industrial sectors. On the route of the 1,556-mile Cotton Belt line through the rich agricultural area from St. Louis to Dallas, Fort Worth, and Gatesville, there are related projects in operation at North Little Rock, Arkansas; Texarkana, on the border line between Arkansas and Texas; Waco, Fort Worth, and Tyler, Texas.

The Tyler Industrial Foundation, organized in 1945, has had such spectacular success that many communities have adopted its methods, in whole or in part, to launch like projects of their own. At that time, with the scheduled postwar closing of nearby Camp Fannin, Tyler businessmen recognized that an important source of employment and payrolls would be lost to their community. The foundation was thus set up as a means of creating a fund to be used to provide sites and plant facilities for industry on a long-term lease-purchase basis. It is a civic, nonprofit operation established under state law for a fifty-year period.

The basic objective of the Tyler Industrial Foundation—and of others that have been modeled after it—is to induce an industry to locate in the community by providing it with sites and with buildings designed and constructed according to its own specifications. The foundation does not actually go out to seek new industries; this is the function of the city's chamber of commerce, and it is in this respect that the Cotton Belt furnishes important aid.

The agricultural wealth of the states traversed by the Cotton Belt is responsible for a large number of important plants located along the railroad's right of way. The area is rich in soy beans, cotton, pulpwood, lumber, petroleum, natural gas, chemical raw materials, and other important natural resources, which have been instrumental in the location of various types of industrial processing plants along the Cotton Belt's main and branch lines. Thus the agricultural richness of the area has aided the industrial growth of the railroad itself and has added to its volume of freight traffic.

The success of such operations as the Trinity Industrial District and the Tyler Industrial Foundation is bringing about a radical change in the face of America. The Urban Land Institute has reported more than one hundred such industrial developments planned or under construction in and around cities from coast to coast, including such widely separated communities as Boston; Teterboro, New Jersey; Atlanta; Kansas City, Missouri; New Orleans; Oklahoma City; Los Angeles; and even in Toronto and Ontario in Canada.

Leading architects, builders, manufacturers, and finance experts now meet regularly with railroad executives to discuss the problems and the possibilities of the "planned industrial district." They have drawn up specifications for the needs of such a district, so that communities planning such projects now have the advantage of learning from the experiences that have been undergone previously. They discuss such questions as how the district helps the industrialist, the importance of correct location, employee transportation problems, design of industrial buildings, zoning restrictions, financing operations, and the proper planning that will make such a district most efficient in terms of railroad operations.

Here, then, is still another example of how the country's railroads work constantly with community officials and American businessmen to move forward to create improved operations of benefit to all.

H. J. McKenzie, a fine railroader and crack engineer, is president of the Cotton Belt and is ably backed up by G. W. Hevermann, who heads the traffic department, and W. H. Hudson, operating vice-president.

CHAPTER XXVIII

SANTA FE

Piggyback and Ribbon Rail

Like many another American railroad that is making its bid to meet the competition of the trucking industry, the forward-looking Santa Fe has instituted and is constantly expanding its piggyback service.

The trailer-on-flatcar operation, which the road began with an experimental run back in 1952 between Wichita, Kansas, and Kansas City, has now been broadened to a service that links two major West Coast cities and joins Chicago with Kansas City and several industrial communities in the Southwest. Shippers can now move their cargo, door to door, to and from points in Los Angeles and San Diego, as well as between Topeka, Hutchinson, Great Bend, Dodge City, Wichita, and Winfield, Kansas; Bartlesville, Tulsa, Ponca City, Enid, and Oklahoma City, Oklahoma; Kansas City; and Chicago.

The Santa Fe is justifiably proud of its cooler-trailer service, inaugurated in August, 1955, between Chicago and Kansas City. Utilizing a specially designed insulated metal unit that holds 600 pounds of dry ice, the cooled trailers facilitate the movement of such perishable commodities as candy, wax paper, vegetable oil products, oleomargarine, and the products of the great meat-packing industry centered in the area served by this unique operation.

Installed in 32-foot trailers, the compact refrigerating unit occupies only 8 square feet, with the interior walls of the trailers themselves having three inches of insulation. Desired temperature, which varies with the nature of the product being shipped

175

in any particular trailer, can be set beforehand, after which a thermostat inside the unit automatically maintains the mercury reading within upper and lower limits that have been assigned to it, guaranteeing maintenance of the proper temperature for the entire journey.

Three fans set on top of the refrigerating unit constantly circulate the interior air, to make sure that all parts of the trailer and its valuable cargo are at all times subjected to the proper degree of cooling.

Batteries securely slung underneath the trailer provide the current necessary to operate the fans. But even these batteries are preserved whenever the trailers are at loading docks, since an extension cord makes it possible to plug into any nearby electrical outlet. Carbon dioxide gas is vented from the trailer by means of a duct that emerges through the vehicle's floor.

The newly fitted trailers provide for year-round shipping of delicate cargo items. During the winter months the entire cooling unit is readily replaceable with a small heater, so that Santa Fe can offer complete protection against extreme outside temperatures to perishable freight commodities, no matter what the season.

George B. Kelley, the road's assistant to the general traffic manager, is enthusiastic about these cooler-trailers. He cites low initial cost, simplicity of design, ease of operation, and portability as their chief assets, which are enabling Santa Fe to widen the scope of its far-flung piggyback service to shippers.

When unusually wide freight objects have to be rolled into or out of a trailer, the refrigerating unit can be quickly moved out of the way to facilitate handling of the bulky cargo. Mr. Kelley points out, too, that there is almost no likelihood that the units will ever suffer any damage en route, because the complete refrigerating box is securely enclosed within the trailer; only the batteries are exposed. Failure of the unit to operate properly is therefore almost impossible.

As an added precaution to assure correct operation, a small light is installed next to the batteries. It flashes on if at any time the temperature within the trailer is not being maintained at the level set by the thermostat. Since this too is outside the trailer, it is always subject to a ready check by railroad attendants.

A load of the famous Brach candy, made by E. J. Brach & Sons, was the first shipment Santa Fe ever made on a cooler-trailer. At the time the railroad had only one such vehicle in operation, and it made two trips each week between Chicago and Kansas City. There are now ten such trailers operated by Santa Fe piggyback service, five that are 32 feet long and five that are 24 feet long. A tape-recording thermometer went along on the first few rides, and it kept a continuous and accurate record of the mercury readings within the trailer for every moment of the entire trip.

The newly expanded piggyback service provides Santa Fe customers with a combination of direct rail or combination rail and truck operation, whichever gives the more dependable service to and from shipping points of the particular cargo. First-morning delivery service is provided between Chicago, Kansas City, and Topeka, and second-morning delivery is in effect between Chicago and the other Kansas and Oklahoma communities served.

Westbound, trailers move on the road's famous freight train, No. 39, leaving Chicago at 6:00 P.M. and arriving at 7:30 the following morning in Kansas City. A new easterly freight train was established to handle piggyback shipments from Kansas City, leaving at 5:30 P.M., to Chicago, where the train arrives the following day at 7:00 A.M.

These early arrivals make it possible for the trailers to be unloaded, attached to prime movers, and delivered to consignees in their respective areas the same day. Flatcars are equipped with special hold-down devices, and carry either two of the 24-foot trailers or one 24-foot trailer with another 32 feet in length.

On the West Coast, piggyback service is in operation between Los Angeles and San Diego on a daily basis, except Saturday southbound and Sunday northbound.

As on the Chicago–Kansas City run, the freight is picked up directly at the shipper's warehouse, hauled to the yards, and loaded onto flatcars. These are run to their destination, where the reverse process is carried out. Delivery is made directly to the

177

consignee at the very same rates and minimums that apply to identical service provided by highway truckers.

The southbound West Coast service leaves Los Angeles at 9:05 P.M., arriving in San Diego less than five hours later, while northbound shipments leave San Diego at 3:15 A.M. and arrive at Los Angeles exactly at 8:00 A.M. the same day. Here too the early morning arrival permits delivery to final consignment point the very same day. As in the Midwest operation, the Los Angeles–San Diego piggyback service is carried on specially equipped flatcars that hold either two 24-foot trailers or one each of the 24-foot and 32-foot variety.

As has been seen, the Santa Fe might well be called "the railroad of forward-looking innovations." Having established a valuable new service for shippers with its expanded piggyback service and its unusual cooler-trailers, the road is now spending great sums of money to improve the riding comfort of its human passengers too.

About one and one-half million dollars has been invested by Santa Fe in relaying a 27-mile stretch of track out in New Mexico between the communities of Rosario and Bernalillo on the New Mexican Division. But it is not ordinary railroad track that has appeared there. It is welded rail that provides a virtually continuous ribbon of track, eliminating the conventional joint that appears every thirty-nine feet and that makes for the proverbial "clickety-clack" of the steel wheels as they hit the slight gap with monotonous regularity.

The new kind of rail is fabricated by a brand-new electric flash method, originally developed in Switzerland and named the Matisa-Schlatter butt welding process, after its inventors. It is a process that not only will make riding quieter for the Santa Fe's passengers, but will, over the years, save the road much time, effort, and funds normally expended on maintenance of conventional track lengths.

Before deciding to install the new electrically welded ribbon rail in this section of its New Mexican division, Santa Fe officials tested trackage brought into one long, continuous ribbon

178

by the more usual acetylene gas process. Riding comfort and reduction of maintenance problems convinced them that welded track represented a real advance, and so it was decided to go ahead with the creation of longer sections of trackage banded together by the new electric method.

By the end of 1955, approximately 63 miles of electrically welded track was in place in scattered areas of the Santa Fe's vast network. Following completion of the 27-mile Rosario-Bernalillo stretch, the specially built Matisa-Schlatter equipment unit of three cars was moved to Santa Fe's Plains Division, where a continuous-weld rail installation of about 7½ miles was made between Curtis and Mooreland, Oklahoma.

Then the railroad's Illinois Division received a section of the new kind of track with the laying of more than 28 miles of ribbon rail between Edelstein and Knox, and in 1956 and 1957 73.7 miles of 136-pound welded rail was laid on the westward track of the first district of the Albuquerque Division. Thus the Santa Fe railroad now has the opportunity to test this track of the future in widely scattered parts of the United States, under their varying conditions of weather, temperature, and traffic pattern.

The new machinery is made up of three cars, which give it a maximum capacity of about fifteen welds per hour. Conventional 39-foot rails are stockpiled in the first car, which also contains the actual welding unit. As it feeds through the other two cars, the ribbon rail goes through all the necessary steps of welding, grinding, and testing.

It emerges in strips 1,440 feet in length, or approximately a quarter of a mile long, and is fed onto a waiting train of thirty-one flatcars, having a total capacity of twelve strings of the long, continuous rail. It is then hauled from its welding point to the site at which it is to be placed into the Santa Fe's service.

Much study has been devoted by the railroad's engineering and metallurgical experts to all facets of creating, transporting, servicing, and maintaining the new kind of rail.

"Something entirely new to American railroading has been adopted," said Vice-President of Operation Clarence C. Tucker, when the first section of new track was placed in operation, "after a great deal of engineering and the outlay of substantial capital costs.

"The end product of it all is that we are proud to have a part in introducing an improvement that under our private management system will result in economies for the public benefit without a single cent of cost to the individual taxpayer."

The nation's railroads, of course, absorb all the costs of maintaining their own rights of way, so that the Santa Fe's important decision to proceed with the laying of more and more ribbon rail will ultimately involve an investment by the road of many, many millions of dollars.

Just how many can be judged by recalling that the nearly half-million-dollar expenditure mentioned above went for materials, welding, and labor costs involved in the change-over from conventional to ribbon rail only in the project undertaken between Rosario and Bernalillo—a total distance of 27 miles!

FROM CHICAGO AND KANSAS CITY TO CALIFORNIA
Trains 59–53

Station	Time	Example Day	Miles	Hours	Amph
Lv. Chicago (CT) . .	11:00 A.M.	Mon.			
Ar. Kansas City . . .	3:00 A.M.	Tue.	447.8	16'00"	30.0
Ar. Los Angeles (PT) .	5:00 P.M.	Thur.	2205.6	80'00"	27.6
Ar. San Diego . . .	11:59 P.M.	Thur.	2284.0	87'00"	26.3
Ar. Bakersfield . . .	10:30 A.M.	Thur.	2192.6	73'30"	29.8
Ar. Fresno	1:05 P.M.	Thur.	2300.1	76'05"	30.2
Ar. Stockton	4:30 P.M.	Thur.	2424.9	79'30"	30.5
Ar. Richmond . . .	7:00 P.M.	Thur.	2494.5	82'00"	30.4

(San Francisco Bay District)

FREIGHT SCHEDULES FROM CHICAGO AND
KANSAS CITY
TO
OKLAHOMA–TEXAS–NEW MEXICO–ARIZONA
Train 39 and connections

Station	Time	Example Day	Miles	Hours	Amph
Lv. Chicago (CT) . .	6:00 P.M.	Mon.			
Ar. Kansas City . . .	7:30 A.M.	Tue.	447.8	13′30″	33.2
Lv. Kansas City . . .	10:00 A.M.	Tue.	. . . . .	. . . . . .	. . .
Ar. Oklahoma City . .	7:30 P.M.	Tue.	793.2	25′30″	31.1
Ar. Ft. Worth . . .	2:55 A.M.	Wed.	997.6	32′55″	30.3
Ar. Dallas	3:00 A.M.	Wed.	1015.5	33′00″	30.8
Ar. Houston	10:00 A.M.	Wed.	1338.7	52′00″	25.7
Ar. Amarillo	1:00 A.M.	Wed.	981.9	31′00″	31.7
Ar. Lubbock	6:00 A.M.	Wed.	1103.5	36′00″	30.7
Ar. Albuquerque (MT)	10:30 P.M.	Wed.	1355.2	53′30″	25.3
Ar. El Paso	6:30 A.M.	Thur.	1548.9	61′30″	25.2
Ar. Phoenix	11:59 P.M.	Thur.	1904.4	78′00″	24.4

CHAPTER XXIX

SOUTHERN RAILWAY SYSTEM

Fast Freight, L.C.L., New Yards, Freight Cars, Car Repair

The changing character of the South's economy is reflected in the altered statistics of the Southern Railway System's freight flow.

Almost all commodities carried by the railroad have increased in volume in the years since the end of World War II, but some of them have assumed greater relative importance than others. Traffic on the Southern is, in general, more balanced today than it was in 1939, for example.

With the exceptions of textiles and other products made from the basic Dixieland cotton crop, the South formerly imported much of its manufactured goods. But today factories located throughout the South make items that are shipped to all parts of the country, and as a result, traffic in manufactured commodities is by way of becoming an evenly balanced two-way operation for the Southern Railway System. It's 8,000 miles of track throughout the Southern states put Southern in a key position to serve the entire area with an all-around freight service.

In addition to its own gateway terminals, Southern interchanges freight loads with other roads at more than 250 points. Southern's freight schedules, based on the runs of more than twenty-four daily time freight trains, are closely synchronized with those of connecting freights and locals serving branch-line points.

Each one of the Atlantic and Gulf port communities served by Southern has at least one scheduled daily freight that connects it with other parts of the South, and through connecting interchanges with the rest of the nation. The busy route between Potomac Yard and New Orleans—via Atlanta, Birmingham, and Meridian—runs two daily freights in each direction.

Some of these scheduled freights have names that are almost as well known, and certainly as descriptive, as those of the road's crack passenger trains: the Clipper, the Eastern Rocket, the Southern Flash, the Jack Pot, the Bean Train. Highly descriptive of its function is the daily Cincinnati-to-Atlanta Automotive Special, which virtually functions as part of the automobile plants' assembly line.

Daily at 6:00 A.M., the Automotive Special—better known as the Spark Plug—moves out of Cincinnati heading south over the Ohio River, its cars loaded with parts that have been picked up in interchange from their points of origin in the Detroit area. Running a schedule that is only slightly less rapid than that of a passenger train, the Spark Plug pulls into Chattanooga within twelve hours, and by midnight it has arrived at the Inman Yard in Atlanta.

Transfer diesels are on hand here to move the cut cars out to Buick-Oldsmobile-Pontiac, Chevrolet, and Ford assembly plants in the Atlanta area. So the daily run of the Spark Plug has again relieved the assembly plants of the necessity of stocking huge inventories of parts.

Throughout Dixie, newly developed cities and manufacturing centers have sprung up off the main routes of the Southern Railway System, and the railroad therefore has had to develop schedules that are integrated with those of connecting runs. Since printed timetables of freight runs are distributed to help shippers plan their product movements, it is essential that Southern meet these schedules as advertised and that fast and dependable transportation be furnished to all shippers, whether their plants are located on the main line or on some branch line. The terminal-improvement program, described in another chapter, has proved of tremendous value to Southern in enabling the railroad to expedite its cargo shipments.

Recognizing that highway carriers have made their greatest

POTOMAC YARD TO ATLANTA-BIRMINGHAM-NEW ORLEANS-MOBILE-MEMPHIS-JACKSONVILLE

No. 153
Lv. Potomac Yard . . . . . 9:00 A.M., ET, Monday
Ar. Atlanta . . . . . 12:45 A.M., ET, Tuesday
Lv. Atlanta . . . . . 12:01 A.M., CT, Tuesday
Ar. Birmingham . . . . . 4:30 A.M., CT, Tuesday
Lv. Birmingham . . . . . 8:00 A.M., CT, Tuesday
Ar. New Orleans . . . . . 6:00 P.M., CT, Tuesday

Mobile Section}
Lv. Birmingham . . . . . 9:00 A.M., CT, Tuesday
Ar. Mobile . . . . . 6:00 P.M., CT, Tuesday

Memphis Section}
Lv. Birmingham . . . . . 6:00 A.M., CT, Tuesday
Ar. Memphis . . . . . 6:00 P.M., CT, Tuesday

Jacksonville Section}
Lv. Charlotte . . . . . 7:00 P.M., ET, Monday
Ar. Jacksonville . . . . . 6:00 A.M., ET, Tuesday

CINCINNATI AND EAST ST. LOUIS TO CHATTANOOGA-BIRMINGHAM-NEW ORLEANS-MOBILE-ATLANTA-JACKSONVILLE

Lv. Cincinnati. . . . . 4:00 P.M., CT, Monday
Ar. Chattanooga . . . . . 12:01 A.M., CT, Tuesday

Lv. E. St. Louis . . . . . 2:00 A.M., CT, Monday
Ar. Chattanooga . . . . . 9:30 A.M., CT, Monday

Birmingham New Orleans Mobile Section}
Lv. Chattanooga . . . . . 12:30 A.M., CT, Tuesday
Ar. Birmingham . . . . . 4:30 A.M., CT, Tuesday
Lv. Birmingham . . . . . 8:00 A.M., CT, Tuesday
Ar. New Orleans . . . . . 6:00 P.M., CT, Tuesday
Ar. Mobile . . . . . 6:00 P.M., CT, Tuesday }

Connects with Potomac Yd. 153 at Birmingham

Atlanta Jacksonville Section}
Lv. Chattanooga . . . . . 1:45 A.M., ET, Tuesday
Ar. Atlanta . . . . . 6:45 A.M., ET, Tuesday
Ar. Jacksonville . . . . . 10:00 P.M., ET, Tuesday

184

NEW ORLEANS–MOBILE–BIRMINGHAM–ATLANTA TO POTOMAC YARD

No. 154

Lv. New Orleans	7:30 P.M., CT, Monday	
Ar. Birmingham	7:00 A.M., CT, Tuesday	
Lv. Mobile	7:00 P.M., CT, Monday	Connects with New Orleans
Ar. Birmingham	7:00 A.M., CT, Tuesday	154 at Birmingham
Lv. Birmingham	11:00 A.M., CT, Tuesday	
Ar. Atlanta	4:00 P.M., CT, Tuesday	
Lv. Atlanta	6:00 P.M., ET, Tuesday	
Ar. Potomac Yard	6:00 P.M., ET, Wednesday	

JACKSONVILLE–MACON–ATLANTA TO CINCINNATI–LOUISVILLE–EAST ST. LOUIS

	No. 154	No. 52
Lv. Jacksonville	7:00 P.M., ET, Monday	5:00 P.M., ET, Monday
Ar. Macon	5:00 A.M., ET, Tuesday	12:30 A.M., ET, Tuesday
Lv. Macon	7:00 A.M., ET, Tuesday	1:30 A.M., ET, Tuesday
Ar. Atlanta	10:30 A.M., ET, Tuesday	5:00 A.M., ET, Tuesday
Lv. Atlanta	12:01 P.M., ET, Tuesday	7:00 A.M., ET, Tuesday
Ar. Chattanooga	5:15 P.M., ET, Tuesday	12:30 P.M., ET, Tuesday
Lv. Chattanooga	5:00 P.M., CT, Tuesday	1:00 P.M., CT, Tuesday
Ar. Cincinnati	6:00 A.M., CT, Wednesday	1:30 A.M., CT, Wednesday
Lv. Chattanooga	5:30 P.M., CT, Tuesday	1:30 P.M., CT, Tuesday
Ar Louisville	7:00 A.M., CT, Wednesday	2:30 A.M., CT, Wednesday
Ar. E. St. Louis	10:00 P.M., CT, Wednesday	

inroads into railroad business because of terminal delays, Southern is continuing its expanded program of terminal modernization.

Coal shipments form an important part of Southern's total freight volume—about 10 per cent of its revenue and about 20 per cent of its tonnage. The railroad owns and operates more than 27,000 open-top cars and constantly keeps its Coster shop at Knoxville busy overhauling, modernizing, and repairing them. The road's Central and Western lines carry most of the road's coal traffic, which originates in five distinct areas—Appalachia, Virginia; the Knoxville-Jellico area in Tennessee and Kentucky; an area between Somerset, Kentucky, and Chattanooga; the Birmingham area; and a section of Southern Indiana. The road's Traffic Department has prepared a coal and coke directory, which sets forth information about all the mines reached by Southern's trackage for the benefit of producers, purchasers, and consumers.

Traffic in iron ore over Southern Railway System's right of way has more than quadrupled during the postwar years, and with heavy loads of imported bauxite ore it moves through the port of Mobile and the Alabama State Docks. To meet this increased volume, Southern has added several hundred ore cars to its rolling stock.

Great increases have also been noted in shipments of construction materials, with tonnages in sand, gravel, and stone now more than four times above prewar levels. Lumber and pulpwood, also reflecting increased Southland production, are increasing not only in the volume carried by the road but in terms of their relationship to total volume carried. On the other hand, cotton, the South's traditional product, has declined in relative importance as a component of Southern's freight totals. The fiber and its products now constitute only about 3 per cent of the road's total annual freight tonnage; yet Southern remains the world's largest carrier of cotton, and the actual volume of cotton and its products transported by the railroad is larger than ever before in history!

Diversification of Southern agriculture is also having a marked effect upon the Southern's operations. Today the area around Spartanburg, South Carolina, is the largest peach-producing center in the world, and of course Southern moves thousands of carloads of the fruit to northern and western markets every year. Tropical bananas unloaded from ships at Charleston, citrus fruits from Florida and Georgia, copra unloaded at New Orleans, and imported sugar taken from ships at the Gulf ports, today make up items of considerable importance in Southern's total freight operation.

At the Chalmette pier in New Orleans, the railroad has constructed and operates special mechanized equipment that moves the copra from the ships and transfers it directly into boxcars. Here too sugar-handling has been completely mechanized, while at Charleston the railroad has built an up-to-date mechanized pier for the handling of bananas.

Southern's concern with improving l.c.l. service, as described elsewhere, has resulted in a movement northward of furniture, textiles, and other manufactured items that now offsets the normal flow of products carried into the South from other parts of the country.

A railroad, it thus is seen, must keep abreast of the technological and industrial developments of the area it serves, with an eternal eye to adjusting its schedules and providing proper service to meet the new order of things.

L.C.L.

When one kind of operation accounts for eight and one-half per cent of a railroad's entire freight revenue, the road's officials know that it pays to devote special attention to it.

That's why Southern Railway System during the postwar years has concentrated on developing and improving the service it offers to its less-than-carload freight-shippers. As early as 1945 the road set up a special department, headed by an assistant to the operating vice-president, to take on the responsibility of devising new ways of providing better service for l.c.l. shippers.

And because a large proportion of all loss and damage claims are always connected with l.c.l. shipments, this new Freight Stations and Transfers Department soon took the railroad's loss and damage prevention work under its wing too.

The particular type of industry that dominates the Southland, combined with the vast network of trackage operated by the Southern throughout Dixie, has made the railroad the second-largest l.c.l. carrier in the entire United States—and Southern is doing everything it can to make of itself the best l.c.l. carrier in the country. This has required a comprehensive, over-all approach to the problem, because those very factors that have contributed to the railroad's large l.c.l. volume are the identical things that have served also to build intense competition from highway carriers.

Southern therefore has worked out a program based upon new, enlarged, modernized stations and transfers, faster schedules, an increased number of through package cars, and improved loading and stowing operations.

An even dozen transfer points handle the predominant part of Southern's l.c.l. traffic, and six of these transfers—Atlanta, Birmingham, Chattanooga, Cincinnati, Sevier (at Knoxville), and Spencer (at Salisbury, North Carolina), are busy enough to remain in operation seven days a week.

These improved yards and terminals, with their modern mechanical equipment and electronic communications systems, make it possible to get goods into consignees' hands with a saving of several days, since a matter of an hour or two saved at a transfer may often result in an earlier connection subsequently made at some transfer or junction point.

The Southern, at its various transfers and freight houses, now has in operation 33 tractors, 27 fork-lift trucks of varying capacities, 4 low lifts for handling live skids, 11 electric load-carrier trucks, and 4,109 four-wheel trucks, more than half of which are fitted with couplers. To make maximum use of this up-to-date equipment, the railroad had to remodel and rebuild many of its stations and had to construct additional trackage and crossover bridges at a considerable number of points.

But undoubtedly the one great improvement that has proved most helpful in expediting l.c.l. service has been Southern's electronic intercommunication system. Its talkback and paging speakers, in use at every large station and transfer, can now accomplish the dissemination of news about the location of cars in a matter of seconds, whereas this operation formerly might have taken as much as twenty minutes.

With the intercom network in use, check clerks and their gangs put in a minimum of lost time, and cars can be loaded more heavily, used longer, and cut out at a few seconds' notice. The foreman, using intercom, can virtually be anywhere at any time for checking purposes, and he can summon machinery and equipment, such as the fork-lift trucks or tractors, to any point at which he finds they are needed.

Southern has developed a unique portable checking booth, mounted on rubber-tired wheels, which, with its glass-paneled walls, enables any one clerk to check two cars at once. Inside each booth are a desk, chairs, and an intercom system that comes complete with two portable talkback speakers.

With one speaker placed in each of the two cars that are being worked by the clerk in the portable booth, a loader can pick up a package and call off to the checker the name of the consignee and the destination marked on it. Checking his records on the desk before him, the clerk then calls back through the portable speaker the proper markings that will transfer the package to its correct outbound car.

One of the major industries of Dixie is that of furniture-manufacturing, and a great portion of Southern's l.c.l. consists of shipments of this household product from the many plants that abound in North Carolina. Much of this l.c.l. volume can be moved in trap cars directly from production lines or warehouses to the modern transfer at Spencer. This is one of the seven-day-operating transfers run by the road, and furniture-shippers are thus furnished with a continuous movement service whose popularity has added to the railroad's extensive l.c.l. volume.

Westbound l.c.l. traffic of all kinds is routed through the Sevier yard, near Knoxville, which handles 105 scheduled cars daily of this type of service. Many of these cars break their cargo for the first time at points west of the Mississippi or north of the Ohio River, so that at least three cars are dispatched from Sevier every day for cities on the West Coast.

Many of the Carolina furniture-manufacturers, as well as a considerable number of textile mills, therefore divide their weekly shipments, dispatching freight consigned to the West direct to Sevier several times each week. In like manner, Spencer sets up separate cars made up solely of individual l.c.l. furniture loads, which are moved on to distant transfer points or ultimate destinations. In addition to furnishing faster service, this method also keeps damage claims down, since heavy furniture is not shipped in the same cars with lighter, more easily breakable commodities.

But even so, Southern officials do not rest content with the important accomplishments that their l.c.l. service has already achieved. The entire pattern of l.c.l. freight traffic is constantly being studied and surveyed, and changing trends in the traffic or in the nature of products being handled is usually swiftly followed by an adjustment in schedules or improvements in equipment designed to make the Southern's l.c.l. traffic service ever faster, more reliable, and more dependable.

New Yards

With the haulage benefits that are inherent in an all-diesel operation, Southern Railway System executives are well aware that inadequate classification yards can prove a bottleneck that will cancel out the gains made by diesel haulage.

Consequently the road is in the midst of a gigantic yard-improvement program, designed to make of these important classification centers not merely holding areas of high capacity, but yards in and out of which cars are kept constantly moving.

Four ultramodern push-button classification yards—Birmingham, Atlanta, Chattanooga and Knoxville—have already been put into operation. With others planned and being worked on, these two pioneers are symbolic of the Southern's modern, forward-looking approach to the entire problem. Like most other American roads, Southern discovered that many of its larger and formerly adequate classification facilities were proving too short to accommodate the long freight trains that diesels can haul; this meant costly, time-consuming "doubling over." In addition, the yards had too few classification tracks to handle the new-type loads, and most of them were planned for flat switching, a process that is slow and expensive when traffic is heavy.

Furthermore, it was realized that no integrated, system-wide planning had ever been applied to yard operations, and that they had merely mushroomed as individual facilities of the several railroads comprising the Southern Railway System. The increase in freight traffic resulting from the South's new industrial development proved to be still another factor in the inadequacy of the classification yards during the years immediately following World War II.

As a result of all these things, freight was being seriously delayed, and competitive facilities—principally the highway truckers—were taking much freight business from the road. The very benefits that were to be achieved through dieselization, new cars, and improved trackage were thus being offset by the inability of antiquated, obsolescent yards to handle the extra available traffic.

Some patchwork yard improvements were made; some tracks were extended, floodlights were installed for round-the-clock operations, radio and loud-speaker communications were set up at some points. But these failed to solve the basic problems, and soon the Southern embarked on a planned, over-all program of complete yard modernization.

Over $50,000,000 has already been invested in this project. The completely rebuilt Norris yard at Birmingham required an investment of $12,000,000 with another $3,500,000 having been spent to modernize the Sevier yard near Knoxville. Today these two represent the most advanced hump facilities to be found anywhere in the United States. About $15,000,000 has been spent at the Inman yard at Atlanta and $12,000,000 at Citico in Chattanooga, while some $600,000 has been poured into basic improvements at the small but important Asheville installation.

The first Southern yard to be worked on was the one at Inman, where grade changes were installed to convert it from flat switching to a "saucer" type of operation. New tracks were added and older ones extended to provide for accommodating an additional 150 cars. The new Inman yard now can handle almost double its former car capacity.

Several thousand cars move out daily from Sevier, an important hub point in the Southern's operation, and the system's engineers soon went to work to redesign and rebuild it. A retarder-hump system was decided upon here, so that cars could be quickly and economically classified into a considerable number of blocks destined for different points. Such preclassification was decided upon as a method of saving work for other yards down the line, with the over-all result that traffic on the entire system can be kept moving at a faster pace. At Norris the same theory was applied.

At both yards trains coming in from any point are moved to a single receiving yard, where they are classified by push-button mechanisms via the hump and automatic retarder devices. Switch engines are then used to make up outbound trains in an adjoining departure yard (Norris has two of these). Electronic developments of the latest type, such as paging and talking setups, two-way radio, radar speed indicators, and electronic weighing, aid the rapid classification work.

Stress at both yards is placed on keeping all cars moving. For example, Sevier humps about 3,400 cars each day, and its combined inbound and outbound car count will average some 3,500 to 4,000 cars daily. Norris, which is slightly larger and has been designed with the expected growth of the Birmingham area in mind, humps some 3,250 cars in each twenty-four-hour period and has a daily combined count of about 3,800 cars.

Modern retarded yards, the Southern quickly learned, have a marked effect far beyond their own confines. Not long after Sevier went into full operation, it was discovered that cars channeled through it were reaching destinations or interchange points an average of eight hours earlier than had been true previously!

At the New Orleans Oliver yard a special problem existed in connection with the need for efficient operation of a "hold" yard where cars might wait for the arrival of an export ship. Here this unit was redesigned for easier access, and a direct connection was laid between it and the New Orleans Terminal line that leads to the Chalmette docks.

Oliver is illuminated for night operation by six 75-foot floodlight towers; photoelectric equipment that measures the intensity of natural daylight serves to turn these lights on and off automatically.

Two new receiving and departure tracks were constructed at Oliver, and all existing tracks were extended. In addition, an important improvement was made with the construction of highway overpasses that eliminate interference with yard operations by street traffic, a major handicap from which the earlier layout suffered. Oliver is controlled from a completely air-conditioned yard-office-tower, and a new diesel-servicing center and rip tracks are located close at hand. The entire rebuilding operation was integrated with an extensive city-wide railroad relocation and grade-separation program that was tied in with construction of New Orleans' new Union passenger station.

To continue the ability to improve its yard service work, the Southern has established a new Yard and Terminal Department, whose personnel continually study operations at the line's major yards, right on the spot. The objectives of this department are to develop methods for making better use of existing facilities and to come up with suggestions for future improvements based on the concept of system-wide operations.

Its value to the system has already been proved by the fact that the classifications established at Norris came about on recommendation of the Yard and Terminal Department, following study of traffic patterns around Birmingham and throughout the Southern's entire system.

Freight Cars

In line with its development as a primary carrier of the products of the new industrial Southland, the Southern Railway System has remained alert to the need for equipping itself with the freight cars required to transport the materials produced in this rapidly growing section of our country.

During the first few years of the postwar period alone, Southern added some 13,000 brand-new freight cars to its total rolling stock, and embarked on a concentrated program of rebuilding and modernizing thousands of its old freight cars. As of December 31, 1957, for example, the railroad owned varying kinds of cars in the following quantities: 24,235 boxcars of all types, 367 stock cars, 9,125 gondola cars, 1,281 flatcars, 31 container cars, 3,871 wood-rack cars, 13,376 hopper cars, 785 covered hopper cars, 796 cabooses, 500 ballast cars, 98 tank cars, and 2,457 miscellaneous and maintenance-of-way cars—a total of 53,071 revenue-producing cars, and an over-all ownership of 55,363 freight cars of all types.

In an area that is expanding at the rate of one new industry every working day, the Southern increased its freight-car ownership by 22 per cent from 1937 to 1953. The repair jobs done at the system's well-equipped shops at such points as Hayne, Spencer, and Meridian have helped make it possible to achieve this level of operation by keeping in service many older cars that would not be suitable for modern haulage tasks without the modernization and rebuilding that have converted them for present-day usage.

Significant in this growth of freight-car ownership are two major factors—an increasing number of larger cars of extended capacity, and the development of a large number of cars built to meet the transportation needs of many of the new Dixie industries. A comparison of prewar statistics with those of the current era will demonstrate the amazing change that has taken place. Where more than half of the Southern's cars had been wooden cars with steel center sills and underframes, and only about 6,000 of them were of all-steel construction, today the situation is completely reversed; there are 28,000 of the 50-ton all-steel type owned and operated by the Southern, and only 2,700 of the old wooden cars are still in service. In addition, the railroad to-day has 10,000 40-ton all-steel cars and 2,300 giant 70-ton cars of the all-steel type.

The special haulage operation, described elsewhere, that en-ables Southern to function virtually as a part of the Detroit automobile manufacturers' regional assembly lines also requires special car construction. Thus there are more than 400 automo-bile box cars, including axle racks, DF loaders, transmission racks, and tractor racks.

The Southern Railway System's new freight cars also reflect new kinds of freight traffic that epitomize the new South and its industrial development. Rayon yarn from the country's biggest textile mills is carried in 74 specially designed rayon spool box-cars. The cement and other building products needed for the new stores, homes, factories, and plants that are mushrooming throughout the Southland move to their destinations in more than 600 brand-new covered hopper cars.

Pulpwood, too, is greatly in demand, and the constant increase in freight of this nature has caused the Southern Railway to experiment with conversion of old flatcars and gondolas to wood-rack cars by fitting them with high ends. As early as 1935 some 70 cars had been converted by this method, and the number has continued to grow ever since.

However, even before the beginning of World War II, at a time when the road owned more than 500 wood-rack cars, it be-came clear that volume of other traffic was growing to such magnitude that it would not long be possible to continue to take flats or gondolas out of service for this conversion operation. Thus a new experiment was undertaken—the rebuilding of old 36- and 40-foot wooden-side boxcars. Today more than 3,200 wood-rack cars constantly travel Southern's extensive lines, car-rying pulpwood for the use of Southern construction gangs. Every one of these has been converted from other types of cars at the Southern's own shops, and at Spencer, North Carolina, about 25 such rebuilt wood-rack cars hit the rails every week.

The boxcars are converted by stripping down the wooden sides and then adding new sills to the underframe. The car ends are retained and cut down to form part of the new end bulkheads.

No freight operation can depend solely on its revenue-producing cars alone. Cabooses, which carry no freight and therefore are classified as non-revenue cars, are nonetheless essential to profitable operations. Southern's Hayne shop recently turned out a fleet of 396 all-steel cabooses with all-view bay windows, each rebuilt of welded and riveted steel bodies on the underframes of obsolete 36-foot boxcars. Many of these new cabooses are radio-equipped too.

Yards like those at Hayne, Coster, Spencer, Sevier, and Norris also have the important responsibility of maintenance operations, whose quick-run repairs make it possible to get maximum rail use of all freight cars with the least amount of idle downtime. The Southern's percentage of bad-order rolling stock, 2.96 per cent, is far below the national railroad average and is a working tribute to the efficient operation of the railroad's maintenance shops.

Tests are continually carried out with the object of discovering which paints and prime coatings will give best and longest-lasting protection to the exteriors of freight cars. Mechanical journal lubricators have been experimented with on local-operation cars, and twenty freight cars used for shipping heavy automobile parts have been equipped, experimentally, with a new nailable steel flooring.

Every boxcar that is used for high-class haulage is thoroughly washed, both inside and out, before being turned over to shippers. Washing stations have been set up at a number of the Southern's more important terminals, with cleaning tracks constructed on a slight incline. After a crew has swept the car clear of any rubbish, nails, or strapping materials that may have accumulated on its last trip, the car is permitted to roll down the inclined rail to the wash station, where a mixture of hot water and detergent is applied to the interior by a high-pressure spray gun.

At the wash station, where this spraying process is applied, the car comes to rest at a point where one rail is on a slightly higher level than the other. Thus the car stands slightly tilted, and the used water and detergent quickly run out of it and drop into a concrete wash ramp constructed just below the rails at that point.

Not only are the Southern's own cars given this scrubbing treatment, but every car in the yard destined to handle Class A lading, regardless of ownership, is thus thoroughly cleaned as well. About twenty-four cars can be washed by this method in a normal eight-hour shift.

Southern's freight cars are thus kept up to the task of hauling the South's ever expanding volume of commerce, through purchase, rebuilding, remodeling, and preventive maintenance.

Car Repair

Mechanization sets the pace in the repair and rebuilding program that the Southern Railway System employs to keep its rolling stock up to a high performance mark.

While there has not been a revolutionary advance in this field comparable to the advent of the diesel engine in the haulage operation, steady improvement and the application of new tools, machines, and methods have aided the road in its maintenance and reconditioning operations. Centralization is the trend, with all heavy repairs and rebuilding concentrated in a limited number of shops.

All the repairing and rebuilding of freight cars undertaken by Southern is accomplished at three shops—Spencer, Hayne, and Coster. Here too cabooses are rebuilt along contemporary lines, wrecked cars are thoroughly reconstituted, and some fabricated parts and assembly components are manufactured.

At Spencer and at Hayne the freight-car shops are in steel-frame sheds, with overhead cranes and with separate facilities for fabricating, blacksmith, pipe, and air-brake operations. A heavy repair shop has been made at Coster out of an old car shed, equipped with overhead crane, a former steam locomotive erecting shop, and machine shops that have been transformed for production car work.

Thus, in an indirect way, dieselization has had its effect upon the road's rebuilding facilities; the end of the need for steam locomotive shop facilities has made it possible to convert the old Coster production shop into a heavy-program car repair unit.

The main building at Coster is 750 feet long and has space for four through tracks, each of which is served by an overhead crane. On a balcony or in areas directly underneath it are sub-assembly shops, washrooms, and locker rooms. What had been boiler and blacksmith shops in adjoining buildings are now units used for fabricating and forging operations.

The most modern of assembly line methods are used for program work in these shops. Cars to be worked on are brought to a halt on track located just outside the shop where the work is to be done. Here they are stripped, sandblasted, and given a coat of primer. Then they are rolled into and through the shop itself, where they are subjected to successive processes during which side and end assemblies, floors, trucks, and appliances are added, until they reach the end of the shop where they are painted and stenciled.

Costs of the over-all rebuilding program have been materially reduced, the Southern has found, both by concentrating all such work in just three locations and by application of the assembly line technique. At the same time, discontinuance of the use of other shops for heavy repair and rebuilding work of this nature has made it possible for the railroad to concentrate the work of those shops on running repair operations, and three new rip tracks have been completed for use in new yards at Knoxville, Birmingham, and New Orleans.

In the same manner, for identical reasons and with like results, wheel shops have also been consolidated and brought up to date. Steel wheel work for both diesel units and cars is done only at Spencer and Chattanooga, while Spencer and Knoxville are assigned to tasks connected with freight-car wheel work.

Each one of these shops is equipped with high-speed hydraulic wheel-mounting presses, axle lathes, latest type boring mills, burnishing lathes with opposed rolls, and Magnaglo test benches. Latest materials-handling equipment, such as monorail and jib cranes, fork-lift trucks, and gravity feed ramps have been combined with assembly line procedures to step up production and bring wasted motion to a minimum.

While in some cases it has been found feasible to increase operating speeds of older machines to take advantage of new carbide tools, in most instances it has proved a better policy to replace the obsolescent units with new, modernized machinery. Some of the new equipment includes, for example, four Watson Stillman mounting presses, two Niles No. 4 profiling car wheel lathes, five Consolidated axle lathes, four Consolidated opposed-roll burnishing lathes, a Consolidated wheel-boring mill, and a number of Hammond roughing and finishing grinders. At Hayne there is a 150-ton press brake which is used with a Travograph cutting machine, while four Unionmelt submerged arc automatic welding units are also in operation at several of the major car shops.

In the railroad's diesel shops most of the tools and machines are new, although some of the equipment used earlier for steam locomotive work has been adapted with success. Machines used in the diesel shops include Magnus Ajadip parts cleaners, Farr or Paxton-Mitchell filter-cleaning machines, valve face and seat grinders, power wrenches, impact wrenches, hydraulic lug presses, electric testing equipment, and various kinds of portable tools.

Most of the larger shops also have their own highway trucks, as well as electrical hoists, platform trucks, and tractors. Gas and electric welding have also proved important factors in producing greater output at lower unit cost. Subassemblies can now be used in locomotive- and car-rebuilding programs, thanks to the employment of submerged arc and Heliarc welders, in combination with cutting machines.

Southern maintains a special mechanical staff whose responsibility it is to tour the various shops for the purpose of discussing new ideas with foremen and workers, leading to the adoption of new machinery or improved methods that will result in increased production or more economical shop operation. The road's management, recognizing the interest and ability of its employees, constantly encourages shop personnel to come up with suggestions for new fixtures, jigs, gauges, and other devices. When such a development proves practical, plans for it are drawn up and distributed to the other shops in the system, and in this manner a friendly and helpful intershop rivalry has been fostered.

For example, not too long ago an electrician foreman at the Citico diesel shop developed a jumper cable test board that makes it possible to effect open, short-circuit, ground, and load tests on each of the twenty-seven wires in a diesel locomotive jumper cable in less than three minutes. The test panel worked out by this shopman consists of receptacles on a panel into which the two ends of the cable are inserted, and a rotary switch that directs the current through each wire in turn as the operator moves it from one contact point to the next. A light bulb signals the condition of each circuit.

Shop employees have worked out dozens of like devices that have helped the road improve its repair, rebuilding, and maintenance operations. Stands and fixtures for traction-motor repairs have been constructed; special gauges have been invented for liners, heads, connecting rods, and baskets.

The Southern's passion for orderliness and cleanliness extends, with notable results, into its repair shops. A standardized color scheme is used to paint each shop; this is a device providing not only for neatness and sanitation but for safety and efficiency as well. Under the plan, all structural steel has an aluminum color finish, with walls and columns in gray. Aisles, railings, switches, and fire-protection equipment are painted yellow, orange, and red. All machinery is finished in green, with important switches, controls, and wheels painted ivory, orange, yellow, or beige in accordance with a standardized code.

All large shops and many of the smaller ones have washing tracks and equipment constantly used to keep diesel units and cars spotlessly clean both inside and out. Leaks and defects are constantly looked for and sought out, to prevent the accumulation of water or oil on locomotive floors.

The mechanization of the Southern's repair, modernization,

and rebuilding operations, combined with centralization and the application of modernized assembly line methods, has resulted in increased output, lower costs per unit, and better service to travelers and shippers alike.

CHAPTER XXX

THE BUDD COMPANY

This Great Car Builder's Innovations Have Meant Much to Many Passenger-carrying Railroads

In this author's series of books on railroads, the reader will find accounts of very few innovations in the railroad industry that have not proved successful. They would have found practically no steam locomotives that were not successful, and it is for this reason the author has never included any of the lightweight toy trains in his writing. But having ridden them and inspected them also in Europe and other countries, he long ago came to the firm conclusion that it was not possible to put the United States public into lightweight, low-slung cars with ballast flying and meals at seats after the efforts of the railroads and car-builders to give them the wonderful dining cars, club cars, private-room sleeping accommodations, coaches, and now the domes to which they have become used. He did not ever consider that these lightweight trains would become a success. It is possible to put a person in a European or South American country in one of these lightweight trains and have him like it. It is probably the only American-made equipment in the country and the only one he will ever ride in. The chances are that this lightweight train has speeded up schedules by many hours, but this is not the case here in the United States. We already have fine fast schedules, and there are very few places where these lightweight trains would do the job. Also you must remember that their availability is poor, that they cannot be used in other services, and that their locomotives have to be used for them and for them alone.

The Budd Company built the original dome, and it is certainly still one of the best with its high type of seating and clear viewing ahead as well as to the rear. Then there are the RDC cars, which have proved tremendously popular and successful on many railroads and have been one of the greatest innovations and comforts for passengers on light-density lines that the roads could possibly provide for them. In my next book, *Railroads of Canada*, I will cover them at great length, as they have meant so much to the Canadian Pacific, but in the United States at many different places they have been a godsend in all-day runs and commuting service. The Budd high-level train is described in the chapter on the high-level El Capitan, and in my opinion it is here to stay. It is a wonderful thing to be able to give the coach passengers semidome rides and to be able to put a ten-car train into eight cars with the new seating arrangement and to give that much space between the seats and better competition for the airplane's sleeperette. The ride is quieter, and any disadvantage of having to go below to reach the toilets is more than compensated to the older person by not having the high steps in boarding the train.

I am definitely sold on the high level in every angle.

The Budd Siesta coach, with its enclosed-room privacy, comfort, and convenience at coach fares, is here to stay. Even though today it has been adopted only by the Burlington and Baltimore & Ohio railroads, it is, I feel, a comer and will be utilized on many railroads when things improve. When you can put forty people and give them berths in a 48-seat coach, losing only eight people, it seems to me that you have something, and there are few who will not happily pay a slight surcharge. A berth and toilet facilities and a private room for a surcharge—who wouldn't use this facility if riding a coach? So far there has been nothing but praise by those who have used it, particularly many of the younger generation and people going skiing, and it has hardly taken anyone from the regular standard Pullman sleeping cars.

The Siesta coach is designed for a type of service to compete more effectively with bus and private automobile. It has a three-fold objective: one, to hold the present level of travel; two, to recapture the passenger business; and three, to create travel—and to do all this by providing comfortable, pleasant, low-cost sleeping accommodations for overnight travel at a profit for the railroads. The last twenty years, of course, have brought changes in the competitive scheme, and transportation changes have taken great chunks out of railroad patronage. The new Siesta coach is built to meet the challenge of modern transportation. It certainly should appeal to the pocketbook-conscious traveler, adding many incentives to those who desire bargain coach fares yet are willing to pay a small premium for its many comforts. It is designed to incorporate many added conveniences to entice the overnight traveler to the rails. In the first five months that slumber coaches were in service, they enjoyed a load factor of more than 70 per cent in a low point of the traffic curve between Chicago and Denver.

The Siesta coach is a stainless steel car of standard 85-foot length and conventional cross section. It provides closed-room privacy for forty passengers. The design calls for twenty-four single rooms and eight rooms for double occupancy. Each single room is provided with a comfortable window seat for daytime travel, a full-length bed 24 inches wide with a foam rubber mattress, sheets, pillows, and blankets, toilet and washstand, full-length mirror, and storage space for three good-sized suitcases. There are individual air-conditioning and heat controls. In the double rooms, which of course are larger, there are two beds and two seats each by the window. The lighting is excellent. Windows are of generous size. Floors are of easy-to-clean rubber tile. There are no doorsills. Beds may be lowered without opening the doors, and toilet facilities are free and clear of the bed at all times. Each bed is in two sections, recessed when not in use into the front and rear walls of the room. At night the passengers simply lower them down to horizontal position. The foam rubber mattress in each section is already covered by contour sheet. The upper sheet and blankets are stowed in the recess at the foot of the bed. The passenger places the pillow at the head of the bed, pulls up the top sheet and the blankets, and the bed is ready for the night. In the morning he rolls the sheet and blankets back in the recess, stows the pillow, raises both halves of the bed into their original position, and the room is ready for daytime occupancy. It seems to me there are many places in the United States where the Siesta coach will be used, making both a profit for the railroads and a better trip for the passenger.

Another fine Budd innovation and a car that should have a great future is the Pioneer III, which combines weight and cost savings on four-wheel trucks with inboard roller bearings and outboard disc brakes and air springs. This car can be turned out in a coach with head-end electric power for 88 passengers; an 88-passenger coach self-contained; a 52-passenger deluxe coach; a 60-passenger diner with an airline type galley; a tavern lounge car; a sleeper with 16 duplex roomettes, 3 single rooms, and a single double room sleeper; and a multiple-unit car with all its motors weighing only up to 82,900 pounds. A 60-passenger diner, for instance, weighs 71,500 pounds. Yet this car is a lightweight car, but at the same time a standard car which can be used anywhere and with all kinds of equipment. Its efficiency is complete. Plastics have been used a great deal in its appointments, particularly in the washroom basins, walls, towel dispensers, etc. Single-piece sections of plastic are used for the car's step walls. The car is built of welded stainless steel and has a standard underframe design. It is a great car that should have a fine future, and the Budd people are to be congratulated on their never-ceasing approach to helping the railroad passenger business.

CHAPTER XXXI

BANGOR AND AROOSTOOK

Maine Potato Mover—This Road Works for the Grower—Searsport, Its Ocean Gateway

Kennebeck, Green Mountain, Irish Cobbler, Katahdin— these are famous names, and they owe at least a good part of their prestige and popularity to the fine work of one of the best small railroads in the country, the Bangor and Aroostook.

For they are well-known varieties of potatoes, called the world's best by experts, and more of them are grown in Aroostook County alone than in any other entire state in the union. That they are of finest quality would not in itself assure their reputation were it not for the fact that the rapid, efficient work of the railroad serving their growing area makes it possible to place them on the tables of America's homes and restaurants to be praised and enjoyed.

Maine—and most particularly the northern part of the state— has a magnificent climate, ideal for the planting and growing of fine potatoes. There is plenty of rain and snow on its ground, instead of cover crop, during the winter months. There are only 110 days in the average year when frost is not assured. There is a high percentage of limestone content in the area's native soil.

Combining these favorable natural advantages with topnotch, scientific farming methods, crop controls, soil rotation, and carefully supervised cultivation of the important potato crop, Aroostook County's farmers produce spuds that are an epicure's delight.

These are potatoes that have proved, year after year, 98 per cent marketable. They are picked from the ground later in the year than in any other section of the country, and usually are not dug up until about mid-October.

Then they go into storage in well-built, well-equipped potato houses, which are located in all parts of Aroostook County, and there they are held until market conditions are most favorable for their move to the nation's major cities. The New York metropolitan area, the big Ohio cities, Detroit, Pittsburgh, and Charleston, West Virginia, are usually the largest recipients of these fine potatoes.

Here it is that the excellently efficient organization of the Bangor and Aroostook Railroad most readily serves the farmers of Maine as well as the nation's diners. For the railroad's preheated cars make it possible to maintain the potatoes at the peak of their quality while shipping them even over long distances.

Well-worked-out connections in Boston bring Aroostook County potatoes to New York's eight million people just about as quickly as the farmers of Suffolk County, Long Island, can transport their crop to the metropolitan area only seventy or eighty miles distant.

All in all, the people of thirty-six states east of the Rockies have the privilege of enjoying the Kennebeck, the Green Mountain, the Irish Cobbler, and the Katahdin. The fine work of the Bangor and Aroostook Railroad is primarily responsible for this wide distribution of a quality product—the Maine potato.

These fine spuds are packed 1,000 bushels to a refrigerator car; in one peak year 73,000,000 bushels were grown in the state of Maine, while the annual average generally runs around 50,000,000 bushels. This would mean a movement totaling fifty thousand freight cars per year, each filled with the products of the state's fine soil and of the efficiency and hard labor of its 4,200 farmers. As part of their modern, scientific farming efficiency, the Aroostook County planters rotate the crops in their ground, or let it rest once in each three or four years. When rotating, they plant some such crop as grain or oats during the off years.

It usually takes the planter about fifteen days of activity to plant his fields and about twenty days to dig up the potato crop. No shortage of labor is ever feared, because of the proximity of

New Brunswick and of Nova Scotia, where additional help is always available if needed. In addition, the county maintains a farsighted policy of starting school earlier in the autumn than is normally done elsewhere in the country. Then, when the crop is ready to be dug late in October or early the following month, the children are given a three-week holiday, which gives them an opportunity to earn some extra money as well as to learn the business of potato farming.

This is an excellent arrangement that works out to the benefit of everyone concerned.

The farsightedness of Bangor & Aroostook President W. Gordon Robertson and Board Chairman Curtis Hutchins has led to the development of the twelve-month ice-free port facilities at Searsport, only twenty-nine miles from the starting terminus of the road's main line.

The port is served daily by through freight trains from North Maine Junction, and incoming loads are classified, while local and switching service is performed here as well. During the high-level activity of the potato move in the early wintry months of the year the great volume of freight and the tremendous number of cars that must be switched at North Maine junction keep crews and switching locomotives busy, and men and locomotives can be seen constantly running in all directions as they pick up and move cars into units of carefully scheduled trains, destined to bring the valued crop to its metropolitan consignees.

Searsport's facilities can also be used for loading potatoes onto outgoing steamers and for transporting incoming coal from freighters to trains. Excellent piers exist for the handling of many other basic industrial items, such as fertilizer, petroleum products, nitrate and phosphate, and other chemical-process products.

Through the rolling stock of the Bangor and Aroostook, under the able management of the road's Sales Vice-President Thomas J. Clark and with the additional impetus provided by the kind of facilities that exist at Searsport, Maine potatoes go almost everywhere.

But in addition to shipping this fine crop to so many points, Aroostook County and other Maine growers have evolved a de-

U.P. Extra 199 east with train of piggy-backs and trailer flats passing East Los Angeles on the Second Sub-div. of the California Div.

Servo hot-box detectors installed on the Southern RR which scan passing trains and flash warning signals of potential trouble to recording units.

Servo hot-box recorder showing tape on operator's desk at B & O Junction, N.Y. on the Lackawanna RR.

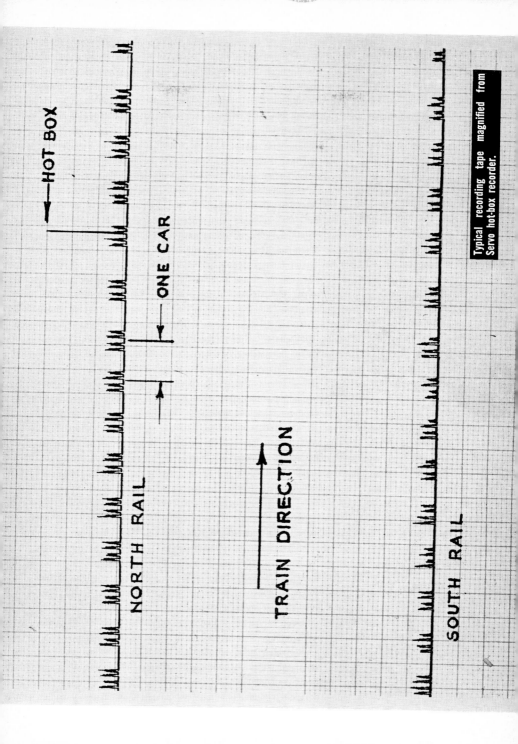

HOT BOX

ONE CAR

NORTH RAIL

TRAIN DIRECTION

SOUTH RAIL

Typical recording tape magnified from Servo hot-box recorder.

Chemical Spray Car, built in Pine Bluff shops, shown in main line vegetation control operation near Camden, Arkansas. Train, drawn by locomotive, consists of seven cars: three tank cars containing chemical weed killer; three tank cars containing water; and the spray unit.

The chemical spray car is manned by an operator and a helper. It can operate effectively at a speed of 15 miles per hour. In main line operation the unit sprays an area seven feet on each side of the track, using an average of 112 gallons of "mix" per mile.

NP Extra 6003 east passing oil well near Fryberg, N.D. This is one of the developments in the Williston Basin, Second Subdiv. Yellowstone Div.

Broken flange detector in front of the hump.

Another inspector in a pit directly under a car watches the axles, breakbeams and under-draft rigging.

Dragging detector at the entrance to C & O's new westbound manifest classification yard at Russell, Ky. used before the cars go over the hump.

As the cars pass over pit inspection point an inspector on each side of the track looks over as much of the running gear as can be seen from that angle.

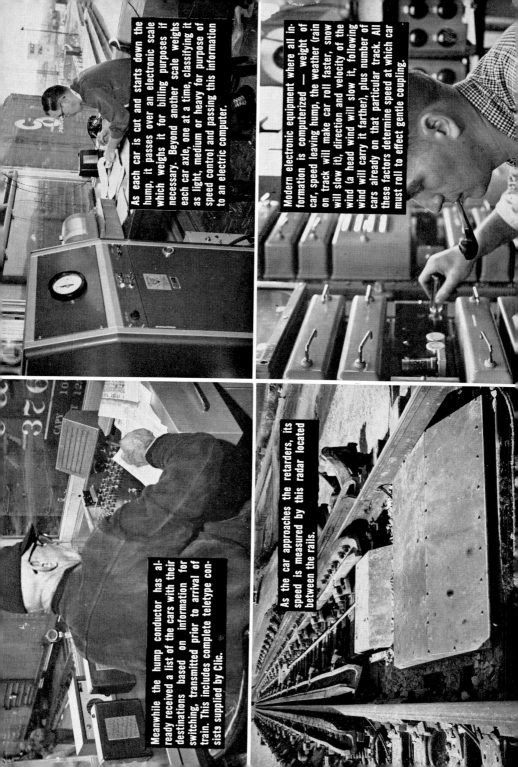

As each car is cut and starts down the hump, it passes over an electronic scale which weighs it for billing purposes if necessary. Beyond another scale weighs each car axle, one at a time, classifying it as light, medium or heavy for purpose of speed control and passing this information to an electric computer.

Modern electronic equipment where all information is computerized — weight of car, speed leaving hump, the weather (rain on track will make car roll faster, snow will slow it), direction and velocity of the wind (a head wind will slow it, following wind will carry it farther), plus number of cars already on that particular track. All these factors determine speed at which car must roll to effect gentle coupling.

Meanwhile the hump conductor has already received a list of the cars with their destinations based on information for switching, transmitted prior to arrival of train. This includes complete teletype consists supplied by Clic.

As the car approaches the retarders, its speed is measured by this radar located between the rails.

From his control point overlooking yard, the yardmaster can talk by radio with the yard engines and by two-way speakers to yard crews and hump office.

South group of 16 tracks is assigned to cars moving thru Cincinnati Gateway; North group of 16 tracks to cars moving thru Columbus Gateway. To illustrate there is one track in this Columbus group to receive cars routed via the Ludington Mich. train ferry — other tracks will receive cars for other Mich. and Ohio destinations.

The computer makes all its calculations in fraction of a second sending its instructions to the retarders telling them how hard and long they should grip the car's wheels. The retarder is powerful enough to bring the heaviest car to a full stop but as each car passes through, the retarder gives its wheels exactly the right squeeze so it will roll gently to its place on classification track.

When hump conductor presses selective track button, switching circuit is activated and automatically sets each switch to guide the car to its assigned track. This means that cars can be released from the apex of the hump with only few seconds headway. The automatic switching system remembers five such programs at a time.

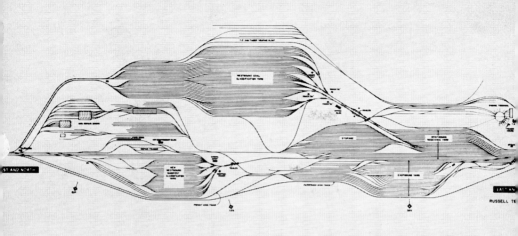

As soon as cars are all classified, yard engine assembles the various cuts into a road train, positioning each cut so it can be most conveniently dropped off at destination.

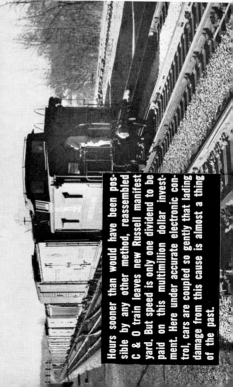

Hours sooner than would have been possible by any other method, reassembled C & O train leaves new Russell manifest yard. But speed is only one dividend to be paid on this multimillion dollar investment. Here under accurate electronic control, cars are coupled so gently that lading damage from this cause is almost a thing of the past.

Aerial view of coal, oil, and fertilizer installation at Searsport, Maine, Bangor & Aroostook dock in foreground. This is their salt water port in Maine.

Specially built Bangor & Aroostook pulpwood cars dumping cordwood at Millinocket, Maine.

U.P. #102, the City of San Francisco, operated by the S. P. west of Ogden and Milwaukee R.R. east of Omaha crossing Devil's Gate Bridge, Utah on the Fourth Sub-div. of the Wyoming Div. enroute to Chicago with 12 cars. Photo by R. H. Kindig.

Southern #38, the Crescent, luxurious streamliner, near Seneca, Ga. on the Charlotte Div.

Southern Pacific 4-unit freight train crossing the famous Pecos River Bridge noted for its great engineering on the Sanderson Subdiv. of the San Antonio Div.

Solid Southern Railway coal train running over the west end of the Birmingham Div.

Closed circuit television in the Southern Railway System's modern yards is used for "picking" car numbers from inbound trains. Time required for the preparation of switching lists and other records is cut to a few minutes. This picture was taken at the new Inman Yard at Atlanta, Ga. Atlanta Div.

Chicago Great Western blinking train order signal at Marshalltown, Iowa.

Board for blinking train order signal on operator's desk in Chicago Great Western's Marshalltown, Iowa Station.

Classifying a freight train in the Southern Pacific's fine new yards at Roseville, Cal. A cut of three cars and a single may be seen going through the retarders while another has just been cut from the train in foreground going over the hump. This yard was built by Union Switch & Signal Co.

Here are three cars headed for three different tracks going over the hump and through the retarders in the Southern Pacific's new yard in Houston, Texas. The city's skyline in background.

mounted on the caboose wall near his desk, and a second handset is at his disposal in the cupola. A University type MM2 loud-speaker is mounted on the cupola wall just above the air gauge.

The two channels available on the Northern Pacific radio net-work are normally used for different purposes. Channel 1 is generally employed only for end-to-end or train-to-train conversa-tions, while Channel 2 is reserved for wayside base stations. It is a simple matter for an engineman to call his conductor: all he need do is pick up his handset, press a button on its handle, and talk. By releasing the button he clears the set for reception of the conductor's reply over the cab's loud-speaker. Of course the conductor can originate the call to his engineman in exactly the same way. Radios in all engines, cabooses, and wayside sta-tions are always kept in operation, so that any incoming call will immediately be heard through the speaker.

Sets installed in cabooses are fitted with switches to make it possible for the conductor to shift his transmitting frequency to Channel 2 for communication with wayside stations. When he finishes such an exchange and hangs his handset back on its hook, his transmitter is automatically switched back to Channel 1 for communication with his own engineman or with a passing train.

By the use of these two separated channels, which can never-theless be hooked into each other by the simple flip of a switch, the Northern Pacific sees to it that end-to-end and train-to-train messages, which do not need to concern base station or dis-patcher operations, can be carried on without interfering with the other network. Train-to-wayside calls, on Channel 2, are not normally heard by trains that are not involved in the particular situation being discussed.

A unique tie-in arrangement between radio and the railroad's telephone circuits makes it possible for the dispatcher to talk to any conductor anywhere along the run. The system, designed and built by Bendix, was conceived in order to minimize the number of pieces of new equipment to be used by NP personnel.

If a conductor wants to talk to the dispatcher, he flips to Channel 2 and tells the operator at the nearest base radio station vice for extending the produce of their state. They ship each year from five thousand to ten thousand carloads of seed to such far-flung points as the eastern shore of Virginia, the Chesapeake district, Nova Scotia, Prince Edward Island, Idaho, and California, and even to that rival potato-growing county, Suffolk County on New York's Long Island.

Here they are planted, cultivated, dug, and shipped to market, and their fine flavor stems largely from the Aroostook County parents from whom the seed is taken. So a potato, no matter in what part of the United States or Canada it may be grown, may very well owe even its existence to the Bangor and Aroostook Railroad.

CHAPTER XXXII

THE SERVO HOTBOX DETECTORS

A New and Important Device for Railroad Operation

When the Lackawanna's fast eastbound manifest freight NE-4 with cars mostly for the New England gateways was stopped by the operator at Linwood, New York, 4.81 miles east of B.&O. Junction, which is 45 miles east of Buffalo on the Scranton-Buffalo Division, the conductor called the operator at B.&O. Junction on the radio and asked why they stopped him there. The operator replied, "You have a hotbox on the twenty-sixth car from the head end, the front box on the rear truck north-side." The conductor asked, "Is that so? How do you know all that?" And the operator answered, "Here at B.&O. Junction we now have an electric hotbox detector system that detects and records hotboxes on passing freight trains at any speed up to sixty miles an hour."

This supersensitive electronic eye had recently been installed by the Lackawanna Railroad at B.&O. Junction. It is known as the Servo-Safe Hotbox Detector. The device is located on the eastbound track of the railroad. It consists of a tube-shaped box containing a highly sensitive lens, which is directed at the outer side of each rail. The lens is covered with a magnetic shutter to protect it from the sun's rays and weather, which automatically opens as a train begins to pass over it. So sensitive is this lens that a trainman's lantern lit and held near it will cause the recording mechanism to begin to operate. As each car passes over the units, the heat from the journal box is picked up by the lenses and is transmitted to the recording machine located at the operator's side at B.&O. Junction. The machine records the information received from the lenses on a paper tape.

The pens on the recording machine make two parallel lines, each indicating one rail. As each journal passes over the hotbox detector, a slight pip appears in these lines. This indicates that the journal is normal. However, when an overheated journal passes over the lens, the pip immediately becomes elongated corresponding to the temperature recorded by the electronic eye. The operator watches the tape as it moves through the machine, and if he sees an elongated pip that indicates a hot journal, he radios the train, or telephones the preceding station, or flags the train to stop for inspection. However, if the inspection tape does not indicate a hot journal, the train continues its normal trip. The elongated pip does not always mean a hot journal. Roller-bearing journals normally run at a higher temperature than conventional journals. This slight increase in heat is distinguished by the recording device when a car with roller bearings passes over the electronic eye. Locomotives also give a slight indication of hot journals as the result of several actions taking place. First, the locomotives are equipped with roller bearings; second, the traction motors run at high temperature; and finally, the heat from the friction of the wheels against the rails can produce such indication. When the operator of the detector notices that the same degree of heat is shown by identical pips in each of the tape's parallel lines, he may assume that the twin elongated pips are due to roller bearings. The Lackawanna's hotbox detector scans over the eastbound train that passes at B.&O. Junction, and the detection of a hot journal in a train before it blazes into a hotbox and burns off the axle naturally may prevent costly derailment and other damage.

The hotbox menace has always been the greatest in railroading outside of that from automobiles and trucks at highway crossings. This hazard has been pretty well licked through automatic gates, wigwags, and other preventive apparatus, as well as the wide-awake carefulness and watchfulness and energy of the engine crew. But the only thing that is going to beat completely the hotbox problem is the adoption of roller bearings. Today practically all the American railroads' passenger equipment uses roller bearings, but of course it is far too great a problem and expense for all the companies to so equip their freight cars. In the years to come we will no doubt see it, but as of today, with cars coming so many miles through all kinds of weather and temperature and particularly during the heat of the summer months, it is most difficult to prevent journals from running hot, even with minute inspection at terminals and frequent oiling. It is also difficult for the train crews to see them from the rear and head ends. Moreover, it is possible for a journal to be hot without any telltale indication on the outside. Therefore the hotbox detector developed by Servo is the first sure-fire method of stopping this destructive and costly menace. It also provides an agency to inspire crews to keep a close watch on their trains.

The hotbox detector consists of six units. The detector and pickups are permanently installed at trackside in rugged weatherproof housings, and their basic designs permit simple alignment with the rails. All major components are readily accessible and easily serviced or replaced. In operation, the train's wheel flanges pass over the first pickup. The ensuing voltage pulse causes the cover detector's Servo-frax lenses to open and activates the recorder. When the wheel flanges pass over the second pickup, located forty feet from the first, the resulting voltage pulses deactivate the recorder styli. In this way only the heat radiated from the terminal box is recorded, so that spurious indications from steampipes or other heat sources are prevented. Also, since the lens cover is always tightly closed except when a train is passing, the detector is protected against sun, dust, and dirt.

Orientation of the detector is essential so that its operation is unaffected by wheel diameters. Also the very small field of view—approximately one square inch—eliminates the problem of lateral movement of the journal box because it accommodates maximum motion in either direction. The infrared radiation of the journal box passes through the Servo-flex lenses which focus it on the sensitive thermistor meter detecting cell of the detector. Fast response and extreme sensitivity allow the meter to operate over a wide range of train speeds and journal box temperatures, so that it is easily suited to this application. Its rugged construction and simple circuit design make it highly stable, virtually unaffected by changes in surrounding temperature. Evacuation of the meter cell excludes dust and dirt and eliminates false indication due to air currents within the cell.

Use of Servo-frax tempered infrared lenses manufactured by Servo Corporation enhances the reliability of the hotbox detector. Widely used in military and industrial applications, this material offers a combination of infrared transmission and weatherproof qualities, strength, and stability that supplies satisfactory performance under all conditions. Servo-frax presents minimum maintenance problems, as it can be cleaned with ordinary tap water. All of this with only six different parts or appliances!

The signal for the detector is fed to the amplifier. When the amplifier outfit is sent to a chart recorder, the height of the pip recorded on the chart is the indicator of the heat from the channel box. Since the signal strength of an overheated journal is approximately five to ten times that of a normal one, it is quite easy to distinguish between the two. Detectors and amplifiers are powered by independent power supplies. The amplifiers and power supplies are housed in a signal case convenient to the location of the detectors. The records are stored in an appropriate location up to four miles from the detector.

And there you have it—one of the most interesting and able devices that the railroads with their forward-looking thinking have applied. Certainly with the speed of freight trains increasing, with hauls getting longer and tonnage growing, there is more need for this device. There are now fewer inspections because of longer nonstop runs, and there is less opportunity for thorough over-all inspection and fewer stops because tighter schedules call for shorter standing time. Shorter stops obviously mean less time for servicing of all journal boxes. Then today's heavier traffic is carried on fewer tracks, so great disruption of operations usually occurs when hotbox troubles do stop trains between terminals. This detector, besides giving warning, also furnishes the permanent chart recording of journal-box behavior, so that such records are available for study and analysis, which helps to find out the basic causes of journal overheating. Several roads have installed detectors just outside of major yards, both on the receiving and leaving tracks.

The Chesapeake & Ohio was the first road to use this great device. Besides the Lackawanna, the Reading now has two in operation; the Boston & Maine, one; the Norfolk & Western, three; the Baltimore & Ohio, one; the Pennsylvania, one; the New York Central, ten; and the Southern has two in operation and has ordered fifty-five. It will not be long before many other roads will have them. One of the biggest troubles is to make the decision where this machine would do the most good—to pick a spot where there may be more hot journals found than in other places.

I have watched the building and tuning up of this machine and seen it in operation on several railroads, and to me it is one of the finest things the industry has ever come up with.

CHAPTER XXXIII

VELAC FOR C&O'S GREAT RUSSELL YARD

Chessie the C&O Cat Can Now Sleep Even Sounder Going Over a New Hump the Road Has Installed

Velac automatic speed control equipment in combination with a programed switching system has served to create one of the most modern classifications in the country, that just completed by the Chesapeake & Ohio Railway at Russell, Kentucky.

Although more coal passes over the hump at Russell than at any similar point in the world, the C&O's program of diversifying its freight ladings, combined with the recent industrial development of the South, brought about new problems of classification at Russell.

The C&O solved these problems by constructing, in about a year and a half, a new manifest classification yard paralleling the westbound coal classification facility. The new yard has a forty-two-cylinder master retarder and four twenty-eight-cylinder group retarders. They feed into thirty-two classification tracks with a total standing capacity of about a thousand freight cars.

Velac automatically controls the retarders, taking into account the weight of each cut, wind and track resistance factors, track capacity, etc., and full automatic operation is provided, since the operator merely exercises supervisory observation and is not required to operate any levers or buttons. Computers take all these measured factors into account, establish leaving speed, and control all retarders, so that the journey of each cut is carried out at proper and safe speeds with minimum risk of damage to either cars or lading.

In combined operation with these controls is a Union Switch & Signal automatic switching system, which takes care of the routing of each cut to its scheduled destination within the new Russell yards. As the cut moves along its route, each switch along the way is automatically set in correct position to direct it properly. Track-destination data is fed into the automatic switching system by means of perforated tape, and the required route is thus set up automatically.

This is but one of many examples of how modern electronic equipment is being used by a major railroad—in this case the C&O—to solve problems of cost, service, and speed that arise out of the natural development of the American economy. Faced with a huge increase in traffic moving through Russell, in addition to the already heavy coal volume, the C&O has found in the Velac automated classification yard the answer to its problem.

The automatic classification yard system is in actuality the working combination of a series of electric, electronic, and mechanical developments, which, when put together at various stages of car movement and placed at appropriate points within a freight yard, make for an over-all automated operation.

Car-retarders, switch machines, yard consoles, switching systems, speed and retarder-control systems, cab signal systems, and other devices all contribute to the operation of the automatic yard. Each has come about as the result of patient experimentation, substantial capital outlay, and a basic understanding of the needs of the railroads for the kind of equipment that will enable them to give faster and increasingly better service to shippers of the nation's goods.

Union Switch & Signal, a division of the Westinghouse Air Brake Company, has made outstanding contributions toward the automated yard. Over an extended period, the company's engineers have conducted a thorough study of thousands of freight cars moving through many different classification yards. With the facts culled from this extensive research, the company has worked out layout designs and control equipment for individual yard problems to handle the indicated volume proficiently and with minimum damage to cars and lading.

The fundamental control device, upon which the whole operation of the automatic classification yard depends, is the car-retarder. This device controls the speed of cars moving down a grade to the classification tracks. It can be controlled manually, semiautomatically, or fully automatically, and generally uses an electropneumatic principle.

Made in units some 6 feet 3 inches long, with individual power cylinders, electropneumatic retarders can be installed on either straight or curved track. Compressed air in the power cylinders acts as a shock absorber, so that any unevenness of the brake shoes or of the car wheels is not transmitted back to the basic electrical equipment that motivates the action.

When installed on a fully automatic basis, the retarder takes into account the speed of the passing car, its load, and the distance it must travel, and then electronically applies just the correct braking pressure to compensate for these factors, so that the car will roll to a gentle stop at precisely its scheduled destination within the classification yard.

Automatic switching systems work hand in hand with car-retarders to direct cuts, through power switches, to their assigned tracks within the yard. Route information is fed into the system by push buttons; as the car advances through the yard, switches are automatically positioned from the information thus set up.

But an even greater advance in this area of operation is the programed switching system, which permits classification of an entire train without the pushing of a single button by an operator. This is essentially how it works:

As the switching list for a string of cars is received in the control tower and printed on a conventional tape printer, it is simultaneously punched on a tape by a reperforator, which cuts in and operates only to record track numbers assigned to each car.

This tape is then fed into a transmitter-decoder, which feeds the track information to a decoding unit. In turn, this code is translated into numbers, which are fed into the automatic switching system, and the required route is set up automatically. The whole system is hooked into a unit located at the "hump," so that as each cut goes over and begins its downhill journey the next set of information is automatically sent to the switch points for proper setting.

To guard against emergencies and to provide for possible changes in car destination orders, a set of push buttons is provided. Use of a "cancel" button by the operator in such a case stops the tape system and allows the operator to make a manual change, following which the tape system resumes control on the pressing of a "start" button by the operator; the system is arranged so that a train can be routed to any specific track by pushing only one button.

Another great contribution toward full automation of classification yard control is the new Velac Automatic Retarder Control system worked out by Union Switch & Signal engineers.

Such information as weight control, wind resistance, tangent-track rolling resistance, curved-track rolling resistance, cut length, track capacity and other factors are fed into an "electronic brain" by various sensing devices installed at points in the yard. With this information, a computer automatically determines correct leaving speed, sets the retarders accordingly, and provides for a correctly timed and routed journey from the hump to the scheduled track position.

The sensitive control equipment is housed in racks, by sections, to facilitate maintenance. Four vertical sections respectively house the tangent-track rolling resistance accelerometer with its storage units, the speed control mechanism for either a master or intermediate retarder, the computer and curved-track rolling resistance accelerometer, and the speed control for a group retarder.

Radio frequency waves are employed to measure the speed of each car as it approaches the retarder, and pressures on the car's wheels are automatically adjusted to conform with the information thus provided. In like manner, change in velocity is calculated to set up necessary speed controls that take into account both tangent- and curved-track rolling resistance factors. Rate of velocity change is influenced, of course, by such factors as weight and grade, and the difference in velocities at various points along the cut's route can therefore be electronically calculated and controlled by automatic settings of retarders set along the route.

A special 7-foot length of track, with a small horizontal slot at its midpoint, is the key to the car-weighing device that is so important a part of the Velac system. Contacts are closed as the car wheels pass over this special rail, and the weight information thus secured is used to select automatically both leaving speed and pressures to be exerted by all retarders involved. At the same time the weight information is transmitted to the computer, where it is used as one factor, along with all the others mentioned, in setting braking pressure for the final retarder through which the cut is scheduled to pass.

Union's classification track Car-pacity system is another important unit in the automation development of the modern freight-classification yard. It automatically counts the cars that enter each classification track and transmits information into the electric computer as to how far each car must travel. As each cars enters the track, the distance needed for the next car changes, and the unit automatically adjusts for this change.

At the same time, this data is fed into a direct reading counter set on the control panel for each classification track. Preset to display the total number of cars that the track will hold, the counter subtracts with each entering car, so that it always displays the total number of cars for which space remains available. Changes in destination can be handled through a manually operated cancellation-add lever, and such changes are also fed into the computer, which determines the leaving speed from the group retarders.

These basic electronic miracles, plus such added devices as yard-track indicator control systems and yard-track indicators, have helped the country's railroads make gigantic strides forward toward the goal of providing better service for their shippers while at the same time instituting modern operational methods that lead to more efficient freight-handling, increased volume of traffic, and greater profits.

CHAPTER XXXIV

NORTHERN PACIFIC RADIO

*How They Operate Over the Main Street of the North-
west*

The 410-mile stretch between Dilworth, Minnesota, and
Glendive, Montana, along which runs the main line of the
Northern Pacific Railroad, is notable for some of the country's
severest winter weather. Heavy snows and icy sleet storms for
years played havoc with the road's trackside telephone and telegraph poles, while adverse weather conditions also often made
it impossible to see hand signals from the head of a train to its
rear.

Now, thanks to modern radio equipment, all that is past. The
NP has installed a complete radio communications network
along the entire length of the four-subdivision run. In addition
to independent transmitter-receiver sets on both ends of thirteen
diesel-electric locomotives and on thirty-five cabooses, there are
eleven base wayside stations, which can be controlled by two
dispatchers, fourteen operators, and three yardmasters.

So interwoven is the network that calls can be initiated either
from train to wayside or in the other direction, between the dispatcher and a conductor on any train, through other wayside
stations along the route, even if those trackside installations are
unattended.

The Northern Pacific began its experimentation with radio
back in 1949, when it installed equipment on freight trains
operating over the difficult Cascade Mountain terrain between
Auburn and Yakima, Washington. It proved effective in reducing train delays, especially expediting the operation of cutting in

helper locomotives on the heavy grades that characterize that majestic Northwest region. In that subdivision, which is 139 miles long, radio resulted in trimming a whole hour from what had in preradio days been an average eight-hour run for through NP freights.

Encouraged by the results of these tests, the Northern Pacific decided to widen its use of radio installation, but indulged in extensive study to determine methods of reducing installation costs and to work out a complete, comprehensive system that would encompass not only end-to-end train communications but also channels for the interchange of information between engineers, conductors, wayside offices, and the dispatcher. The system now in effect resulted from that series of studies and investigations.

Daily traffic schedules on these four subdivisions include four through passenger trains and as many scheduled through freight trains, with two to four extras depending upon volume of tonnage. Automatic block signaling is in service throughout, with passenger trains limited to seventy miles per hour and freight trains restricted to fifty miles per hour. The thirteen diesels used on the freight runs in these subdivisions, which have been fitted with radio equipment, are assigned out of a pool operation and ordinarily do not run beyond Dilworth on the east and Glendive on the west.

The new radio installations continuously prove their value to the Northern Pacific's operations, even under completely normal conditions. On one run, for example, between Dilworth and Jamestown, North Dakota, the radio was put into service nineteen times for end-to-end communications, twice for messages from the train to the dispatcher, once for the dispatcher to get information from the conductor, and twice for point-to-train communications about cars picked up.

End-to-end calls checked air in the lines when the diesel hooked on to begin the run at Dilworth, and the train moved out when the conductor gave the engineer the highball via the air waves. As the caboose cleared the final yard switch onto the main track and the yard departure switches were closed, the engineer was able to open his throttle without delay, for he had the news instantaneously from the conductor.

All along the route, flagging delays were avoided whenever the engineer encountered a "stop then proceed" signal, because he could immediately tell the conductor, verbally, what was happening. Across the Red River of the North from Dilworth, the train stopped to pick up loaded cars at West Fargo, North Dakota, and here again radio saved time. On curves, with the trainmen in the caboose and the engine crew up front watching, as they normally do, for hotboxes or other conditions spelling possible trouble, end-to-end radio immediately reported that all was clear. A normal twenty-minute ground crew inspection, with the train moving slowly, was reduced to twelve minutes by means of radio communication of instructions.

En route, the train moved into a siding. On the move in, and again on the move back to the main line, there was no estimating of time or distances to be done by the engineer. Riding the caboose, the conductor kept him up to the minute, via radio, as to how many cars were still to clear the switch and when he was finally completely in the clear.

Passing Bismarck, the conductor notified the yardmaster at Mandan, directly across the Missouri River that here marks the boundary between North Dakota and Montana, of their position. "No. 603 passing Bismarck with eighty-five loads" drew the immediate radioed response, "Track 4"—a communications operation that saved a minimum of five minutes, which would usually be required for the head brakeman to call the yardmaster after the train had arrived at the entrance to the yard.

But it is in abnormal weather conditions that the comprehensive radio network installed by the Northern Pacific has proved its tremendous worth to the road. During a January snowstorm, with the temperature well below zero, Extra 6002, going west, came to a dead stop on the main track, blocking four important street crossings in the busy city of Fargo. The blizzard conditions that prevailed at the time made it impossible for the four-unit diesel locomotive to get the train under way again.

But radio saved the day. The crew of an incoming eastbound

train was directed by the dispatcher to cut off their locomotive, switch over, and couple it onto the rear of the stalled westbound freight. Then the two engineers, speaking directly to each other from opposite ends of the long string of cars, were able to co-ordinate their efforts and get the freight started smoothly, without a break anywhere along the line.

Track men were replacing a broken rail on a hill somewhere farther along the route, causing the same Extra 6002 to come to a halt once again. Here snowy conditions, coupled with the incline, for a second time prevented the train from getting started. It was planned to cut the train in two and move half of it up the grade at a time, then to recouple on level ground farther on, but radio conversations between the crew and the dispatcher made this operation unnecessary.

Because of weather conditions, a snowplow was at work not too far from where the delay to Extra 6002 had taken place. The dispatcher, therefore, quickly and easily communicated with the engineman of the locomotive attached to this plow, and directed him to lend pulling power to the stalled freight. This operation not only got the freight into operation again but served to clear the right of way for two scheduled passenger trains, both of which might have been seriously delayed had the line continued to be blocked.

On another occasion a telegraph operator at Casselton saw a defective wheel on a car near the rear of a passing westbound freight. He immediately telephoned the dispatcher, whose radio contact with the conductor made it possible to bring the train to a stop for inspection purposes. Such radio conversations also keep the dispatcher at all times informed about unscheduled or unusual train delays, and let him know when trains get under way again. With this kind of information instantaneously available, he can plan train meets with great accuracy and can give arrival times and crew calls based on up-to-the-minute knowledge of the position of every train.

Base radio stations also make it possible for the Northern Pacific to keep in close touch with many branch-line operations, a by-product of the main-line installation system that has developed since the basic network was established. A branch line that runs from Fargo to Streeter now can be cleaned of its impeding snowdrifts with much greater speed than formerly, because radio base stations at Jamestown and Cleveland on the main line can keep in touch with radio-equipped cabooses attached to snowplows on the branch run. A recent stalled train on the Linton branch had its rerailing and clearing operations directed from the dispatcher's office by way of the base mainline radio installation at McKenzie.

When the NP's main line was washed out on the Montana side of the Missouri River, a result of spring thaws sending tons of melting snow down the mountain sides, work trains were employed on both sides of the broken line for a three-day period. With radio, it was possible to coordinate the work of the repair crews approaching one another, although they were physically separated by hundreds of feet of rushing water. During this period, many hours were saved also in bringing strategic equipment and needed materials to the scene of the repair work, since they could be requested and dispatched with a minimum of delay.

One of the exceptionally practical features of Northern Pacific's radio installation is the use of identical units on all locomotives, cabooses, and land stations. This means, of course, that the entire network reflects an unusual flexibility, since all units are readily interchangeable. They package the transmitter, the receiver, and the power supply unit all in one chassis, and will operate on either of two frequencies, 161.25 megacycles or 161.01 megacycles. All Northern Pacific radio units are the Bendix type MRT-5B.

There is a complete and independently operated radio unit on each end of every freight locomotive, which is made up of four diesel-electric units. The NP found that the cost of installing these two separate units in each of a locomotive's two A cabs was little more than it would have been to install only one broadcasting and receiving unit and then to wire together individual speakers and mikes at opposite ends of the four-unit diesel.

In addition, the use of two independently operated units in each locomotive keeps radio service intact even when diesel units are interchanged; it guarantees dependable service, since the failure of one unit will not affect operation of the other in the rear end of the diesel. Furthermore, when a head brakeman or a trainmaster is riding the diesel, he can employ radio communications without interfering with the engineer's use of his own equipment.

A bracket on the engineer's controller carries the handset and control panel in the cab of each diesel A unit. A University type MM2F speaker is mounted on a wall of the passageway leading to the engine nose, and is so angled that its sound is reflected off the opposite wall and can easily be heard anywhere in the cab. There is a specially built shelf in the upper left corner of the nose compartment on which sits the transmitter-receiver unit, which receives its 115-volt AC power from a Cornell-Dubilier vibrator-convertor, that in turn operates on 64 volts DC out of the locomotive's starting battery.

The entire unit, including power supply equipment, cost the Northern Pacific merely $1,600 each, completely installed and ready to operate. To avoid lost time on operations, installation was made in installments during regular layover time between runs.

Caboose installations came to a total of about $2,400 each, a figure considerably under the $5,000 per unit that marked the NP's first experiments with radio on the Yakima-Auburn run in 1949. The new system uses two Exide 6-volt storage batteries, hooked in series, charged by a Leece-Neville alternator-rectifier, which is mounted on the floor of the car and is driven through an axle pulley by a Dayton V belt drive. The 115-volt AC that runs the radio in each caboose is furnished by a Cornell-Dubilier vibrator-convertor, such as is used in the diesel installation, but run from the hooked up batteries. All this equipment, including the radio unit itself, is installed under one of the bunks in the end of the caboose and occupies a total space only 2 feet 6¼ inches wide, 6 feet 6¼ inches long, and 15 inches deep.

The conductor's radio control panel and the handset are

—on the Dilworth-Mandan run, no train is ever out of touch with a base station. The operator then throws a small toggle switch that connects his radio receiver into the dispatcher's telephone circuit. It is that simple: only the movement of this small switch is needed to transform the normal wire circuit into a combined radio-wired line to complete conversations between the dispatcher's office and any moving train anywhere in the radio-equipped division.

Electronic devices installed at base stations that are unattended for some part of the day make it possible for the dispatcher or for the conductor of any train to call through the station by means of an automatic control that hooks up the radio-wire circuit just as the operator would do if he were on duty. All that is required in this case is the pressing of an additional small button in the caboose transmitting unit or in the dispatcher's office. When conversation is concluded, the two circuits automatically disconnect.

The base station transmitter-receiver unit at Fargo has been installed atop a ten-story office building some distance from the railroad. Through remote control devices, this unit can be used at any given time by any one of four men: the operator in the telegraph office at Fargo; the dispatcher, by connection through this telegraph office; the operator in the telegraph office at the Dilworth yard, which is nearly five miles east of Fargo; the yardmaster in the Dilworth yard office.

With this base set subject to use by four separate individuals, a control system had to be worked out to eliminate confusion. In the telegraph offices at both Fargo and Dilworth, the loudspeakers are set up to receive any calls coming through the Fargo receiver, normally on Channel 2, as are all the wayside stations. But the telephone equipment on the desks of these two operators is usually hooked into the regular telephone dispatching circuit.

When they wish to use radio, therefore, these two operators must plug into conventional jacks, which immediately hook them into Channel 2, but a flip of a toggle switch makes it possible for either of them to operate on Channel 1 if necessary.

The yardmaster, if he wishes to talk on Channel 1, must continuously hold down a push button installed for that purpose; as soon as he releases it, his transmitter-receiver automatically reverts to Channel 2.

This arrangement makes it impossible for the yardmaster to leave his set tuned into the wrong channel. Safeguards against having this kind of error made by the two telegraph operators are provided through means of a small electric light at each telegrapher's set, which displays a visual signal at all times, showing to which channel the set is tuned.

The entire installation now consists of seventy-two complete units—in engines, cabooses, and wayside base stations. Spare units are kept in reserve all along the line, at Fargo, Dilworth, Jamestown, Mandan, and Glendive. The Northern Pacific has established a radio repair shop at Mandan, which is centrally located in the Fargo-Glendive run. Whenever a defective unit is removed from service it is placed in a specially prepared shipping box, built for maximum protection, and transported to the Mandan shop.

Equipment inspectors continuously cover the territory in motor trucks and inspect and test the wayside station equipment. Since all of the units are made in easily-plugged-in panel style, it is a relatively simple matter for these traveling crews to replace improperly working units. However, failures are extremely rare in the NP's experience. On the few occasions that major repair work is found to be needed, the mobile crews can call upon the help always available from a special radio repair man assigned to the Mandan shop.

Three Northern Pacific engineering executives are mainly responsible for the completeness and flexibility of this unusual railroad communications network. F. L. Steinbright, superintendent of communications, supervised the forces that planned and constructed the installation; F. B. Childs, radio inspector, analyzed and designed the mobile equipment and the base station antennas; while development and installation of remote-control and base-station apparatus was the responsibility of the road's telephone inspector, M. N. Zeller.

CHAPTER XXXV

SOUTHERN PACIFIC'S TERMINALS

Houston Yard

The growing volume of traffic that characterized all railroad operations immediately following World War II taxed the terminal facilities of the Southern Pacific, as it did all American roads. Long-range planning offered the only solution, and in the years since 1946 the SP has been involved in a series of modernizing and rebuilding operations that have resulted in expansion and improvement of its many key yards throughout the western half of the United States.

The hub of the road's Pacific lines is located at Roseville, near Sacramento, California. Here four great lines meet: the Overland Route coming west from Ogden, Utah, the lines running eastward from Oakland and other points in the San Francisco bay area, the San Joaquin Valley line, which runs southward through the lush California country to Los Angeles, and the Shasta route coming in from Portland, Oregon.

With four flat yards at Roseville handling all the switching from the merging lines, SP officials decided that one modern push-button-controlled gravity yard would serve their needs better by increasing Roseville's capacity, and that it would further aid the work of other yards through improved blocking services it could render.

Consequently a dual-hump yard has been constructed and is now in operation at this great California freight center. It is so arranged that either of its tracks can be used to hump all forty-nine classification tracks at one time. When this is not necessary, one hump is used to serve twenty-one westbound classifications, while the other is used to make twenty-six classifications east-bound and to serve two repair classifications. A diamond cross-over provides each track with access to the entire yard, while electropneumatic retarders control impact speed and remote-control power switches set up the route of the humped cars. The modernized yard at Roseville, complete with its talk-back speakers, paging speakers, and switch-engine–to–tower radio, has served as many as 3,774 cars in a single twenty-four-hour period.

This modern yard also boasts the largest railroad car ice plant in the world, used to ice the reefers carrying perishables that are being moved from the San Joaquin Valley to the east.

Other yards at Bayshore (near San Francisco), Fresno, and West Oakland back up the SP's Roseville operations. The latter serves an industrial area of growing importance, and its lines extend to the Sacramento valley for the Overland and Shasta routes and to the San Joaquin Valley and the Coast routes. Its car capacity is 4,643.

Bayshore yard, with its capacity of 3,788 cars, serves the needs of shippers and consignees in the San Francisco industrial area, while Fresno is actually divided into two yards which function as assembly points for the perishables moving up out of the valley.

A similar radiation of vital rail lines in the Southern Pacific's vast system exists at Houston, Texas, from which point lines of the road's Texas and Louisiana operation extend in every direction. They run westward through San Antonio and El Paso to Los Angeles; they run north to Austin, Dallas, Fort Worth, and Denison; they go northeast to Shreveport, Louisiana, and to St. Louis; they move eastward to New Orleans, south to Galveston, and southwest to Corpus Christi and the lower Rio Grande valley. Trains from eight subdivisions move in and out of the new Englewood yards at Houston.

Actual contact between the SP's two great sets of lines—the Pacific line and the Texas and Louisiana lines—is made at El Paso. This two-unit yard, with its total capacity of 5,450 cars, is also a junction point for the famous Golden State Route running to Tucumcari, New Mexico, and here too interchange is made with the Texas & Pacific, with the Santa Fe, and with the

National Railways of Mexico. The capacity and the servicing facilities of this important El Paso yard are currently being increased and improved through installation of a gravity-type yard.

After Roseville and Englewood, the third of the SP's modernized gravity classification yards is located directly within the city limits of Los Angeles. Located between the Los Angeles River and the San Fernando Road, Taylor Yard, as it is known, was thoroughly modernized as early as 1949. Together with its support yards in the immediate vicinity, it now has a capacity of 7,163 cars.

With its up-to-date towers and lighting equipment, Taylor can hump some 2,800 to 2,900 cars each day. There are sixteen tracks in the receiving yard, which can handle 1,993 cars; a twenty-one-track departure yard holds 1,297 cars; and the classification tracks accommodate 1,157 cars.

But, even after 1949 modernization operations, the SP found that Taylor was still greatly overworked, so a new 24-mile bypass line was constructed, running from Firestone Park, which is on the line to the Los Angeles–Long Beach harbor area, to the main line near Puente. This construction relieved traffic congestion by breaking the bottleneck previously existing as a result of heavy eastbound shipments from the harbor.

The 24-mile bypass also facilitates interchange with the Pacific Electric. Five grade separations and one principal stream crossing had to be built, but only 8¾ miles of new line construction was needed. Rails of the Union Pacific were employed for a 6.5-mile stretch, and a branch line of the SP was used for another 8¾ miles. Centralized traffic control is used to regulate train movements over part of the new bypass.

Further relief for heavy operations in the Taylor Yard was provided for by construction of Los Nietos yards in 1953. Here a thousand cars are classified each day, and some solid trains are made up, although major operations here are fills for trains out of Taylor or for main-line trains at Puente. Another yard at Los Angeles, Aurant, is used for main-line classifications, whereas the other yards in the area are restricted to local consists.

The modernization project at Taylor brought into being a new hump for gravity switching, replanned track groupings, and the installation of power switches, floodlights, car inspection facilities, and modern methods of communication. As a result, the yards in this area are now able to do a great deal of the blocking and classification task that intermediate terminals cannot accomplish, so this modernized yard has its effect upon operations all along the line.

Expedited freight schedules, more efficiently serving the Los Angeles industrial area, have been placed in effect as a result of the Taylor modernization program. For example, it is no longer necessary for crews to stop at outlying points along the route to reswitch cars for set-outs, since the expanded facilities at Taylor make it possible for cars to be lined up in proper set-out order.

In a further attempt to raise the efficiency level at the yard, the SP is experimenting here, too, with closed-circuit television, so that any point in the two-mile-long classification yard can be observed from the central tower.

At Brooklyn (near Portland), and at Eugene, Oregon, are located the two major yards serving the northern extremes of the SP's Pacific lines. The latter is used as a concentration point for lumber shipments that originate in the great woods of the Pacific Northwest, and its cars are usually reblocked to move either into California or over the Siskiyou line.

Another recently enlarged and improved yard is that at Ogden, Utah, where the SP makes contact with the Union Pacific. Cars are interchanged here with the UP, the Denver & Rio Grande, and a short-line connection. Operated by the Ogden Union Railway and Depot Company, this two-unit yard has a capacity of about 3,360 cars and serves a major re-icing point for eastbound perishables.

A significant factor in the redesign and development of the Southern Pacific's various classification yards has been the railroad's concentration on the problems of l.c.l. operations. A coordinated rail-truck service has played an important part in making it possible for the SP to operate l.c.l. handling at a minimum number of stations, thus making the mechanization of cargo-handling a feasible project.

Southern Pacific's l.c.l. transfer stations are located at a number of points from fifty to more than a hundred miles apart, with pickups made throughout the intermediate territory by trucks owned and operated by the Pacific Motor Trucking Company or the Southern Pacific Transport Company, both subsidiaries of the railroad. Between major centers, the SP loads freight for local delivery on cars separate from those used for traffic destined for delivery beyond the transfer point. In this way, l.c.l. for delivery by truck beyond a major center can be dispatched for early delivery, and local l.c.l. delivery is also ready for pickup by truck early each morning.

Small packages consigned to a single destination are consolidated by loading them into a palletized container, which in turn can easily be loaded into a merchandise car by modern materials-handling equipment, such as hand lifts or fork trucks. This method of handling l.c.l. is so rapid that it has given rise to a new problem: sufficient time no longer exists for the normal routine of handling bills of lading. In many cases the billing must be completed after a train has left its point of origin, and information must be sent by teletypewriter to its destination.

Another special problem arose at Houston, where constantly increasing traffic loads and a series of narrow platforms were leading to serious congestion. SP engineers, after studying the situation, came up with the answer in the form of a link belt towline trailer system, which channels freight along predetermined paths at a set speed.

About seven hundred tons of freight each day are towed by this 2,030-foot link chain line and its fleet of 375 trailers. Hooks are set at intervals of 15 feet along the entire length of the chain, which takes nineteen minutes to complete its circuit. The system can handle an average load of 135 platform trailers carrying fifteen hundred pounds each. Trailers are easily added to or taken off the moving chain by handlers at appropriate points along the loading zone.

In the face of constantly increasing traffic loads, the need for improved yard, rail, and car facilities is a factor to which railroad executives must always be prepared to devote attention.

233

Constant improvement of such facilities continues to be the goal at the Southern Pacific.

Houston Yard

A freight classification yard costing $7,000,000 and controlled by an electronic brain and a radar device is the Southern Pacific's curtain-raiser to its second century of American railroading service.

In 1855 the first line of track was laid in California by the Sacramento River Railroad, which soon became part of the rapidly developing Southern Pacific system; in 1955 the SP completed reconstruction of its amazing new automatic yard at Houston, a fitting climax to the road's first one hundred years of operation and a dramatic introduction to what science will contribute to railroading during the century that lies ahead.

At the Englewood yard in Houston, an electronic brain that remembers and thinks makes it possible to put a car over the hump every twelve seconds a full twenty-four hours each day.

Unguided by any human brain or hand, a fully loaded, heavy steel boxcar rolls down the hump, gathering speed of its own momentum as it moves forward. But suddenly there is a perceivable slowing of its progress, in direct response to an order from the electronic device that controls its movements. Having recorded the weight of the car, measured its speed by radar, and noted the distance it must still travel before reaching the line of Chicago-bound cars to which it has been assigned, the electronic brain has already computed the maximum speed at which the car must be allowed to travel in order to avoid a damaging contact with the last car in the line awaiting it. As a result, automatic retarders lining the sides of the rails have reached in and applied pressure to the car wheels.

As the car proceeds at its carefully governed speed, the electronic brain orders its automatic hands to throw the proper switches that will guide the moving boxcar to its proper destination in the great classification yard. Once again science has been put to use in a practical application that completely eliminates all possibility of human error.

Englewood, the key yard on the SP's busy Sunset Route, blocks trains for eight of the road's subdivisions in its Texas and Louisiana operations. It also feeds seven other nearby yards and a great many industrial sidings in this expanding Houston area. Almost every train that moves into this great center is subject to reclassification; the only exceptions are California–New Orleans runs, perishable blocks to St. Louis, and two westbound consists that run through to San Antonio, where they consolidate with the Southern Pacific's Motor Special.

Months of research, examination of other yards, and careful planning went into the creation of the modernized, automatic Englewood yard. Engineers assigned to the task of designing and creating the new classification center decided that a gravity yard was essential to handle the huge volume of traffic scheduled to flow through it. But, they recognized, efficient operation of this type of yard is thoroughly dependent upon continuous operation of the hump; this recognition, in turn, practically dictated the need for a pull-back, saddle-type yard.

As a result, a forty-eight-track yard was constructed, allowing for future expansion to sixty-four tracks. Two receiving yards flank it, one on each side, a type of design that lends the name "saddle-type" to the yard. The "pull-back" part of the description arises from the use of two leads, one from each of the receiving yards, extending to points far behind the hump. Each train is pulled around the hump over one of the two pull-back tracks, allowing for a continuous operation in which, while a switch engine is pulling a train back, another is pushing a string of cars over the hump. The use of saddle-type design keeps the operation at full use at all times, since the side tracks can be used to prevent congestion on the hump by other trains.

The automatic retarders, with their radar control, make it possible to classify cars of varying weights and different loads safely and efficiently. Where the conventional push-button type of yard is brought almost to a standstill during weather conditions accompanied by poor visibility, radar is unaffected by such inclemency. Regardless of temperature, snow, moisture, wind, or darkness, the radar beams pick up each car as it approaches the retarders and set electrical control circuits to apply the correct rate of retardation.

Electric power, governed by electronic devices, does the greatest share of the work. All the tower operator has to do is to press a button indicating the track to which he wants each car to be assigned; the electronic brain, controlling the automatic switching system, does the rest of the job.

A three-story tower is the nerve center of this amazing operation. The crest conductor, located on the second floor, merely pushes a button to route each car to its assigned classification track. As many as four complete routings can be punched at any one time, since the brain remembers these and sets up the desired route, through its control of the automatic switches, for each car as it rolls down the hump.

On the top floor of the control tower, the yardmaster is in position of vantage to observe the entire operation and to issue whatever instructions he deems necessary to keep things rolling at a satisfactory pace.

A unique scale, operated by electronic equipment, is located on the ground-level floor of the tower. With equipment manufactured by the Cox & Stevens Aircraft division of Revere Corporation of America, it weighs each car as it rolls down the first 3 per cent slope off the hump. This track scale is 92 feet long, and is supported by eight load cells.

The electronic brain, heart of the entire system, checks on a group of factors affecting the movement of every car that rolls down the hump. A fairly simple system is employed to check car weight and to apply necessary retardation. Immediately ahead of each trackside retarder a weight-detecting device is located; it consists merely of a treadle working against a heavy spring, so that as the car passes over it, the treadle is depressed to a greater or lesser degree, depending upon the total weight of the car and its contents. This information is flashed back to the electronic brain through electrical contact points, and the retarder is automatically applied to the degree necessary.

Speed of the rolling car is also a factor that the electronic brain must be told about in order to apply the retarders properly. This operation is taken care of by a radar control device on an instantaneous basis. A radar antenna unit, affixed at the end of each retarder, beams ultrahigh-frequency waves right on the approach end of the retarder. As a car enters the area, the beam hits it and is reflected back to the antenna unit, thus changing the frequency of the reflected wave from its original rate. The difference between the two frequency rates is a measure of the car's speed, which the electronic brain interprets. It then sets up the retarder unit to control the speed at which it will permit the car to continue.

This is the most technical and most involved part of the automatic yard classification system, since large numbers of varying factors must be taken into account by the electronic brain in determining just what is the optimum speed for each car. The rollability of the car and the track resistance it is scheduled to encounter—this varies with the route selected—are two of the most important things the brain must consider. Longer tracks with greater curvature offer a different amount of resistance than short, straighter rail lengths; several coupled cars, rolling as a unit, show different rolling characteristics than does a single car.

Rollability is checked by the computer by recording the increase in speed for each car between the time it leaves the hump retarder and the time it checks in at the group retarder. While this computation is going on electronically, the automatic switching system informs the computer of the switching pattern and the track route that have been set up for the car. The use of continuous radar installations makes it possible for the SP to control the speed of each car from beginning to end of its yard journey, and to make automatically and electronically any corrections in speed that may be necessary as the car moves from the hump to its proper place in the yard.

The retarder operator in the tower, however, maintains at all times human control over the operation of the electronic system. He must set the important control that tells the electronic brain whether the car has a long or short distance to roll to its waiting

237

consist, and he is expected to use his judgment in exercising control over car speeds under unusual weather conditions. At any time he is in position to take over from the electronic brain and to impose manual control over the car-braking operations and the switching pattern.

When SP engineers began laying out the new Englewood yard, they decided it was necessary, in view of the traffic pattern that dominates operations there, to locate the hump east of the classification tracks. Further calculations showed that the exact location of the hump would be directly over the main tracks of the Houston Belt & Terminal Railway, a consideration requiring construction of a 27-foot-high crest and a lead-off grade of 5.9 per cent. This unusually steep decline created additional problems of retardation.

A municipal requirement also made it necessary to provide for ample clearance over a superhighway four lanes wide, and the main crest is therefore built on a concrete-and-steel-ballasted deck structure resting on spiral welded pipes that are concrete-filled. The entire humping operation is speeded and fast clearance is provided for by the use of lap switches to shorten distance between the top of the hump and the clearance points to the group retarders. Additional design problems were created by the realization that part of the master retarder, located on the crest, would fall on a bridge that spans Hunting Bayou, so it was necessary to provide construction features that would permit the bridge to resist braking action safely.

Key buildings in the yard are air-conditioned. They include, in addition to the crest control tower, a power and retarder equipment structure, general yard office, interlocking control tower, inspection stations, and five locker rooms. All in all, Englewood has three tower structures and twenty-four miscellaneous buildings.

To serve the yard's communications needs, thirty-one miles of underground cables were laid. There are 38 paging speakers and 238 talk-back speakers, all manufactured by the Electronic Communications Equipment Company. The system includes a bank of six teletypewriters, a PAX dial telephone system, Ampex electric hi-fi recording equipment, and a battery of PBX phones.

Waybills and messages are carried from point to point in the yard by means of a total of 24,000 feet of pneumatic tubing. All yard switch engines are equipped with two-way radio to enable enginemen and supervisory personnel to remain in constant, instantaneous, direct communication, and a closed-circuit television system is being installed to help yard employees see what is going on in portions of the vast classification operation that may not be clearly visible by direct line of sight.

Key points and trackage are provided with block signaling and interlocking systems. Eastbound entering switches are all power operated, under the control of a tower-stationed employee who enjoys clear visibility over the entire complex of the yard's western entrance. In both the interlocking and crest towers there are track-occupancy panels that indicate clearance conditions on all receiving tracks. The yardmaster can flash on a trackside panel the number of the track to which he has assigned a westbound train.

There is a ground-level inspection station so positioned that the eye level of the car inspector is exactly at the top of the rail, and there is also a high-level station for observing the tops of the cars.

The longest of Englewood's tracks can hold 132 cars. Total capacity of the classification tracks is 2,975 cars; receiving and departure tracks hold 3,015 cars; repair and shop tracks, 505; miscellaneous-purpose tracks, 110; bringing the entire yard to an over-all total of 6,605 cars.

The Southern Pacific, through design and construction of the highly scientific, fully automated Englewood yards, has provided safer, better, and faster service for its shippers. But, perhaps of greater significance, it is making a real contribution to all of American railroading, for the superior facilities that exist here for blocking cars and classifying consists bring in their wake improved rail operations by all other lines with which the SP functions through its interchanges.

CHAPTER XXXVI

THE SOUTHERN RAILWAY'S DIESELS

Availability and Mileage, Radio Communications, Training Schools

A completely dieselized railroad system serves the Southland today.

With 854 diesels at work, the Southern Railway System is one of the largest railroads anywhere in the world whose trains are hauled entirely by diesel-powered locomotives. Historically, this gigantic conversion is significant in itself, since it marks the end of 123 years of steam locomotive operation on these lines, but complete dieselization holds much more than mere historic interest. The change-over makes it possible for the Southern to move all of its trains more smoothly, more comfortably, and faster, and through concurrent elimination of the old steam locomotive service shops, enables the road to effect great economies in its over-all operations.

As recently as 1939 Southern operated 1,550 steam locos; today it does a greater transportation job, hauling more freight and a greater number of passengers more miles in less time, with only 854 diesels! The conversion required an investment of $140,000,-000 for the locomotives themselves, in addition to many more millions of dollars spent for repair shops and varying types of newly required servicing facilities.

But the investment of these huge sums has more than paid off for the Southern. In 1941, for example, steam locomotives hauled 99 per cent of the road's total freight-ton miles and registered for the year 38 billion ton miles, 26 million train miles. Sixteen years later, diesels hauled 47 billion gross ton miles

NP Extra 7000 east hauled by 7000 h.p. diesel west of Missoula, Mont. on the Sixth Subdiv. of Rocky Mt. Div.

New modern mechanical PFE reefer owned jointly by the U.P. and S.P. rolling through the retarder at North Platte, Neb. — Nebraska Div.

U.P. new freight yard at Kansas City has 4,500 ft. mechanized icing dock which can accommodate 100 cars on either side and is equipped with a chain conveyor system for supplying ice on each of its two decks. This new yard was built at a cost of $4,000,000 to handle eastbound traffic. Its 34 tracks have capacity of 2,460 cars.

Southern Pacific Extra 6190 east at Crystal Lake on a typical winter day in the Sierra Nevadas. The westward track is on the right. Mountain Subdiv. of Sacramento Div.

Looking from control tower at the new hump at C & O's yard at Russell, Ky. showing Union Switch & Signal Co.'s retarder machine.

Lackawanna HB-7 crossing the Delaware River Bridge approaching Slateford Junction near the New Jersey-Pennsylvania state line.

Rear end of Lackawanna HB-9 west of Slateford Jct. on the Scranton and Buffalo Div. entering the Delaware Water Gap showing one of the road's fine new all-steel radio equipped cabooses. Note the marvelous track for which this road has always been famous.

New Northern Pacific Pig Palace cars rolling through Livingston, Montana, headed west. These double-deck livestock cars are equipped with movable shutters that can be completely or partially closed for cold weather protection, roller bearings, and have aluminum paint on roofs and ends of cars to reflect the hot rays of the sun in summer.

Northern Pacific #661, local freight on the Pullman Wash. Branch on the Second Subdiv. of the Idaho Div. near Cheney hauled by EMD 1500 h.p. diesel.

Santa Fe # 2, the new San Francisco Chief with diesel 308 crossing the Muir, Cal. trestle at the top of the 1% grade between Maltby and Muir. This is on the Third Dist. and is the ruling grade for the entire Valley Div.

Santa Fe #17, the Super Chief, in Apache Canyon near Canyoncito descending Glorieta Pass on the Third Dist. of the N.M. Div. Photo by R. H. Kindig.

Impact Recorders are used extensively by the freight protection department. When set, this device will operate over a period 16 to 20 days with a chart speed of 1½ inches per hour.

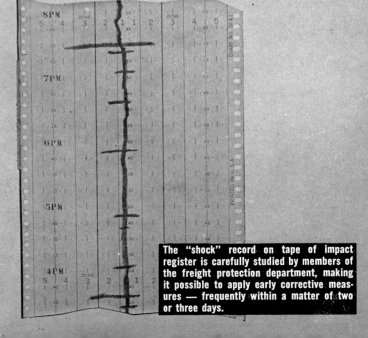

The "shock" record on tape of impact register is carefully studied by members of the freight protection department, making it possible to apply early corrective measures — frequently within a matter of two or three days.

while moving 100 per cent of the total system traffic. Yet this record was accomplished at the end of only 16 million train miles, which means that the new diesel units carried almost 10 per cent additional cargo while actually moving some 38 per cent less distance. Gross ton miles per train hour in 1941 were 25,790, against an 84 per cent gain to 47,378 in 1952.

Statistics indicate that even with the tremendous increase in Dixie's industrial activity since the end of World War II and the great gain in volume this has meant for Southern, the railroad would have had difficulty staying in the black, because of parallel increases in costs of labor, supplies, and equipment, had it not been for the tremendous operating economies gained through the use of all-diesel power.

The Southern Railway System, while not the first road in the United States to employ diesel units, had been in the forefront in uncovering methods and techniques for getting a maximum of useful mileage out of its new prime movers and in developing efficient, low-cost maintenance techniques.

Local passenger service was the first level of Southern operations to reap the benefits of dieselization, when in 1939 six 750-horsepower Fairbanks Morse streamlined cars, each with a matching streamlined coach, were placed in operation. Four trains inaugurated this new kind of service, running between such points as Tuscumbia and Oakdale, Chattanooga and Meridian, Columbus, Mississippi, Birmingham, and Mobile, and Atlanta and Brunswick, and bearing such romantic names as the Joe Wheeler, the Golden Rod, the Vulcan, and the Cracker.

During the war years these four trains often operated with as many as four cars each and displayed a remarkable ability for economical operation, while showing average repair costs of about one-third those normally expected of a steam locomotive. With this experience, Southern acquired eight varied-sized diesel yard switchers in 1940 and assigned them to yards at Macon, Atlanta, and Jacksonville. Nine 2,000-horsepower passenger units were soon added; three of these were operated as single units for the then recently streamlined Southerner, while six were

241

organized into three two-unit locomotives to haul the Tennessean, the Crescent, and the Ponce de Leon.

The Southern system can lay claim to being the first railroad ever to acquire and operate a road freight diesel locomotive, as a result of its acquisition, in 1940, of the Electro-Motive 103, a four-unit diesel, which was used by the manufacturer as a demonstrator. That locomotive is still being used today, as No. 6100, in a Southern freight pool out of Birmingham, although now it is officially CNO&TP property.

With the acquisition and use of this famous four-unit mover and the impressive performance it delivered, there came the real impetus to dieselization on the lines of the Southern Railway System. Wartime restrictions prevented the purchase and addition of any really substantial number of new diesels for freight use, but the period did provide the railroad's officials with a great opportunity to learn how to operate the new locomotives and to experiment with techniques for getting maximum usage from them. By the end of the war, therefore, the road had built up a good pool of employees who knew and understood diesel operation, and it had already established the nucleus of a scientific maintenance setup.

Immediately after the cessation of hostilities, many new diesels were delivered to the road, so that diesel-hauled ton miles jumped from 16.7 per cent in 1946 to 33.2 per cent a year later, while passenger car miles during these same two years went from 22.97 per cent to 52.54 per cent. Acquisition of thirty road switchers in 1952 added to Southern's diesel power.

These road switchers have proved to be versatile performers, and they have been used for all kinds of work on the railroad's secondary and branch lines throughout Dixieland. They have been used for freight haulage, for passenger service, and for pulling mixed trains to provide dependable service for both shippers and travelers.

Southern officials keep in close touch with engineering developments in the diesel market, and the road's shops are kept busy modernizing the older units in accordance with latest design features. The railroad has also constructed, in its own shops, five booster units for hump operation at the Sevier, Norris, and Lynchburg yards. These were built by taking a ballasted frame and superstructure from a steam locomotive tender, which had been equipped with cooling fans and freight-type diesel trucks. This unit was then coupled between two yard switcher diesels, with the two motors on each truck hooked up in series with the four motors of a locomotive.

This coupling provides the high traction at low speeds needed in hump operations, by providing six motors that are supplied with the current from each locomotive. The units are also furnished with an automatic speed-control device that permits the maintenance of constant speeds without attention from the engineer while humping cars.

Problems of operation, scheduling, maintenance, and personnel have followed rapidly in the wake of the Southern's policy of full dieselization, but they have been tackled and solved energetically. Every department—from shops and service centers through communications and yards—has had its part in developing methods to provide fullest use of and extra major advantages from the use of diesel power.

The use of full dieselization and the changes it has brought about on every level of railroad operation have made the Southern one of the world's most completely modern railroads.

Availability and Mileage

How the Southern Railway System has planned its diesel movements to obtain highest possible mileage results from their use is a story in itself.

To operate at a level of greatest profit to the road it serves, the diesel engine, unlike the steam locomotive, must be kept to a minimum of idle time, and its great haulage powers and potential must be available for the most complete employment. To work out railroading schedules that take this need into account is a newly developed art, which can be practiced only by discarding all traditional concepts of motive-power operation.

Applying new theories to a new kind of operation, Southern transportation and mechanical personnel have provided the railroad with mileage records that would have been an impossibility in the days of steam locomotives. The average steam locomotive, back in 1941, traversed some 5,000 miles monthly over Southern's trackage; ten years later, the road's diesels averaged about 9,000 miles each month! And these freight mileage statistics are more than balanced by what diesels are accomplishing in providing motive power for the Southern's passenger fleet: they average some 14,000 miles per month, a gain of some 300 per cent over the steam locomotives they replaced.

Yard diesels, too, in a ten-year period, showed a 136 per cent increase in average hours of operation, recording about nineteen hours per day or seven thousand hours each year.

Many new concepts had to be accepted by the road's executive and operating personnel in order to accomplish such achievements. One of the first new ideas brought into play was that of dispatching and maintaining the new-type locomotives on a regional basis, rather than on the restricted division basis employed with steam. From this it became but a step to plan operations in terms of the entire system, because the long-range abilities of the diesel unit make it feasible to extend its operations over parts of all three of the road's operating regions and over a half-dozen or more divisions.

This new concept was put into actual practice along with the original acquisition of Southern's first diesels, back in 1941, when the new engines were assigned to such comparatively long runs as Washington to Atlanta, Washington to New Orleans, and Bristol to Memphis.

At the beginning this concept was not applied to the operations of the freight diesels. In the same year, the road's first two four-unit engines were assigned to a run of only 138 miles, between Danville and Oakdale on the CNO&TP. However, as additional freight diesel units were ordered and delivered, it became possible to apply the new theory of long-range assignment, and soon diesels were hauling long lines of freight cars as far as from

Cincinnati to Chattanooga, to Birmingham, to New Orleans, and eventually on to Atlanta and beyond.

Cooperative effort is maintained between the transportation and mechanical departments, with the aid of the traffic department, to get the maximum mileage out of the Southern's fleet of diesel-powered units. For the ability to achieve such productive activity falls somewhere between keeping the individual diesel at the head of a moving train as many hours as possible and permitting it adequate idle time for the maintenance that is essential if it is to be kept in condition to provide that vital mileage in the first place! Thus, in operating its diesels, the Southern uses both the planned cycle and the "first in–first out" system in its maintenance and repair work. Which method is employed depends upon local circumstances, with the scheduled rotation plan being used where a number of daily trains move through permanent maintenance areas.

On the road's Eastern Lines, the largest diesel maintenance center is located at Spencer, North Carolina; on the Central Lines, at Knoxville; on the Western Lines, at Chattanooga. But important supplementary maintenance points are also kept in continuous operation.

Columbia, South Carolina, is the focal point for a large fleet of road switchers used on the Eastern Lines for both freight and passenger runs, while passenger diesels additionally are given maintenance service at Alexandria, Virginia. Atlanta and Memphis are pool centers for both freight and local passenger units operating over the Central Lines, while Birmingham, Ludlow, Kentucky, and New Orleans operate shops that supplement Chattanooga activities for diesels working the system's Western Lines.

A typical operation out of Chattanooga will serve to show how planned cycle maintenance gets maximum mileage out of each diesel unit, yet permits it to spend adequate maintenance and check-up time in the shop. Working a three-cycle schedule, a unit will arrive back in Chattanooga for inspeciton once in about every ten days.

On its first cycle, the locomotive will haul a freight train from Chattanooga to Cincinnati, from there to Atlanta, and then back to Cincinnati again via Chattanooga. From the Queen City it moves to Oakdale, Tennessee, back north to East St. Louis via Danville, Kentucky, south again to Oakdale, and on once more to Cincinnati. The diesel then makes a trip to New Orleans, following which it returns to the Chattanooga maintenance shop, having completed some 4,100 miles in ten days.

The same unit takes off on its second cycle after fourteen hours in the maintenance shop. This time it heads first for New Orleans, returns to Chattanooga, and keeps going right on to East St. Louis. Its return to Chattanooga then permits it to be assigned, if advisable, to return to its first-cycle journey.

Another freight cycle operated out of Chattanooga accounts for some 2,300 miles of operation in about seven days. This run sends the diesel to Louisville, from which point it hauls its freight cars all the way to Jacksonville, Florida. Here it picks up a GS&F train, which it carries to Macon, then powers another train from that city to Chattanooga. A round trip to Cincinnati completes the cycle, which is a typical interregional diesel operation, since the Chattanooga-Jacksonville portion is run over rails of the Central Lines.

To maintain these regular cycles the Southern operates twenty-one diesels out of Chattanooga, plus additional units which do not run on regular schedules but nevertheless keep moving. A so-called "mountain pool," running between Chattanooga and Oakdale, Danville, and Cincinnati, employs the services of no less than eleven diesels at all times. On some operating cycles the diesels handle both freight and passenger trains, the units being equipped with steam generators for these purposes.

Typical of this kind of operation is a two-unit locomotive that leaves Cincinnati at the head of passenger train No. 3, the Royal Palm, after having been inspected and maintained at Ludlow, Kentucky. This unit arrives next day in Jacksonville, is detached from its passenger cars, and picks up a local freight, which it hauls to Valdosta, Georgia. The following morning it is moving to Macon, hauling mixed train No. 26; during the night it returns to Jacksonville on through freight No. 59, arriving there early in the morning. From this point it returns to Cincinnati at the head of passenger train No. 2, and completes a cycle that encompasses two regions and three divisions.

On the Eastern Lines, Spencer, North Carolina, is maintained as the main pooling point for the Southern's diesel power. All freight traffic operating between Washington and Atlanta (638 miles over the Washington, Danville, and Charlotte divisions) is handled by seventeen locomotives, which are not split except when power is needed for extra passenger trains. At Spencer these units are operated on the first in–first out method.

There are a great many branch and secondary lines radiating out of the Southern Railway System's main lines, and these have presented a problem in obtaining maximum benefits from diesel power. Southern officials are constantly studying the problem, and while they have already achieved astounding results, they are all confident that continual application will result in new methods of use, changes in scheduling, and operational improvements that will enable them to keep their diesels on the move in the future even more efficiently than they have already done.

Meanwhile, of course, they note with pride and satisfaction the work of their diesel units on the Charleston and Columbia divisions. Maintained at Columbia, they handle the yard work at Charleston, every single freight run on both divisions, and local freight trains on the Charlotte division. There are 41 units assigned to this work, and they accomplish what was formerly done by 150 steam locomotives!

Radio Communications

Supplementing full dieselization and the rebuilding of its classification yards, the Southern Railway System has embarked on an extensive program of radio installations, designed to facilitate its handling of a huge volume of freight.

About $1,000,000 has been spent by the road to put end-to-end radio in operation through installations in some four hundred diesel locomotives and cabooses, to purchase about three hundred portable handie-talkie units, and to expand yard and terminal radio communications systems at key points. Radio-equipped and radio-controlled freight trains are thus in operation today on almost every foot of Southern's vast 8,000 miles of trackage.

Yard radio service was inaugurated at the Sevier yard, Knoxville, in 1948; train service radio began with an experimental installation in 1951 on the St. Louis–Louisville division, between Danville and East St. Louis. Motorola FMTU equipment was used on nine cabooses at that time.

Today, fifty-seven diesel "A" units are radioized for operations on the St. Louis–Louisville division. Polled at Chattanooga's Citico yard, actually only a small part of this total is used in that territory at any one time. The units employ a Cornell-Dubilier vibrator convertor which changes the 64-volt DC locomotive power to 117-volt AC, and a mounting rack is provided for the Motorola transmitter, receiver, and power pack.

Both locomotives and cabooses have Motorola "firecracker" antennas. The railroad's Mechanical Department, which has responsibility for maintenance of this equipment, made the fixed installations on the locomotives and cabooses; maintenance of the radio equipment itself is taken care of by the Southern's Communications Department.

The power-supply units on locomotives are mounted in the nose of the diesel "A" unit, with the radio apparatus rack set underneath the cab floor on the fireman's side. This can be made available for inspection and maintenance merely by removing the stairs that lead from the fireman's side to the engine room.

Danville is headquarters for radio maintenance. Originally, before every "A" unit had been supplied with radio, the equipment was simply slipped into place on the rack of each locomotive as it left Danville westbound, and removed from returning units.

Still another unusual device was tried out on the St. Louis–Louisville division, where each train was furnished with two portable units in addition to the regular permanent installations.

248

These handie-talkie sets were for the use of rear trainmen and the head brakeman.

As total installation progressed on the Southern, the standard set by the experimental installations on the St. Louis–Louisville division was extended. This provides for complete interchange of equipment, with the same receivers, transmitters, and power packs installed on every "A" unit. Since diesel operation offers the advantage of using any engine anywhere, this interchangeability makes it possible to provide flexibility and maximum use of the system's radio network.

In extending its radio operations, Southern placed what is believed to be the largest single order for train radio equipment— $500,000 for components to be installed by the Mechanical Department and an additional $120,000 for handie-talkies, spare parts, and testing instruments of various types.

A series of radio shops has been set up at strategic points along the system's lines. Each such shop has a standing force of two technicians and is fully stocked with everything necessary to test, repair, and align every radio—oscilloscopes, frequency meters, signal generators, etc. Adjustment rooms are completely screened to fend off possible interference from nearby electrical installations.

Dependable operation of the system's radio equipment has made it unnecessary to schedule any regular cycle of maintenance and repair, and radio apparatus is attended to only when, as it infrequently does, it requires overhauling or repairing. Standardization of installations makes this a relatively simple task, since it becomes merely a matter of removing the faulty equipment and replacing it with a workable unit.

However, to insure fresh battery sets for use with the handie-talkies, these portable units are removed and replaced every time a locomotive or caboose passes through a radio maintenance point.

Three different types of radio installations are employed in the Southern's yards and terminals. There is the general coverage radio, which has its base station in the tower office tuned in to mobile units on all of the switch engines that are operating within that yard. Installations of this type operate at Cincinnati, Chattanooga, Meridian, New Orleans, Birmingham, Atlanta, and Knoxville.

The so-called "Dick Tracy" setup, first experimented with at Atlanta's Inman yard, has now been extended for use at Birmingham, Knoxville, Asheville, and Charlotte. With this system, instructions broadcast by the switch conductor over a portable transmitter are heard both on the locomotive radio and through loud-speakers mounted on poles at specific locations throughout the yard. In this way all members of a switch crew can hear whatever the conductor says, while at the same time the speakers pick up whatever the engineman says in reply to the conductor's instructions.

At Sevier, Citico, Inman and Norris, still a third type of network is employed, in which the humpmaster and the hump locomotive engineer are in constant direct communication.

Interference is avoided by having each of these three systems operate on a separate frequency. Locomotive radios are so equipped as to enable the engineer to switch to whichever frequency he desires.

Training Schools

One way to guarantee a future supply of well-trained, properly equipped executives is for a railroad to train and school such men itself. This is precisely what the Southern Railway System does, and as a result many of its present officers can look back on their early days with the railroad as a continuation of their classroom work.

Almost forty years ago Southern began a recruiting and training program in its Operating Department. Today each of the system's many departments conducts its own training course so that its junior employees are assured of sound grounding in the Southern's way of doing things.

The Traffic Department, for example, which runs a very effective selection and on-the-job training program, is extending this sphere of activity to classroom operations, while since the advent of the diesel engine the railroad has broadened its efforts to attract graduate mechanical and electrical engineers.

Transfer of promising young employees from point to point at periodic intervals is a company policy too. This gives each junior staff member an opportunity to watch railroading at work under varying conditions of topography, climate, and cargo, and provides a valuable base of experience for future executive decisions that may have to be made by that same individual.

Selection of trainees is the very first step in the employment pattern at the Southern, and careful discretion is exercised. Study of scholastic records, investigation of character references, check into leadership potentialities, and the like are thoroughly gone into, and reports by the Southern's interviewers are closely scrutinized and discussed.

The applicant is made to realize that the railroad's standards are high in all things. He is told exactly what his training will be like, what he is expected to contribute, and what his prospects are with the company. For example, even though he may be executive material for the long pull, it is made clear to him that, at least during his trainee period, he will have to work with his hands and use tools. He may work and live with the section gangs. He is impressed with the fact that his aptitude for working with people and for getting along well with them is at least as important as the technical abilities he has learned at school.

During training, detailed reports are required of him on every phase of work to which he is assigned. Supervisory officers study and grade these papers as a check on the progress being made by the student; and, as a further aid to him, the trainee is informed of the nature of the supervisors' reactions to his reports.

For development of all-around personnel, a trainee also receives some assignments in departments other than the one for which he is being prepared. A maintenance-of-way trainee, for example, may find himself working at one time or another with freight agencies or traffic solicitors, in a locomotive or car repair shop, in the Southern's personnel department, or in a classroom studying train operations.

251

A trainee normally will consume about two years in this kind of apprenticeship before finding himself installed at the bottom of the supervisory personnel ladder. As a result of this kind of training and of the over-all policy it represents, the Southern has not been compelled for many years to look outside of its own ranks when top-level jobs were to be filled.

Off-the-job study is also encouraged for those employees who enter the railroad's service from outside channels, and about half of the company's present officers have made the grade in this manner. But the success of the system's internal schooling program is amply attested by the fact that today the president of the Southern Railway System, the operating vice-president, three general managers, and well over a hundred other officials are graduates of the first program that began so long ago in the railroad's Operating Department.

In addition, five graduates of the Southern Railway System's executive training program are today presidents of other railroads. They are Clark Hungerford of the Frisco, Fred W. Okie of the Union Railroad and the Bessemer & Lake Erie, Earl L. Keister of the Tennessee Central Railway, O. B. Keister, Jr., of the Tennessee, Alabama & Georgia Railway, and Carroll W. Ashby of the Kentucky & Indiana Terminal Railroad.

Not too many schools can point to such a distinguished and accomplished list of graduates.

Yes, the Southern truly serves the South and President Harry A. DeButts can really take a bow. DeButts was operating vice-president when a great deal of the preceding effort was accomplished, and he has been ably followed by D. W. Brosnan, a great all-around railroad man, and by W. Mason King, the traffic vice-president, and one of the country's best.

CHAPTER XXXVII

LACKAWANNA

Fast Freight BH-4, and Radio

At a scheduled time every afternoon a Lackawanna freight train pulls into the passenger station at Binghamton, New York, and comes to a halt there. In a split second the diesels that have pulled it from East Buffalo that morning are cut off, and a waiting switch engine removes the leading freight cars and returns within a few minutes with other cars, which it backs into place. The diesels return, a final check of connections is made, and the Lackawanna freight is off again.

What has happened is that BH-4, a freight train making the run from Buffalo to Hoboken, has made its daily connection with "the Capitol District Perishable Block," exchanging its lead cars of fruits and vegetables, consigned to Albany, New York by D&H, for other cars bearing tons of newsprint bound for the New York metropolitan area.

Connections are as important to the shipper of cargo as they are to the passenger who is trying to get from one city to another and doesn't want to be kept waiting for several hours at some way station. In the case of perishable foods or of merchandise that a store has promised to a customer, good dependable connections are vital. That is why Lackawanna runs BH-4 and its other symbol freights with precision and attention to detail aimed always at seeing to it that the train is at the right place at the right time.

BH-4 leaves Lackawanna's big East Buffalo yard at 8:15 each morning, carrying with it merchandise that in some cases started its journey on the Pacific Coast a few days earlier. After leaving

Binghamton it hurries on to Scranton, where it has a 5:00 P.M. date with switch engines, other freight cars, and a crew of eager-eyed inspectors. Here there is a fast series of moves that may include the cutting out or the addition of some cars, the changing of a caboose, and perhaps getting a new set of diesels.

While these changes are being made, four car inspectors each walk half the length of the train—two on each side start from the front and two others from the rear as they work toward each other—carefully checking running gear, car seals, and the visible portions of the train's cargo. But BH-4 has other important appointments down the line, so this work must proceed with efficiency and speed.

At Port Morris there are exchanges to be made with the Lehigh & Hudson, where cars are cut off and shipped to eastern New York State, Connecticut, and Massachusetts. Meat and other commodities must continue with BH-4 on its journey into Hoboken in time to be picked up on floats and hauled across the Hudson River by Lackawanna's fleet of tugs, so that they will arrive early enough to be distributed throughout the great city's markets.

Throughout the daily run of BH-4, Lackawanna officials are aware of how many people are dependent upon the train's doing its part to keep the wheels of America's commerce moving steadily and smoothly. The emphasis today is upon speed in the movement of merchandise; much effort has been put forth in creating a demand for the shippers' products, and this effort and the money invested in it is entirely lost if Mrs. Housewife cannot find the advertised goods when she asks her storekeeper for them. A sale can easily be lost if the new washing machine fails to arrive on the day the dealer has promised that it will, and the failure of a railroad to keep a connection date by as little as an hour can lose that sale.

The manifest of a typical day's run by BH-4 is a summary of the nation's geography and economics. With its 4,500-horsepower diesels easily handling a typical cargo of seventy-eight loads amounting to some 3,500 tons, BH-4 might leave Buffalo some morning with waybills covering almost anything and everything imaginable.

There might be vegetables on their way to Albany from the fertile fields near Guadalupe, California; a builder in Unionbury, New Jersey, would be ready to receive shingles from Port Angeles, Washington, and the tractors from Peoria, Illinois, that BH-4 is hauling for him; that night a family in South Kearny, New Jersey, might enjoy a delicious cut of beef that had arrived in the market that same morning from Pueblo, Colorado.

Or there might be hogs on their way from Detroit to Secaucus, hams from Toronto to Jersey City, floor polish from Racine to Kingsland, evaporated milk from Manitowoc to Netcong, oranges from Riverside to Boston, butter from Bemidji to Cambridge, tobacco from Louisville to Brooklyn, and copper bars from Garfield, Utah, to a seagoing freighter in New York harbor.

All these and more are moved, on schedule, by BH-4, exchanging its cars with those of such connecting railroads as the Nickel Plate, Wabash, Chesapeake & Ohio, Michigan Central, Pere Marquette, Canadian National, Erie, Pennsylvania, Baltimore & Ohio, and South Buffalo.

Furniture, washing machines, cereal, fuel oil, flour, carrots, cattle, wall board, sheet iron—all the products of American industry, commerce, and agriculture are moved daily by such fast-moving, dependable freight trains as Lackawanna's BH-4, providing service that manufacturer and consumer alike can depend upon completely.

The extended use in recent years of radio as a means of instant and clearly understandable communications between train crews is one of the factors that has helped make trains like BH-4 such dependable movers of the nation's merchandise. Two-way radios installed in BH-4's caboose and locomotive cab insure reliable communications and eliminate the need to rely upon hand or light signals, whether starting, stopping, or under way. While the train is moving, conductor and engineer can quietly and calmly confer about any matter concerning its operation.

In addition, radio makes it possible for train crews to send or receive important information to or from stations along the way. It provides instant warning in emergency cases such as the development of hotboxes, and enables the conductor to coordinate the starting of lead and pusher engines. It permits the train to get under way with a minimum of wasted time when the flagman returns to the caboose after a stop, and it makes it possible for the conductor to give instructions to the engine crew when cars are being switched.

After extensive tests and experiments with many types of equipment, Lackawanna has decided to install Bendix equipment on BH-4 and its other symbol freights. Dual-channel units are used, operating on VHF bands, as required for this kind of operation by the Federal communications system; Lackawanna's assigned channels are 161.37 megacycles and 160.83 megacycles. VHF is ideal for this kind of task because it is far less subject to outside interference than normal wave lengths and consequently furnishes clearer reception.

One assigned channel is used for end-to-end train communication, while the Lackawanna uses the other for contact between trains and wayside stations. These stations are located at Bath, Owego, and B.&O. Junction, New York, and at New Milford, Pennsylvania, where power is obtained from regular commercial sources available at those points.

A total of thirty-nine diesels have been equipped with radio installations. Should any one of the fitted diesels be assigned to another run or sent to a shop for repair or overhaul, radio sending and receiving units can easily be removed and installed in another locomotive.

The chassis for the locomotive radio unit is specially shock-mounted on a platform built in for this purpose. The loudspeaker is placed directly in the center of the cab, right above the windshield, where the engineer is assured of the highest and clearest degree of audibility. Added to the normal components of the engineer's control stand are a radio handset and a control panel, while the antenna is strung on the roof of the cab. A 12-volt DC motor generator supplies the needed power.

A unique installation in the caboose provides for power to be supplied from storage batteries, which in turn are charged by means of an axle-driven alternator-generator. This means that just so long as the wheels of the caboose are turning—no matter in which direction—the battery-charging process continues, so that the caboose does not have to be detached and turned around at the end of each run.

The chassis in the caboose is also shock-mounted and is set in a compartment under the seat in the cupola, while the speaker is mounted on the ceiling of the cupola. In the aisle below are the control box and the handset.

The Lackawanna was the first railroad in the world to experiment with wireless communication between a fixed point and a moving train when on November 13, 1913, a message was actually transmitted and received between the Lackawanna Limited and towers that had been specially erected at Hoboken, Scranton, and Binghamton. Up till this time Guglielmo Marconi, inventor of the wireless, had held to the theory that his new invention would work properly only over water, believing that minerals in the earth's surface would prevent the signal from reaching its destination.

The route of the Lackawanna proved ideal for a test, since it ran through mountainous terrain that would certainly have stopped effective reception if Marconi's theory had been correct. However, the Italian inventor had revised his thinking along these lines, and late in 1913 he received the cooperation of the Lackawanna railroad when he was ready to test his altered theories.

An interesting footnote to history is furnished by the fact that one of the men who played an important part in this early-day experiment was an employee of the Marconi company named David Sarnoff. Today, Brigadier General Sarnoff is president of the Radio Corporation of America.

The invention of the vacuum tube two years later by Dr. Lee DeForest brought radio equipment to the Lackawanna Limited and to the road's wayside stations. At that point in history, the two inventions had not yet proved reliable enough for train-dispatching purposes, but wireless communications among the three wayside points continued to be used with great success for many years. The Hoboken station in 1921 attempted to broadcast the Dempsey-Carpentier fight for the entertainment of passengers aboard the Lackawanna Limited, but this proved not too successful an operation.

Installation of modern radio equipment in twenty-four of Lackawanna's new all-steel cabooses has led also to other important improvements. The need for electric power to operate the radios now makes it possible for the Lackawanna to eliminate the romantic and traditional, if generally impractical, oil lamps that have always been an integral part of the caboose, and to replace them with the up-to-date illumination provided by electric lights.

A new safety feature has also developed as a by-product of radio and the electric wiring it requires: electric markers have been installed, each of which is open on its underside, so that the steps of each caboose are now adequately lit for night operations.

The magic of radio thus helps BH-4 and the other Lackawanna symbol freights to carry out their important assignments of running on time and of meeting their schedules so that vital interchanges of cars with other roads can take place when and where they are supposed to, so that the nation's commerce may run on schedule.

Lackawanna officials know that a railroad has only its service to sell to a shipper. For that reason they realize that every move must be made to count, and that terminal time as well as road time must be kept to the minimum that can be achieved through the use of the most modern available scientific devices and methods.

The Lackawanna is always on the alert for ways to improve its service, and freight trains like BH-4, with their reliable end-to-end and train-to-wayside instant communication, represent the best that is possible in service today; and what is more, President

EASTWARD MANIFEST TRAIN SCHEDULE
THE TIME SHOWN CONVEYS NO TIME TABLE AUTHORITY

Station		BH-2 Daily	A/BH-4 Daily	NE-2 Ex Fr Sa	BH-4 Daily	BS-2 Daily	No.20 Ex Fr Sa Su	NE-4 Daily	NE-6 Daily	BH-8 Daily	BH-12 Daily
EAST BUFFALO (R.T. East Buffalo-Elmira)	Lv.	1.00 AM 5'50"	4.30 AM 5'00"	5.15 AM 4'15"	8.15 AM 4'15"	10.30 AM 4'30"	5.00 PM 3'30"	6.45 PM 3'35"	8.00 PM 4'45"	9.15 PM 4'45"	—
ELMIRA	Ar.	6.50 AM 55"	9.30 AM 30"	—	12.30 PM 30"	—	8.30 PM 10"	10.40 PM 20"	12.45 AM 10"	2.00 AM 30"	—
ELMIRA (T.T. Elmira; R.T. Elmira-East Binghamton)	Lv.	7.45 AM 2'00"	10.00 AM 1'30"	—	1.00 PM 1'15"	—	8.40 PM 1'10"	11.00 PM 1'05"	12.55 AM 1'50"	2.30 AM 2'15"	—
EAST BINGHAMTON	Ar.	9.45 AM 45"	11.30 AM 45"	11.30 AM	2.15 PM 30"	8.00 PM 30"	9.50 PM 1'25"	12.05 AM 25"	2.45 AM 15"	4.45 AM 30"	10.30 AM 2'00"
EAST BINGHAMTON (T.T. East Binghamton; R.T. East Binghamton-Scranton)	Lv.	10.30 AM 3'15"	12.15 PM 1'30"	—	2.30 PM 1'45"	8.30 PM 2'00"	—	12.30 AM 1'25"	4.00 AM 2'00"	5.15 AM 2'00"	10.30 AM 2'00"
SCRANTON	Ar.	1.45 PM	1.45 PM 45"	—	4.15 PM 30"	10.30 PM	11.15 PM 25"	1.55 AM 35"	6.00 AM	7.15 AM 1'30"	12.30 PM 2'00"
SCRANTON (T.T. Scranton; R.T. Scranton-Stroudsburg)	Lv.	—	2.30 PM 3'10"	—	4.45 PM 2'45"	—	11.40 PM 2'30"	2.30 AM 2'55"	—	8.45 AM 5'15"	2.30 PM 3'30"
STROUDSBURG (R.T. Stroudsburg-Port Morris)	By.	—	5.40 PM 1'20"	—	7.30 PM 1'00"	—	2.10 AM 55"	5.25 AM 1'20"	—	2.00 PM 2'35"	6.00 PM 3'40"
PORT MORRIS	Ar.	—	7.00 PM	—	8.30 PM 30"	—	3.05 AM 10"	6.45 AM	—	4.35 PM 40"	9.40 PM
PORT MORRIS (T.T. Port Morris; R.T. Port Morris-Secaucus)	Lv.	—	7.30 PM 1'30"	—	9.00 PM	—	3.15 AM	—	—	5.15 PM 2'00"	via Wash.
SECAUCUS (R.T. Port Morris-Hoboken)	Ar.	—	1'30"	—	1'30"	—	—	—	—	7.15 PM 45"	7.15 PM 45"
HOBOKEN	Ar.	12.45 PM	9.00 PM	6.15 PM	10.30 PM	12.00	5.00 AM	9.00 AM	10.00	8.00 PM	12.10
Elapsed Time		12'45"	16'30"	6'15"	14'15"	12'00"	12'00"	14'15"	10'00"	22'45"	12'10"

Revised 4/27/58

WESTWARD MANIFEST TRAIN SCHEDULE
THE TIME SHOWN CONVEYS NO TIME TABLE AUTHORITY

Station		EB-1 Ex Sa & Su	2/EB-3 Ex Sa & Su	BH-5 Daily	EB-8 Ex Sa & Su	BH-7 Ex Mo	BH-9 Ex Mo	BH-3 Daily	EB-3 Ex Mo
HOBOKEN (R.T. Hoboken-Port Morris)	Lv.	6.00 AM 1'15"	8.00 AM 1'25"	9.30 PM 1'31"	10.45 PM 2'30"	4.00 AM 3'15"	—	—	—
PORT MORRIS	Ar.	7.15 AM 55"	9.25 AM 55"	11.01 PM 54"	1.15 AM 45"	7.15 AM 30"	—	—	—
PORT MORRIS (T.T. Port Morris; R.T. Port Morris-Stroudsburg)	Lv.	8.10 AM 1'50"	10.20 AM 2'00"	11.55 PM 50"	2.00 AM 1'00"	7.45 AM 1'20"	10.40 AM 1'00"	—	—
STROUDSBURG (R.T. Stroudsburg-Scranton)	By.	—	12.20 PM	12.45 AM 2'00"	3.00 AM 1'20"	9.05 AM 2'40"	11.40 AM 1'40"	—	—
SCRANTON	Ar.	10.00 AM 15"	2.35 PM 15"	3.00 AM 2'10"	4.20 AM 10"	11.45 AM 1'30"	1.20 PM 25"	—	—
SCRANTON (T.T. Scranton; R.T. Scranton-East Binghamton)	Lv.	10.15 AM 1'15"	2.50 PM 1'10"	5.10 AM 1'30"	4.30 AM 4'30"	1.15 PM 2'15"	1.45 PM 1'30"	11.30 AM** 2'00"	—
EAST BINGHAMTON	Ar.	11.30 AM 30"	4.00 PM 10"	6.40 AM 1'45"	9.00 AM	3.30 PM 45"	3.15 PM 30"	1.30 PM 30"	—
EAST BINGHAMTON (T.T. East Binghamton; R.T. East Binghamton-Elmira)	Lv.	12.00 1'10"	4.10 PM 1'10"	8.25 AM 1'00"	—	4.15 PM 1'45"	3.45 PM 1'15"	2.00 PM 1'45"	12.30 PM*** 1'20"
ELMIRA	Ar.	1.10 PM 10"	5.20 PM 10"	9.25 AM 1'30"	—	6.00 PM 30"	5.00 PM 20"	3.45 PM 25"	1.50 PM 20"
ELMIRA (T.T. Elmira; R.T. Elmira-East Buffalo)	Lv.	1.20 PM 3'40"	5.30 PM 3'45"	10.55 AM 5'30"	—	6.30 PM 5'31"	5.20 PM 3'55"	4.10 PM 4'50"	2.10 PM 6'50"
EAST BUFFALO	Ar.	5.00 PM	9.15 PM	5.00 PM	—	12.01 AM	9.15 PM	9.00 PM	8.00 PM
Elapsed Time		11'00"	13'00"	18'15"	10'15"	20'01"	10'35"	9'30"	7'30"

Revised 4/27/58

*—Departs from Taylor.
**—Departs from "YO" Yard.

259

Perry M. Shoemaker, one of the country's outstanding all-around railroaders, and Operating Vice-President W. G. White, another crack operator, know only one kind of railroading, and that is to give service that typifies this "Railroad of the Hour."

CHAPTER XXXVIII

SOUTHERN PACIFIC

Fine Shops, and Two-Level Commuter Cars

Dieselization of the Southern Pacific's motive power has brought about streamlined methods and installation of revolutionary new machinery in the railroad's service shops on both its Pacific and its Texas-Louisiana lines.

Heavy diesel maintenance has replaced the old steam erection bays at both Sacramento and Los Angeles, and new machine tools have been set up to take the place of older steam equipment. At both Los Angeles and Roseville, modern diesel engine houses have been constructed at a cost of more than $2,500,000. A modern diesel-serving facility has been made out of the old Houston engine house, and all along the line division-point engine houses have been converted in the same way.

Dieselization brings in its wake economy and efficiency not only in hauling consists but in servicing facilities as well; many old engine houses and shops have been closed, and diesel repair work on the Texas-Louisiana lines is now concentrated at but two locations—Houston and San Antonio. On the SP's Pacific lines two separate mechanical jurisdictions have been established. The northern district, with its general shops at Sacramento, takes in the area enclosed by Portland, Ogden, and Oakland, while the southern district, whose general shops are located at Los Angeles, comprises the territory within the triangle formed by San Francisco, Los Angeles, and El Paso. There are five operating divisions within each of these areas, as well as its general shop.

The Sacramento shop carries on a considerable volume of

manufacturing in addition to the conventional shop duties that it performs. Car wheels are produced there, as well as track frogs and jobs for the road's Stores Department, and there is a brass and iron foundry located there too.

Periodic maintenance and running repairs of diesels take place at the Los Angeles Taylor yard, while major heavy repairs are assigned to the general shops in that city. Although truck repair work is undertaken at Taylor, the electrical shop at Sacramento is used for work on traction motors.

At Los Angeles there are six inspection pits each 215 feet long, and seven elevated platforms running between them. Each of the lengthy pits can accommodate a four-unit diesel locomotive. There is also a drop table that serves two pit tracks, and it can handle a locomotive truck or a single pair of wheels. A wheel-truing machine, duplicates of which are also in operation at Roseville and San Antonio, makes it possible to return work wheels to efficient operating conditions without removal from the locomotives; worn flanges are aligned by the machine's cutting tools while the drivers turn.

Light repairs and running maintenance operations are handled at other major yards and terminal points, such as Roseville, Bayshore, West Oakland, Dunsmuir, and Bakersfield, California; Sparks, Nevada; Ogden, Utah; Eugene and Brooklyn, Oregon; El Paso, Texas; and Tuscon, Arizona.

A long-range planning and schedule program for repair is established at the road's San Francisco headquarters, and over-all maintenance-of-equipment budgets are allocated monthly to shops and divisions on the basis of this program. The shops themselves, however, assign the necessary man power and materials to carry out the schedule; they follow up on the work being done and they check on delivery of necessary materials.

Since 1946, the SP's Pacific lines has invested $3,850,000 in the purchase of shop machinery and tools. Included were such equipment items as a new tracer lathe at Los Angeles for machining all types of diesel engine liners and a modern air-tracer at Sacramento for shaping diesel locomotive axles, which reduces machining time from eight hours to one hour per axle. This latter machine, using carbide tools, machines the collar, journal, dust guard, and wheel seat of an axle all in a single pass.

To cover the scope of necessary maintenance operations at varied calendar intervals, the Southern Pacific has issued circulars to its shop personnel. They set forth the road's premise that preventive maintenance is the keynote of the program; supporting it is a complete program of parts-testing to anticipate and detect incipient failures.

To eliminate the possibility of excessive removal of diesel units from active service, swing stocks of parts are used at both Houston and San Antonio, including spare engines, main generators, cylinder heads, liners, piston and rod assemblies, fuel and water pumps, traction motors, radiators, blowers, and pumps. Such parts are reconditioned in advance of a call for their use and are always ready to be installed when replacement of an active part becomes necessary.

Many newly developed scientific approaches to maintenance and repair work are incorporated in the SP's shop activities, as well as ingenious expedients worked out by experienced shop hands. They range from ultrasonic inspection for possible metal flaws to the use of high-intensity black light in locating fuel leaks, and on through such devices as turning diesel generator commutators on boring mills.

Modernization of passenger cars is carried out in a separate shop located at Sacramento. In a one-year period this unit constructed seven full-dome lounge cars and performed work on the conversion of fourteen conventional dining cars, eight coffee-shop lounge cars, and two articulated units, changing them into twenty-six hamburger-grill cars!

This Sacramento area also includes an additional number of specialized shop units, and it is acknowledged that the SP's combined shops in this community constitute one of the largest and best-equipped facilities in the United States. For example, in addition to the important electric shop, the railroad has also established both a traction motor shop and a special battery shop here. There is a sawmill owned and operated by the Southern Pacific at Sacramento which processes more than a million board feet of lumber every month; an iron and wheel foundry casts 2,800 brake shoes every day and up to 304 chilled, cast-iron freight-car wheels each twenty-four hours. The brass foundry casts 800 journal brasses per day and also turns out aluminum parts for diesel engines.

The Southern Pacific's modernized shops perform the many duties required to keep a modern railroad running at top efficiency, and they use shop job planning techniques, improved machinery, and the latest scientific developments to keep pace with modern railroading and to anticipate the needs of the future.

Two-Level Commuter Cars

Modernization in Southern Pacific operations applies not only to repair and maintenance work on existing rolling stock but to the acquisition of equipment designed to do the job that present-day problems require.

In the San Francisco suburban area, for example, the SP has met a problem peculiar to its short-run, high-density operations through the purchase of a new type of passenger car, a two-level commuter car. Each of these new units is 85 feet long, 10 feet wide, and 15 feet 8 inches above the rails. This added height provides ample room for comfortable passenger seating on two levels; each car has a total capacity of 145, with 94 passengers on the lower level and 51 on what commuters like to call "the balcony."

Sliding doors, controlled by automatic door mechanisms, are wide enough to permit three passengers at a time to enter or leave each car. Lower-level seats are the conventional double type, while those on the upper level are singles, except those located at the extreme ends of each car. All parcel racks are enclosed, and those for the use of lower-level passengers are underneath their seats. A protective glass and metal guard rail running the length of the car offers additional comfort and security to passengers walking the balcony.

Seats are of foam rubber with plastic covering. The seats, by Heywood-Wakefield, are of the throw-over type, so important for avoidance of turn-around operations in a heavy commuting train schedule.

The cars were built to SP specifications by Pullman-Standard; each weighs some 145,000 pounds empty and about 166,750 pounds when loaded with its capacity of passengers. They are of all-welded girder-type construction, with their structural members made of high-strength, low-alloy steel. Hyatt 6 by 11 roller bearings are used. The cars are fully air-conditioned, with a Detroit diesel supplying the drive for a thirty-kilowatt generator that provides the necessary power for both air-conditioning and lighting. Two overhead evaporators, each with about an eight-ton refrigerating capacity, are mounted in a chamber over the vestibule of each of SP's ten new two-level commuter cars.

CHAPTER XXXIX

NORTHERN PACIFIC

Diesel Pools and Manifest Freight Schedules

The Main Street of the Northwest, the Northern Pacific, has always had a very fine record for diesel power availability ever since the first of the new locomotives reached the railroad.

You can read for yourself how they do it in both freight and passenger service. Mile after mile, in all kinds of weather conditions—wind, dust, rain, and snow—they service them well enough to set up these daily records. At the end of this chapter you may read the type of expedited fast freight trains they are hauling and what it means to the shipper.

There are 190 road freight units regularly assigned to the freight pool. In addition to handling through freight, these units also provide power for four unit helper on the Cascade Mountains, local and assigned time freight trains on the Tacoma, Rocky Mountain, and Lake Superior Divisions.

In addition to the road freight units, nineteen GP-9 units equipped with twenty-four RL or main-line brake equipment, radios, and dynamic brakes are available for service in the freight pool, work trains, locals, or switch engines as required.

The road freight units consist of forty-four FT 1,350-horsepower units, eighty-five F-3 and F-7 1,500-horsepower units, and sixty-one F-9 1,750-horsepower F-9 units.

There are forty-three F-3 and F-7 1,500-horsepower and nine 1,750-horsepower F-9 passenger units regularly assigned to the passenger pools.

ASSIGNMENT OF THREE-UNIT PASSENGER DIESEL ENGINES
BETWEEN ST. PAUL AND SEATTLE

Effective January 10, 1957

	Time	Day	Train	Dead	Road	Cum.	Road	Cum.
				HOURS			**MILES**	
Lv. St. Paul	6:40 P.M.	1	#25					
Ar. Seattle	7:50 A.M.	3	#25		39'10"	39'10"	1892	1892
				4'40"		43'50"		
Lv. Seattle	12:30 P.M.	3	#408					
Ar. Portland	4:30 P.M.	3	#408		4'00"	47'50"	186	2078
				1'00"		48'50"		
Lv. Portland	5:30 P.M.	3	#407					
Ar. Seattle	9:30 P.M.	3	#407		4'00"	52'50"	186	2264
				10'55"		63'45"		
Lv. Seattle	8:25 A.M.	4	#6					
Ar. Spokane	6:50 P.M.	4	#6		10'25"	74'10"	392	2656
				12'35"		86'45"		
Lv. Spokane	7:25 A.M.	5	#5					
Ar. Seattle	6:10 P.M.	5	#5		10'45"	97'30"	392	3048
				6'50"		104'20"		
Lv. Seattle	1:00 A.M.	6	2/680					
Ar. Portland	8:30 A.M.	6	2/680		7'30"	111'50"	186	3234
				10'00"		121'50"		
Lv. Portland	6:30 P.M.	6	1/679					
Ar. Seattle	1:30 A.M.	7	1/679		7'00"	128'50"	186	3420
				12'00"		140'50"		
Lv. Seattle	1:30 P.M.	7	#26					
Ar. St. Paul	6:40 A.M.	9	#26		39'10"	180'00"	1892	5312
				26'00"		206'00"		
Lv. St. Paul	8:40 A.M.	10	#1					
Ar. Seattle	7:40 A.M.	12	#1		49'00"	255'00"	1894	7206
				13'55"		268'55"		
Lv. Seattle	9:35 P.M.	12	#2					
Ar. St. Paul	10:30 P.M	14	#2		46'55"	315'50"	1894	9100
				20'10"		336'00"		
Lv. St. Paul	6:40 P.M.	15	#25					

14 Engines   650.7 miles per day

ASSIGNMENT OF PASSENGER UNITS TRAINS 3 AND 4 BETWEEN ST. PAUL AND GLENDIVE

Effective April 14, 1957

Cab Unit				Hours	Miles
Lv. St. Paul	9:30 P.M.	Sunday	No. 3		
Ar. Glendive	5:05 P.M.	Monday	No. 3	20'35"	657
At Glendive				16'10"	
Lv. Glendive	9:15 A.M.	Tuesday	No. 4		
Ar. St. Paul	7:25 A.M.	Wednesday	No. 4	21'10"	657
At St. Paul				14'05"	
Lv. St. Paul	9:30 P.M.	Wednesday	No. 3		
Ar. Glendive	5:05 P.M.	Thursday	No. 3	20'35"	657
At Glendive				16'10"	
Lv. Glendive	9:15 A.M.	Friday	No. 4		
Ar. St. Paul	7:25 A.M.	Saturday	No. 4	21'10"	657
At St. Paul				38'05"	
Lv. St. Paul	9:30 P.M.	Sunday	No. 3		
		Total Hours	168'00"		
		Total Miles	2628		

Booster Unit					
Lv. St. Paul	9:30 P.M.	Sunday	No. 3		
Ar. Mandan	12:01 P.M.	Monday	No. 3	14'30"	451
At Mandan				4'15"	
Lv. Mandan	4:15 P.M	Monday	No. 4		
Ar. St. Paul	7:25 A.M.	Tuesday	No. 4	15'10"	451
At St. Paul				14'05"	
Lv. St. Paul	9:30 P.M.	Tuesday	No. 3		
Ar. Mandan	12:01 P.M.	Wednesday	No. 3	14'30"	451
At Mandan				4'15"	
Lv. Mandan	4:15 P.M.	Wednesday	No. 4		
Ar. St. Paul	7:25 A.M	Thursday	No. 4	15'10"	451
At St. Paul				14'05"	
Lv. St. Paul	9:30 P.M.	Thursday	No. 3		
Ar. Mandan	12:01 P.M.	Friday	No. 3	14'30"	451
At Mandan				4'15"	
Lv. Mandan	4:15 P.M.	Friday	No. 4		
Ar. St. Paul	7:25 A.M.	Saturday	No. 4	15'10"	451
At St. Paul				38'05"	
Lv. St. Paul	9:30 P.M.	Sunday	No. 3		
		Total Hours	168'00"		
		Total Miles	2706		

TYPICAL FREIGHT DIESEL POOL RUNS—EASTERN DISTRICT

Four F-7 Units	Time	Day	Train	Hours	Miles
Lv. Northtown	10:30 A.M.	1	1/603		
Ar. Livingston	1:10 P.M.	2	1/603	27'40"	983
At Livingston				6'50"	
Lv. Livingston	8:00 P.M.	2	Fruit		
Ar. Northtown	9:00 P.M.	4	Fruit	48'00"	983
At Northtown				5'00"	
Lv. Northtown	2:00 A.M.	5	Exa. West		
Ar. Dilworth	5:00 P.M.	5	Exa. West	15'00"	232
At Dilworth				2'30"	
Lv. Dilworth	7:30 P.M.	5	No. 635		
Ar. Mandan	8:00 A.M.	6	No. 635	12'30"	204
At Mandan				4'30"	
Lv. Mandan	11:30 A.M.	6	Exa. West		
Ar. Laurel	1:00 P.M.	7	Exa. West	25'30"	446
At Laurel				7'00"	
Lv. Laurel	8:00 P.M.	7	No. 607		
Ar. Livingston	12:01 A.M.	8	No. 607	4'00"	100
At Livingston				1'00"	
Lv. Livingston	1:00 A.M.	8	No. 612		
Ar. Laurel	6:00 A.M.	8	No. 612	5'00"	100
At Laurel				9'00"	
Lv. Laurel	3:00 P.M.	8	No. 612		
Ar. Northtown	5:00 P.M.	10	No. 612	49'00"	882
At Northtown				4'30"	
Lv. Northtown	9:30 P.M.	10	No. 631		
Ar. Dilworth	6:30 A.M.	11	No. 631	9'00"	232
At Dilworth				13'00"	
Lv. Dilworth	7:30 P.M.	11	No. 632		
Ar. Northtown	4:30 A.M.	12	No. 632	9'00"	232
At Northtown				7'30"	
Lv. Northtown	12:01 P.M.	12	2/603		
Ar. Livingston	2:00 P.M.	13	2/603	27'00"	983
At Livingston				7'45"	
Lv. Livingston	9:45 P.M.	13	No. 602		
Ar. Northtown	8:00 P.M.	15	No. 602	45'15"	983
At Northtown				18'30"	
Lv. Northtown	2:30 P.M.	16	No. 605		
Ar. Laurel	4:30 P.M.	18	No. 605	51'00"	882
At Laurel				9'00"	
Lv. Laurel	1:30 A.M.	19	BL Mfst.		
Ar. Livingston	5:30 A.M.	19	BL Mfst.	4'00"	100
At Livingston				2'30"	
Lv. Livingston	8:00 A.M.	19	2/612		
Ar. Laurel	1:00 P.M.	19	2/612	5'00"	100
At Laurel				5'00"	
Lv. Laurel	6:00 P.M.	19	2/612		
Ar. Northtown	8:00 P.M.	21	2/612	49'00"	882
At Northtown				14'30"	
Lv. Northtown	10:30 A.M.	22	1/603		
			Total	504'	8324

TYPICAL FREIGHT DIESEL POOL RUNS—WESTERN DISTRICT

Four FT or F-9 Units	Time	Day	Train	Hours	Miles
Lv. Auburn	2:00 P.M.	1	No. 640		
Ar. Pasco	5:00 A.M.	2	No. 640	15'00"	228
At Pasco				3'00"	
Lv. Pasco	8:00 A.M.	2	Fruit		
Ar. Livingston	7:15 P.M.	3	Fruit	34'15"	664
At Livingston				5'45"	
Lv. Livingston	1:00 A.M.	4	No. 607		
Ar. Missoula	12:15 P.M.	4	No. 607	11'15"	242
At Missoula				14'45"	
Lv. Missoula	3:00 A.M.	5	Exa. West		
Ar. Yardley	11:00 A.M.	5	Exa. West	9'00"	283
At Yardley				1'30"	
Lv. Yardley	12:30 P.M.	5	Exa. West		
Ar. Auburn	10:30 A.M.	6	Exa. West	22'00"	377
At Auburn				7'30"	
Lv. Auburn	6:00 P.M.	6	No. 642		
Ar. Pasco	8:00 A.M.	7	No. 642	14'00"	377
At Pasco				6'30"	
Lv. Pasco	2:30 P.M.	7	No. 602		
Ar. Livingston	9:00 P.M.	8	No. 602	29'30"	664
At Livingston				9'00"	
Lv. Livingston	6:00 A.M.	9	BL Mfst.		
Ar. Pasco	5:00 A.M.	10	BL Mfst.	24'00"	664
At Pasco				10'30"	
Lv. Pasco	3:30 P.M.	10	No. 612		
Ar. Livingston	12:30 A.M.	12	No. 612	32'00"	664
At Livingston				13'00"	
Lv. Livingston	1:30 P.M.	12	1/603		
Ar. Auburn	7:30 P.M.	13	1/603	31'00"	892
At Auburn				5'30"	
Lv. Auburn	1:00 A.M.	14	No. 600		
Ar. Pasco	12:01 P.M.	14	No. 600	11'00"	228
At Pasco				5'30"	
Lv. Pasco	5:30 P.M.	14	Exa. East		
Ar. Yardley	11:30 P.M.	14	Exa. East	6'00"	149
At Yardley				2'30"	
Lv. Yardley	2:00 A.M.	15	No. 612		
Ar. Livingston	3:00 A.M.	16	No. 612	24'00"	515
At Livingston				11'30"	
Lv. Livingston	2:30 P.M.	16	2/603		
Ar. Auburn	7:30 P.M.	17	2/603	30'00"	892
At Auburn				18'30"	
Lv. Auburn	2:00 P.M.	18	No. 640		

Total Hours 408
Total Miles 6839

MONTHLY STATEMENT OF ROAD FREIGHT DIESEL
UNIT MILEAGE

Month	Units in Service		Average Mileage per unit		Average Mileage per day	
	1955	1956	1955	1956	1955	1956
January	151	159	9630	10277	311	332
February	154	160	9347	9858	334	340
March	154	179	10786	9771	348	315
April	157	180	10039	9596	335	320
May	161	175	9806	10211	316	329
June	158	178	9663	9808	322	327
July	153	176	10546	10155	340	327
August	151	177	10351	10041	334	324
September	158	176	10531	10065	351	335
October	157	176	10985	10268	354	331
November	157	178	10108	9635	337	321
December	159	176	9921	10069	310	324
Yearly Average	156	174	10120	9979.5	333.5	327

MANIFEST FAST FREIGHT TRAIN SCHEDULES
SCHEDULE OF WESTBOUND TRAIN 603-B AND BB—EFFECTIVE JUNE 15, 1955

Will be operated from Northtown daily in two sections. *Advance Section "B"* will handle cars Pasco and (including S.P.&S.) Yakima, Auburn, and beyond loads, also cars to Laurel for Billings and stations between Laurel and Spokane. Hogs and perishables requiring ice will be handled in this train. *Second Section "BB"* will handle all remaining and late loads same as advance section, except hogs and perishables.

DAY

Lv. Northtown	10:30 A.M.[1]	1st	SUN	MON	TUE	WED	THU	FRI	SAT
Ar. Staples	1:30 P.M.	"	"	"	"	"	"	"	"
Lv. Staples	1:50 P.M.	"	"	"	"	"	"	"	"
Ar. Dilworth	4:20 P.M.	"	"	"	"	"	"	"	"
Lv. Dilworth	4:40 P.M.	"	"	"	"	"	"	"	"
Ar. Jamestown	7:00 P.M.	"	"	"	"	"	"	"	"
Lv. Jamestown	7:20 P.M.	"	"	"	"	"	"	"	"
Ar. Mandan (CST)	10:05 P.M.	"	"	"	"	"	"	"	"
Lv. Mandan (MST)	9:25 P.M.	"	"	"	"	"	"	"	"
Ar. Dickinson	12:01 A.M.	2nd	MON	TUE	WED	THU	FRI	SAT	SUN
Lv. Dickinson	12:15 A.M.	"	"	"	"	"	"	"	"
Ar. Glendive	3:00 A.M.	"	"	"	"	"	"	"	"
Lv. Glendive	3:20 A.M.	"	"	"	"	"	"	"	"
Ar. Forsyth	6:35 A.M.	"	"	"	"	"	"	"	"
Lv. Forsyth	6:50 A.M.	"	"	"	"	"	"	"	"
Ar. Laurel	9:50 A.M.	"	"	"	"	"	"	"	"
Lv. Laurel	10:20 A.M.	"	"	"	"	"	"	"	"
Ar. Livingston	1:10 P.M.	"	"	"	"	"	"	"	"
Lv. Livingston	1:30 P.M.	"	"	"	"	"	"	"	"
Ar. Helena	5:10 P.M.	"	"	"	"	"	"	"	"
Lv. Helena	5:30 P.M.	"	"	"	"	"	"	"	"
Ar. Missoula	9:10 P.M.	"	"	"	"	"	"	"	"
Lv. Missoula	9:30 P.M.	"	"	"	"	"	"	"	"

[1] Advance Section B Manifest. Second Section BB Manifest will depart approximately 2 hours after the Advance Section.

Southern Pacific Extra 5405 west, the Northwest Special, rounding the Horseshoe Curve between Indian Camp and Likely, Calif. on the Alturas Subdiv. of the Salt Lake Div.

Bangor & Aroostook #8, the Potatoland Special, at Northern Maine Jct. Southern Division.

View from dome of #26 eastbound North Coast Limited looking towards rear end of the spectacular limestone outcropping in Jefferson Canyon west of Logan, Mont. on Second Subdiv. Rocky Mt. Div.

Compartment in one of all-room Pullmans on NP North Coast Lim. showing made-up lower berth. There is also upper berth, upholstered chair, wardrobe locker, enclosed toilet and washstand. Built by Budd.

Santa Fe fast freight the CTX east climbing 1.25 grade with 2 unit helper in Abo Canyon on the Second Dist. of the Pecos Div. This is the ruling eastward grade on the Santa Fe low grade Southern Dist. line all the way from Belen to Chicago. C.T.C. Territory.

C & O coal train hauled by diesel 7084 running along Levisa Fork, Ky. on the Big Sandy Subdiv. of the Ashland Div. This train originated at Prestonburg, Ky.

C & O fast time freight, the Expediter, #90, near Fort Lee, Va. on the Peninsula Subdiv. of the Richmond Div.

Chicago Great Western ice loading machine in operation on the new ice dock at Oelwein, Iowa. This fine time-saving machine was built by the Link-Belt Co.

Interior of Chicago Great Western's new iceplant at Oelwein, Iowa.

Southern Railway Extra 4171 east solid coal train, passing thru June's Mill Gorge, Va. Knoxville Div.

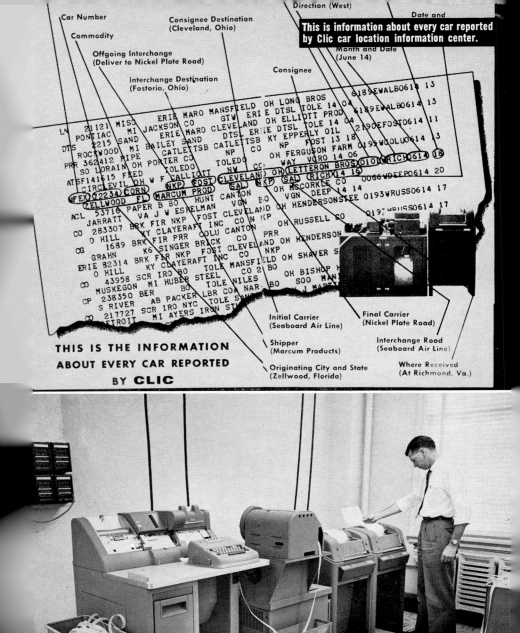

This is information about every car reported by Clic car location information center.

Car Number

Commodity

Consignee Destination (Cleveland, Ohio)

Offgoing Interchange (Deliver to Nickel Plate Road)

Interchange Destination (Fostoria, Ohio)

Direction (West)

Date and

Month and Date (June 14)

Consignee

Initial Carrier (Seaboard Air Line)

Shipper (Marcum Products)

Originating City and State (Zellwood, Florida)

Final Carrier (Nickel Plate Road)

Interchange Road (Seaboard Air Line)

Where Received (At Richmond, Va.)

THIS IS THE INFORMATION
ABOUT EVERY CAR REPORTED
BY CLIC

& O's new car location information enter (Clic) in Huntington, W. Va. is served y one of world's largest railroad teletype etworks — 30,000 miles of circuits con- ecting 338 teletype installations.

U.P. Fast Freight 2-257, the CB-NWF-29 and KC-NWF-28 the Council Bluffs and Kansas City northwest manifest combined with 99 loads and 11 empties, 3,587 tons, at M.P. 51 west of Wyeth, Ore. on the Fourth Sub-div. of the Oregon Div. in the Columbia River Gorge.

Chicago Great Western's fine new modern depot and office building at Des Moines, Iowa.

CHICAGO GREAT WESTERN

Chicago Great Western are great believers in mobile maintenance equipment. They have 3 of these fine truck cranes, 1 stationed at Oelwein, Iowa, 1 at St. Paul, Minn. and 1 at Council Bluffs, Iowa.

Southern Railway's Royal Palm #3 crossing the New Cumberland river bridge at Somerset, Ky. on the CNO & TP Div.

Southern Pacific Extra 6268 east with perishables passing historic Donner Lake on the Mountain Subdiv. of the Sacramento Div.

U.P. DLS (Day livestock) crack roller-bearing stock train which operates from Ogden and Salt Lake to Los Angeles and handles all livestock originating at or moving thru Odgen and Salt Lake to Los Angeles and southern California at St. John on the Second Sub-div. of the Utah Div.

Retarder operator in four story tower at Santa Fe's new Corwith automatic freight yard at Chicago works the new Union Switch & Signal Co.'s compact control console on which is complete diagram of yard's 32 tracks with indicating lights reflecting operation of entire system.

"Hump" conductor at Santa Fe's new Corwith yard has charge of route selection panel containing 1 pushbutton for each of yard's 32 tracks. Built by Union Switch & Signal Co.

Santa Fe stock car passes thru master retarder at road's new Corwith automatic classification yard in Chicago. This yard is capable of putting 4 cars per minute over the "hump" and the installation was made by the Union Switch & Signal Co.

Southern Pacific's 2nd 75, Los Angeles-San Francisco Fast Freight running as 2nd sect. of its crack overnight Lark crossing Steiner Creek viaduct climbing the 2.2 grade at Hathaway, Cal. on Santa Margarita Hill running over the Subdivision of that name on the Coast Div. in CTC territory.

Ar. Paradise (MST)	12:20 A.M.	3rd	TUE	WED	THU	FRI	SAT	SUN	MON
Lv. Paradise (PST)	11:35 P.M.	"	"	"	"	"	"	"	"
Ar. Yardley	4:20 A.M.	"	"	"	"	"	"	"	"
Lv. Yardley	5:00 A.M.	"	"	"	"	"	"	"	"
Ar. Pasco	9:00 A.M.	"	"	"	"	"	"	"	"
Lv. Pasco	11:15 A.M.	"	"	"	"	"	"	"	"
Ar. Yakima	1:35 P.M.	"	"	"	"	"	"	"	"
Lv. Yakima	1:55 P.M.	"	"	"	"	"	"	"	"
Ar. Auburn	7:30 P.M.	"	"	"	"	"	"	"	"
Ar. Seattle	9:00 P.M.	"	"	"	"	"	"	"	"

Note: Advance Section "B" will pick up hogs at West Fargo and hogs received from C&NW at Oakes will be picked up at Jamestown. Set-outs will be made at Laurel for hogs and perishables and at Missoula for hogs only. Second Section "BB" will pick up hogs and perishables at Laurel and hogs at Missoula which were set out by Advance Section "B." No set-outs by either section will be made except as noted or except cars account bad order.

(CST) Central Time   (MST) Mountain Time   (PST) Pacific Time

SCHEDULE OF WESTBOUND TRAIN 605-G AND W—EFFECTIVE JANUARY 28, 1955

Will be operated daily from Northtown to handle cars for Red River Branch; cars for Canada via Pembina, North Dakota; cars for Fargo and points Valley City, North Dakota, to Laurel, Montana, inclusive.

		DAY							
Lv. Northtown	2:30 P.M.	1st	SUN	MON	TUE	WED	THU	FRI	SAT
Ar. Staples	6:15 P.M.	"	"	"	"	"	"	"	"
Lv. Staples	7:15 P.M.	"	"	"	"	"	"	"	"
Ar. Dilworth	11:15 P.M.	"	"	"	"	"	"	"	"
Lv. Dilworth	12:15 A.M.	2nd	MON	TUE	WED	THU	FRI	SAT	SUN
Ar. Jamestown	3:45 A.M.	"	"	"	"	"	"	"	"
Lv. Jamestown	8:00 A.M.	"	"	"	"	"	"	"	"
Ar. Mandan (CST)	1:00 P.M.	"	"	"	"	"	"	"	"
Lv. Mandan (MST)	2:00 P.M.	"	"	"	"	"	"	"	"
Ar. Dickinson	8:00 P.M.	"	"	"	"	"	"	"	"
Lv. Dickinson	8:45 P.M.	"	"	"	"	"	"	"	"
Ar. Glendive	2:45 A.M.	3rd	TUE	WED	THU	FRI	SAT	SUN	MON
Lv. Glendive	3:45 A.M.	"	"	"	"	"	"	"	"
Ar. Forsyth	9:45 A.M.	"	"	"	"	"	"	"	"
Lv. Forsyth	10:30 A.M.	"	"	"	"	"	"	"	"
Ar. Laurel	4:30 P.M.	"	"	"	"	"	"	"	"

(CST) Central Time   (MST) Mountain Time

Note: "G" Manifest includes cars for Red River Branch and Canada. "W" Manifest includes all other loads. "G" and "W" Manifests will be handled in one train—the "G" Manifest loads being set out at Lake Park.

SCHEDULE OF WESTBOUND TRAIN 607-C—EFFECTIVE JUNE 15, 1955

Will be operated from Laurel with business for stations Laurel to Spokane which will include cars handled to Laurel in 603 trains.

		DAY							
Lv. Laurel	8:00 P.M.	1st	SUN	MON	TUE	WED	THU	FRI	SAT
Ar. Livingston	12:01 A.M.	2nd	MON	TUE	WED	THU	FRI	SAT	SUN
Lv. Livingston	1:00 A.M.	"	"	"	"	"	"	"	"
Ar. Helena	6:30 A.M.	"	"	"	"	"	"	"	"
Lv. Helena	7:30 A.M.	"	"	"	"	"	"	"	"
Ar. Missoula	12:15 P.M.	"	"	"	"	"	"	"	"
Lv. Missoula	2:15 P.M.	"	"	"	"	"	"	"	"
Ar. Paradise (MST)	5:45 P.M.	"	"	"	"	"	"	"	"
Lv. Paradise (PST)	5:05 P.M.	"	"	"	"	"	"	"	"
Ar. Yardley	11:00 P.M.	"	"	"	"	"	"	"	"

(MST) Mountain Time   (PST) Pacific Time

274

SCHEDULE OF EASTBOUND TRAIN NO. 602-B—EFFECTIVE JUNE 15, 1955

Operates from Pasco daily and handles business only for Twin Cities and beyond. Loads from West Coast points will be assembled and classified at Pasco and will be handled from Auburn in extra trains and scheduled Train No. 600 daily to connect with Train No. 602-B. Exception: Livestock shipments may be handled to and from any subdivision terminal or scheduled stop.

				DAY							
Lv. Auburn		2:30 A.M.	1st	SUN	MON	TUE	WED	THU	FRI	SAT
Ar. Yakima	Train	8:30 A.M.	"	"	"	"	"	"	"	"
Lv. Yakima	No. 600	9:15 A.M.	"	"	"	"	"	"	"	"
Ar. Pasco		12:01 P.M.	"	"	"	"	"	"	"	"
Lv. Pasco		2:30 P.M.	"	"	"	"	"	"	"	"
Ar. Spokane		8:15 P.M.	"	"	"	"	"	"	"	"
Lv. Spokane		9:30 P.M.	"	"	"	"	"	"	"	"
Ar. Paradise (PST)		3:00 A.M.	2nd	MON	TUE	WED	THU	FRI	SAT	SUN
Lv. Paradise (MST)		4:30 A.M.	"	"	"	"	"	"	"	"
Ar. Missoula		8:00 A.M.	"	"	"	"	"	"	"	"
Lv. Missoula		9:00 A.M	"	"	"	"	"	"	"	"
Ar. Helena		2:30 P.M.	"	"	"	"	"	"	"	"
Lv. Helena		3:15 P.M	"	"	"	"	"	"	"	"
Ar. Livingston		9:00 P.M.	"	"	"	"	"	"	"	"
Lv. Livingston		9:45 P.M.	"	"	"	"	"	"	"	"
Ar. Laurel		1:15 A.M	3rd	TUE	WED	THU	FRI	SAT	SUN	MON
Lv. Laurel		2:45 A.M.	"	"	"	"	"	"	"	"
Ar. Forsyth		7:00 A.M.	"	"	"	"	"	"	"	"
Lv. Forsyth		7:30 A.M	"	"	"	"	"	"	"	"
Ar. Glendive		12:01 P.M.	"	"	"	"	"	"	"	"
Lv. Glendive		12:45 P.M.	"	"	"	"	"	"	"	"
Ar. Dickinson		4:45 P.M.	"	"	"	"	"	"	"	"
Lv. Dickinson		5:15 P.M.	"	"	"	"	"	"	"	"
Ar. Mandan (MST)		9:00 P.M.	"	"	"	"	"	"	"	"
Lv. Mandan (CST)		11:15 P.M	"	"	"	"	"	"	"	"
Ar. Jamestown		3:15 A.M.	4th	WED	THU	FRI	SAT	SUN	MON	TUE
Lv. Jamestown		4:00 A.M.	"	"	"	"	"	"	"	"
Ar. Dilworth		7:45 A.M.	"	"	"	"	"	"	"	"
Lv. Dilworth		8:45 A.M.	"	"	"	"	"	"	"	"
Ar. Staples		1:00 P.M.	"	"	"	"	"	"	"	"
Lv. Staples		2:30 P.M	"	"	"	"	"	"	"	"
Ar. Northtown		8:00 P.M.	"	"	"	"	"	"	"	"
Ar. Park Junction		5:00 A.M.	5th	THU	FRI	SAT	SUN	MON	TUE	WED

(PST) Pacific Time   (MST) Mountain Time   (CST) Central Time

SCHEDULE OF EASTBOUND TRAIN NO. 612-C—EFFECTIVE
JUNE 15, 1955

Will handle business from Pasco destined Spokane, Missoula, Laurel, and east thereof. Cars destined east of Missoula to and including Livingston will be cut out for forwarding on other trains. Loads from West Coast points will be assembled and classified at Pasco and will be handled from Auburn in extra trains and scheduled Train No. 600 daily to connect with Train 612-C. Exception: Livestock shipments may be handled to and from any subdivision terminal or scheduled stop.

			DAY								
Lv. Auburn ⎤		2:30 A.M.	1st	SUN	MON	TUE	WED	THU	FRI	SAT	
Ar. Yakima ⎟ Train	8:30 A.M.	"	"	"	"	"	"	"	"	
Lv. Yakima ⎟ No. 600	9:15 A.M.	"	"	"	"	"	"	"	"	
Ar. Pasco ⎦	12:01 P.M.	"	"	"	"	"	"	"	"	
Lv. Pasco		3:30 P.M.	"	"	"	"	"	"	"	"	
Ar. Spokane		9:30 P.M.	"	"	"	"	"	"	"	"	
Lv. Spokane		11:00 P.M.	"	"	"	"	"	"	"	"	
Ar. Paradise (PST)		5:00 A.M.	2nd	MON	TUE	WED	THU	FRI	SAT	SUN
Lv. Paradise (MST)		6:30 A.M.	"	"	"	"	"	"	"	"	
Ar. Missoula		10:00 A.M.	"	"	"	"	"	"	"	"	
Lv. Missoula		11:30 A.M.	"	"	"	"	"	"	"	"	
Ar. Helena		5:30 P.M.	"	"	"	"	"	"	"	"	
Lv. Helena		6:30 P.M.	"	"	"	"	"	"	"	"	
Ar. Livingston		12:30 A.M.	3rd	TUE	WED	THU	FRI	SAT	SUN	MON
Lv. Livingston		1:30 A.M.	"	"	"	"	"	"	"	"	
Ar. Laurel		6:00 A.M.	"	"	"	"	"	"	"	"	
Lv. Laurel		4:30 P.M.	"	"	"	"	"	"	"	"	
Ar. Forsyth		9:00 P.M.	"	"	"	"	"	"	"	"	
Lv. Forsyth		9:45 P.M.	"	"	"	"	"	"	"	"	
Ar. Glendive		3:00 A.M.	4th	WED	THU	FRI	SAT	SUN	MON	TUE
Lv. Glendive		4:00 A.M.	"	"	"	"	"	"	"	"	
Ar. Dickinson		8:00 A.M.	"	"	"	"	"	"	"	"	
Lv. Dickinson		8:45 A.M.	"	"	"	"	"	"	"	"	
Ar. Mandan (MST)		1:00 P.M.	"	"	"	"	"	"	"	"	
Lv. Mandan (CST)		3:30 P.M.	"	"	"	"	"	"	"	"	
Ar. Jamestown		8:00 P.M.	"	"	"	"	"	"	"	"	
Lv. Jamestown		9:30 P.M.	"	"	"	"	"	"	"	"	
Ar. Dilworth		2:30 A.M.	5th	THU	FRI	SAT	SUN	MON	TUE	WED
Lv. Dilworth		4:00 A.M.	"	"	"	"	"	"	"	"	
Ar. Staples		9:30 A.M.	"	"	"	"	"	"	"	"	
Lv. Staples		11:30 A.M.	"	"	"	"	"	"	"	"	
Ar. Northtown		5:00 P.M.	'	"	"	"	"	"	"	"	
Ar. Park Junction		5:00 A.M.	6th	FRI	SAT	SUN	MON	TUE	WED	THU

(PST) Pacific Time   (MST) Mountain Time   (CST) Central Time

276

SCHEDULE OF "F" MANIFEST EASTBOUND TRAIN—EFFECTIVE JUNE 15, 1955

This train originates at Yakima or Pasco. Operates when required for handling perishable business. Schedule guaranteed to Twin Cities and connections at Twin Cities.

		DAY							
Lv. Yakima	1:15 A.M.	1st	SUN	MON	TUE	WED	THU	FRI	SAT
Ar. Pasco	5:00 A.M.	"	"	"	"	"	"	"	"
Lv. Pasco	8:00 A.M.	"	"	"	"	"	"	"	"
Ar. Yardley	2:30 P.M.	"	"	"	"	"	"	"	"
Lv. Yardley	4:30 P.M.	"	"	"	"	"	"	"	"
Ar. Paradise (PST)	11:00 P.M.	"	"	"	"	"	"	"	"
Lv. Paradise (MST)	12:15 A.M.	2nd	MON	TUE	WED	THU	FRI	SAT	SUN
Ar. Missoula	4:30 A.M.	"	"	"	"	"	"	"	"
Lv. Missoula	5:30 A.M.	"	"	"	"	"	"	"	"
Ar. Helena	12:01 P.M.	"	"	"	"	"	"	"	"
Lv. Helena	12:45 P.M.	"	"	"	"	"	"	"	"
Ar. Livingston	7:15 P.M.	"	"	"	"	"	"	"	"
Lv. Livingston	8:00 P.M.	"	"	"	"	"	"	"	"
Ar. Laurel	11:45 P.M.	"	"	"	"	"	"	"	"
Lv. Laurel	2:45 A.M.	3rd	TUE	WED	THU	FRI	SAT	SUN	MON
Ar. Forsyth	6:45 A.M.	"	"	"	"	"	"	"	"
Lv. Forsyth	7:15 A.M.	"	"	"	"	"	"	"	"
Ar. Glendive	12:01 P.M.	"	"	"	"	"	"	"	"
Lv. Glendive	12:45 P.M.	"	"	"	"	"	"	"	"
Ar. Dickinson	4:45 P.M.	"	"	"	"	"	"	"	"
Lv. Dickinson	5:00 P.M.	"	"	"	"	"	"	"	"
Ar. Mandan (MST)	8:30 P.M.	"	"	"	"	"	"	"	"
Lv. Mandan (CST)	10:45 P.M.	"	"	"	"	"	"	"	"
Ar. Jamestown	2:45 A.M.	4th	WED	THU	FRI	SAT	SUN	MON	TUE
Lv. Jamestown	3:30 A.M.	"	"	"	"	"	"	"	"
Ar. Dilworth	7:30 A.M.	"	"	"	"	"	"	"	"
Lv. Dilworth	9:45 A.M.	"	"	"	"	"	"	"	"
Ar. Staples	2:15 P.M.	"	"	"	"	"	"	"	"
Lv. Staples	3:45 P.M.	"	"	"	"	"	"	"	"
Ar. Northtown	9:00 P.M.	"	"	"	"	"	"	"	"
Ar. Park Junction	5:00 A.M.	5th	THU	FRI	SAT	SUN	MON	TUE	WED

(PST) Pacific Time   (MST) Mountain Time   (CST) Central Time

277

SUPPLEMENTAL SCHEDULES
(Daily unless otherwise shown)

DULUTH

627		628	TWIN CITIES
7:30 P.M.	Duluth	5:00 A.M.	
4:00 A.M.	St. Paul	9:45 P.M.	

DULUTH

623		624	STAPLES
6:00 P.M.	Duluth	1:00 A.M.	
10:50 P.M.	Brainerd	7:20 P.M.	
12:20 A.M.	Staples	6:00 P.M.	

TWIN CITIES

621				622	INTERNATIONAL FALLS
10:15 P.M.	Ex. Sun.	Northtown	11:00 A.M.	Ex. Mon.	
3:45 A.M.	Ex. Mon.	Brainerd	6:00 A.M.	Ex. Mon.	
4:45 A.M.	Ex. Mon.	Brainerd	2:15 A.M.	Ex. Mon.	
8:40 A.M.	Ex. Mon.	No. Bemidji	10:30 P.M.	Ex. Sun.	
3:00 P.M.	Ex. Sat.	No. Bemidji	9:00 P.M.	Ex. Sun.	
11:00 P.M.	Ex. Sat.	Intl. Falls	5:00 P.M.	Ex. Sun.	

DILWORTH

632				631	TWIN CITIES
4:30 A.M. Daily	Northtown	9:30 P.M.	Ex. Sat. Sun.		
12:01 A.M. Daily	Staples	1:30 A.M.	Ex. Sun. Mon.		
11:00 P.M. Daily	Staples	2:30 A.M.	Ex. Sun. Mon.		
7:30 P.M. Daily	Dilworth	6:30 A.M.	Ex. Sun. Mon.		

DILWORTH

635				MANDAN
7:00 P.M.	Ex. Sat. Sun.	Dilworth		
2:30 A.M.	Ex. Sun. Mon.	Jamestown		
8:00 A.M.	Ex. Sun. Mon.	Mandan		

YARDLEY

661		662	LEWISTON
7:45 P.M.	Yardley	6:35 P.M.	
2:10 A.M.	Lewiston	12:45 P.M.	

RED RIVER BRANCH

633	
# 9:00 P.M.	Lake Park
2:30 A.M.	E. Grand Forks
5:00 A.M.	E. Grand Forks
8:45 A.M.	Pembina
7:00 P.M.	Winnipeg

Connection No. 605.

LIVINGSTON — BUTTE

	607-651	652
Laurel	8:00 P.M.	
Livingston	12:01 A.M.	
Livingston		10:15 A.M.
Butte		6:30 A.M.
Livingston	1:15 A.M.	
Butte	6:00 A.M.	

S.P.&S.

	275	276
Pasco	11:50 A.M.	9:00 A.M
Portland	9:30 P.M.	10:00 P.M.

AUBURN

	675
Auburn	7:30 A.M.
Sumas	2:00 P.M.

SUMAS

	676
Auburn	11:59 P.M.
Sumas	5:00 P.M.

PORTLAND

	1/679	2/679
Portland	6:30 P.M.	10:30 P.M.
Seattle	1:30 A.M.	5:30 A.M.

SEATTLE

	1/680	2/680
Portland	4:30 A.M.	8:30 A.M.
Seattle	8:30 P.M.	1:00 A.M.

TACOMA

	695		
Tacoma	10:30 P.M.	Ex.	Sat.
Centralia	1:00 A.M.	Ex.	Sun.
Hoquiam	3:45 A.M.	Ex.	Sun.

HOQUIAM

	696		
Tacoma	11:00 P.M.	Ex.	Sun.
Centralia	9:00 P.M.	Ex.	Sun.
Hoquiam	6:00 P.M.	Ex.	Sun.

CHAPTER XL

CHESAPEAKE & OHIO

Diesels—The Greenbrier, White Sulphur Springs

In the relatively short period of time that has elapsed since the end of World War II, the Chesapeake & Ohio Railroad—a line whose base of operations lies in America's large Eastern coal fields—has become virtually 100 per cent dieselized.

The C&O enjoyed its first operating experiences with diesel locomotives back in 1947, when it merged with the Pere Marquette, a road that was then using diesels to a considerable extent. Examining the operations of this new kind of mover with considerable interest, C&O officials saw enough to warrant placing their first diesel on their own Chicago division in September, 1950; since then the growth of diesels as the C&O's prime movers has been rapid and continuous.

Diesels on the C&O now total one thousand eighty units. Today there are only about a hundred steam locomotives remaining on the railroad in standby service.

Moving largely through rugged, difficult mountain country, the C&O has found that diesels can haul increased gross ton loadings without the use of helper service. This has led to the replacement of a large fleet of steam locomotives—many of which stood by idly for much of the time waiting to be called in for brief helper duties—by diesels, with great reductions effected in maintenance, fuel, and repair costs. Substantial economies have been noted, too, in costs for lubricants, water, and engine houses.

The railroad's operating ratio, reaching an all-time high of 80.1 per cent in 1949, has steadily declined with the use of diesel engines, dropping to 72.2 per cent in 1953, while gross ton miles per freight train hour rose between 1950 and 1953 from 58,139 to 68,468. With full dieselization of entire divisions or even of districts, such costly facilities as ash pits, loading facilities, and water tanks have been completely eliminated.

With this new kind of motive power at its disposal, the C&O management began to indulge in a new kind of thinking about scheduling; a system of cycles and power pools was worked out to provide for maximum usage and minimum repair-shop or other idle time. Each engine now runs up high monthly mileage totals and yet is in position to fit into flexible schedules that must be worked out to meet unexpected assignment shifts.

In the mountain districts, with their steep grades, and on special sections of track that carry speed restrictions, dynamic braking on the diesel units quickly proved its value. Time between terminals has been reduced, as have delays. Long trains, running in heavy traffic territory and over CTC trackage, can move more freely with the security of dynamic brakes. And this provides a self-improving advantage: faster movement between points not only expedites freight and passenger delivery but also increases the available utilization time for each locomotive.

Several types of diesels have been used on C&O runs. In 1946 what was then still the Pere Marquette road placed 2,000-horsepower E-7's in service between Grand Rapids and Detroit, and followed this with the purchase of 14 dual control BL-2 units. Since then, the C&O has acquired only general-purpose diesel locomotives, and today it owns no strictly road engines at all, with the exception of passenger units.

The Southern Region operates a wide range of types, running from a single 44-ton General Electric unit through road locomotives to the heavy six-motor Alcos and Baldwins. On Canadian trackage between Sarni, Ontario, and Buffalo, the C&O uses diesels built in Canada by the London GMC plant.

Higher and higher utilization is constantly being achieved on the road through the continuous development of special pools and operating cycles. On the main line of the Southern Region, for example, passenger locomotives are operated on an eleven-day cycle, spending ten days on the road and the eleventh in the maintenance shop. Eleven two-unit engines are used in this cycle, and on the second day of the operation of each, it is broken into two one-unit locomotives, each of which performs one round trip, after which the two are again reassembled. This cycle is in effect from Huntington, West Virginia, to Cincinnati, Washington, Detroit, and Newport News.

Freight units on this division are pooled at various points, where the first unit in becomes the first locomotive out. A pool at Russell, Kentucky, handles 105 road freight units and 23 freight-passenger units. Runs are scheduled from this point over the Cincinnati-Chicago division, Hocking division, Huntington division, Logan subdivision, Hinton divison, Clifton Forge division, Big Sandy subdivision, and Lexington and Louisville subdivisions.

Another pool is maintained at Clifton Forge, Virginia, where 76 general-purpose units are assigned to runs over the Hinton division, the James River subdivision, and the Mountain subdivision. Thirty road freights run from Clifton Forge to Russell and to Peru, Indiana.

At Peru there is a pool comprised of 10 general purpose units and 36 road freight units. The former handle freight runs from Peru to Chicago and return, while the road units operate to Russell, Columbus, Toledo, and Clifton Forge.

Freight units on this Southern regional operation average about nine thousand miles per month. Because of their ability to make long runs, with limited stops necessary only for fuel, freight units often will run over other divisions besides the one to whose pools they are assigned.

Passenger diesels on the C&O's Northern Region are pooled at Grand Rapids, Michigan, where the region has its shops. Toward Chicago, they operate with two units; to Detroit and to Petoskey, Michigan, they run as single units.

All freight locomotives in the Northern Region are of the general-purpose type and operate on a cycle entirely different from that which has been described above for Southern Region freight operations. Here a seven-day cycle is used, beginning each

Monday with two-unit locomotives on the manifest trains, which run light during the early part of each week. Extra units are added later in the week as the manifest runs become heavier.

The cycle repeats each week, but is so arranged that each individual locomotive works its way back to Grand Rapids once a month for inspection and scheduled repairs. Shorter runs are the rule in this region, with freight locomotives averaging some 7,500 to 8,000 miles per month, while passenger diesels hit close to 9,000.

Saint Thomas, Ontario, is the periodic inspection and heavy overhaul headquarters for Canadian locomotives. An eight-stall roundhouse here has been converted to handle diesel units.

Operating cycles are not employed on either regional operation for road switchers or transfer locomotives, but instead the units are stationed at a central operating point. At Walbridge, Ohio, for example, there is a pool of nineteen Alco transfer units, which are assigned to service between that point and the coal and ore docks at Presque Isle, near Toledo. They are also used in yard service and on interchange runs. Four such units operate for the Huntington division for switching and mine run service, while three are assigned for switching duties at Russell.

The flexibility of diesels is one of the operating advantages that the C&O has found to be so beneficial. Many of the locomotives can thus be used in more than one kind of service, depending upon schedule and need. While freight-passenger units are regularly assigned to the road's heavy freight service, they can be called upon to serve extra main-line passenger trains. Four E-7 2,000-horsepower passenger units are used in the freight pool as well. General-purpose locomotives, well named as they are, see service in such varied operations as switching, humping, local freight runs, through freight schedules, helper duties, and passenger service.

Off-line runs also benefit from the use of diesels, and it is now possible for the C&O to run trains from Cincinnati or Detroit straight through to Washington without changing engines, even though the run from Louisville to Lexington is over Louisville & Nashville trackage and the section from Orange, Virginia, into Washington is over Southern Railway tracks.

The Greenbrier

But the Chesapeake & Ohio Railroad is not all coal and freight, not all industry and commerce. On its main line, at White Sulphur Springs, West Virginia, in the heart of the awesome Allegheny Mountains, lies one of the great show places of America—the famous Greenbrier.

Consisting of a famous old hotel and a series of fine cottages, the Greenbrier has been the property of the C&O since 1910. It has been promoted by the railroad, as a means of building passenger revenue and as a convention place and meeting headquarters for many of the country's major industrial and business groups. It is truly a luxury operation, deliberately maintained and operated as a show piece for the railroad, where C&O efficiency and service are constantly on display for the benefit of the commercial leaders who make many of the decisions about the nation's freight business.

More than 60 per cent of the Greenbrier's convention and meeting business is repeated from year to year, and some organizations have already made their reservations for conferences that will not be held until well into the 1960's. In a recent year 318 groups, ranging from ten to eight hundred persons in attendance, met at the Greenbrier.

Operated at the hotel is a famous institution, the Greenbrier Clinic, to which 52 companies sent 1,325 of their executives for a physical checkup in one year. Included in this group were more than 200 from a single steel company. On the clinic's advisory staff of specialists there are twenty-three of the nation's leading medical practitioners. The facility has been in operation since 1948, to provide a place where businessmen could go for an annual physical checkup in an atmosphere that is quite different from that usually found in the traditional clinic or hospital.

Businessmen attending meetings at the Greenbrier enjoy the

use of four ranges for trap or skeet shooting, three golf courses, five tennis courts, a bridle path, and an indoor swimming pool. A $2,000,000 addition to the hotel has been completed, including a new wing that houses a thousand-seat auditorium, a four-hundred seat theater, and smaller meeting and banquet rooms, all of which can be used by groups of varied size without interfering with the privacy or activities of the hotel's other guests.

Because of its new policy of catering largely to organizations, the Greenbrier now enjoys the benefits of year-round business, no longer being subject to the "off-season" slack that affects most resorts. A complete redecorating job, under the supervision of Dorothy Draper, was accomplished in 1948, when the C&O took back title to its property; during the war years, the hotel and grounds had first been used as an internment camp for enemy diplomats and later as an army hospital. Today the Greenbrier is acknowledged to be more attractive and beautiful than at any time in its previous history, since its stately traditional architectural lines have been cleverly enhanced by its new cloak of modern color and design. President Walter J. Tuohy, one of America's best-liked railroad officials, has constantly turned in a great leadership job heading this improved property and is ably backed up by Traffic Vice-President J. E. Doyle, Coal Traffic Vice-President G. S. Dune, Operating Vice-President M. I. Dunn, other fine staff officers, and a forward-thinking board of directors.

CHAPTER XLI

UNION PACIFIC

New Cheyenne Stockyard

Hogs, sheep, and calves are happier walking up ordinary stairs than they are trying to climb the traditional chute filled with cleated ramps.

This fact, learned out of observation and experience, has been used by the Union Pacific Railroad in building and placing into service an ultramodern stockyard and feeding station at Cheyenne, Wyoming, to add to a whole chain of servicing stockyards along the system's entire right of way.

The new Cheyenne yard is divided into two sections: a group of covered stock pens adjacent to the track and ten large open pens located just south of the covered unit. Of fire-resistive construction, the building is 110 feet wide and 400 feet long and includes ten double-deck rail chutes. The chutes are spaced for servicing UP's new-type 40-foot 7-inch stock cars, and the stair-type construction makes it possible to load lower and upper decks of the new cars simultaneously. The arrangement of these chutes not only speeds up the loading and unloading processes but prevents the damage that may occur to livestock when the animals are crowded against the sides of the chutes.

Well-thought-out laws govern the handling of livestock in transit. One of them requires that all such animals be unloaded every twenty-eight hours for purposes of feeding, watering, and rest; special permission may be obtained from the owner to extend this period to thirty-six hours, but not even the owner can grant an extension beyond that time limit.

So the Union Pacific, like other railroads engaged in long-distance livestock haulage, must provide efficient, up-to-date stopping places at intervals along its right of way. These stockyards must be large enough to accommodate the livestock cargo of the road and capable of feeding and watering them quickly enough to prevent any kind of bottleneck as new loads arrive at the yard.

The new Cheyenne yards were thus planned and built by the UP to upgrade capacity by 20 per cent—either by handling the same amount of animal traffic in one-fifth less time or by servicing 20 per cent more stock in the same amount of time than could be done in the old yards. Capacities had to be worked out in accordance with another legal requirement that cattle and sheep must remain off cars for five hours or more at each interval, while hogs must have at least one and one-half hours off cars for water.

The largest volume handled by the new Cheyenne yards consists of hogs moving westward; from markets in the Missouri River valley they are carried to the West Coast in four days, for slaughter on the fifth morning. An increasing volume of westward-bound cattle is also being moved by the UP, and Cheyenne must service them too, in accordance with the law's requirements and the railroad's schedule for a fourth-evening delivery from Omaha to either the West Coast or the Pacific Northwest area.

There are three narrow pens at each end of the covered portion of the Cheyenne building, plus fifty-one other pens of various sizes. Most pens have individual troughs, but in any event the troughs are so arranged that livestock, no matter where assigned, has access to at least one. Near the track side there are larger pens that are designed to serve hogs, and these are equipped with two troughs, each of which serves two of the big pens.

In the south-central portion of this building the weighing area is located. It consists of two large and two small pens, each with access to a Fairbanks-Morse self-registering stock scale that can weigh an entire carload of livestock at one time; its mammoth platform is 36 feet long and 10 feet wide.

The scale is so situated that stock can be brought to it from any or all of the ten large outside pens on the south side of the building, moved across the platform for weighing, and then either returned to the same pens from which they were brought or sent on through the inside pens to be loaded on stock cars. Stock from any pen can thus be weighed and returned to the same pen or moved to any other pen, an arrangement that both speeds up the weighing operation and protects the stock from damage through overcrowding.

Of unique interest is the nature of the pen building's construction. It is of Stran-Steel Nailable-frame type, with the distinctive feature of the "nailing groove," a design device that is said to provide a holding power comparable to that of more expensive construction methods. This groove exists in all joists and studs and is created by welding two or more specially formed steel parts back to back. The small space between these parts is so designed that when a nail is driven into it, the nail is not only gripped by steel but becomes deformed, to provide an unusually high degree of holding power.

Other materials thus can be attached to the steel framework with the application of nothing more complicated than ordinary hammer and nails. Sheet-metal screws, bolts, nails, or welding methods can be used to assemble the basic framework itself.

Roof, sides, and ends of the steel framework are enclosed with 26-gauge corrugated galvanized sheeting. The floor is of concrete and is elevated about one foot above the level of the car floor, or about two feet nine inches above rail top. Only the inside pens and chutes are of wood, with every other part of the building constructed of steel and concrete, thus assuring a high degree of fire resistance. The roof is supported by Nailable-steel wall studs and by four rows of Stran-Steel columns, which are so spaced as to form two 20-foot bays parallel to the walls with a 30-foot bay in the center.

The Union Pacific recognizes the importance of fast, efficient movement of its huge livestock cargo day after day. That is why such new stockyards as this one at Cheyenne have been designed to provide maximum movement, combined with safety, under conditions that permit the important loads of cattle, sheep, and hogs to dine in grand style as they take their mandatory off-car rest periods.

CHAPTER XLII

GREAT WESTERN'S ICING FACILITIES

Fabulous Installation at Oelwein Takes Care of System's Perishables—Industrial Development

A map of the routes of the Chicago Great Western railway looks roughly like a huge plus sign. The crossbar is the run between Chicago on the east and Omaha on the west, while the somewhat bowed vertical stroke is the north-and-south line between Saint Paul–Minneapolis and Kansas City.

The road's key division point is at Oelwein, Iowa, where these two major lines cross. The dozens of communities that the CGW serves in northern Illinois, southern Minnesota, northern Missouri, and through the heart of Iowa represent a vital sector of the agricultural and meat-producing industries, and the railroad is called upon to transport fresh meat and perishable farm produce from America's great plains areas to the four major cities that lie at the ends of its lines.

These are the products that must be delivered daily to their destinations without loss through spoilage, and thorough, proper refrigeration of the cars that carry them is an absolute must.

That is why one of the world's most modern, efficient, and rapid car-icing operations can now be found at the Chicago Great Western's Oelwein hub.

A new ice house, capable of manufacturing sixty-two tons of ice a day and with a storage capacity of four hundred tons, functions as a unit along with a 700-foot icing dock, a self-propelled dock-type car-icer, and a series of conveyor systems to insure rapid, push-button-controlled re-icing of the many hundreds of bunker cars that enter and leave Oelwein every day, loaded with their precious cargoes.

The new ice house is one of the most modern and efficient manufacturing and storage buildings that can be found anywhere. It produces ice in blocks weighing 300 pounds each, which are automatically moved to the storage room as they are produced. When needed, the blocks are moved mechanically to a belt conveyor running along the dock. This conveyor, in turn, serves the self-propelled car-icer that does the final job of icing and salting the bunkers.

All the equipment used in this marvel of mechanical and engineering ingenuity is the product of the Link-Belt Company, of Chicago. Rivetless chains, link chains, the car-icer itself, gear motors that are employed throughout the various stages of the process, generators, conveyors, and elevator equipment were all designed and then built to specifications by this great industrial organization.

The icing dock is 700 feet long, and there is provision for an additional 700-foot extension, which would then give it a total capacity of fifty bunker cars. It is the key to the operation, and is built between two lines of track, on which the bunker cars to be iced are halted. The icing car, which rides the top of the dock, can work either side.

The process of re-icing starts when a chain conveyor moves ice from the storage room to another conveyor atop the dock. This dock conveyor, 685 feet long, travels at the rate of 180 feet per minute and has ice-pushing attachments every ten feet of its length. It is driven by a 25-horsepower motor.

The dock-type car-icer is a self-propelled device that travels along the dock on rails and is capable of both bunker-icing and bunker-salting in one operation; in addition, it is equipped with an ice crusher-slinger, so that it can produce very finely crushed snow-ice for use as a top layer on perishable farm products.

As an ice block travels down the dock, riding its conveyor, it is intercepted by an inclined pickup conveyor that is part of the car-icer. It is then carried up the incline to another conveyor, this one of the reversible-slat apron type, which in turn feeds it into an ice-crusher. The crusher consists of three steel rolls with picks of hardened steel, and is adjustable, so that the size of ice chunks it will produce can be regulated by manipulating the positions of the rolls.

The crushed ice then falls into a reversible distributing conveyor that runs at right angles to the line of the dock, and can then be discharged at either side of the dock into a boom chute leading directly to the hatches of the bunker car. The operator of the car-icer can direct the flow of crushed ice to either the inboard or outboard bunkers of any car by controlling hydraulically operated bypass gates.

Meanwhile salt is carried right along with the car-icer on a trailer attached to it, using the same tracks atop the dock. Every second, ten pounds of salt are fed by screw feeders into the boom chutes, and timing controls measure how much salt is going into each bunker.

A stationary tank near the end of the icing dock is used to store the salt, and it is delivered to the car-icer's salt trailer when needed by conveying and elevating equipment. Originally it reaches its storage tank through the use of a power unloading scoop that removes it from the boxcars delivering it. The entire operation is mechanical, and CGW has found that the elimination of manual handling has resulted in halting losses that were formerly encountered due to spillage. The use of the mechanical scoop also makes it possible to unload cars of their salt cargo the day they arrive, thus quickly releasing them for other functions.

The icing machine, operated by one man through a series of push buttons, handles chunk ice to the bunkers at the rate of 18 cakes a minute, which amounts to 162 tons each hour. Top icing for the proper preservation of fresh produce is accomplished by reversing the apron conveyor, again through the pressure of a finger on a button, sending the ice into the ice crusher-slinger, where it is reduced to very fine particles resembling snow.

It is then directed uniformly by the operator over and between the tiers of farm-produce containers, and it blankets them completely. In this manner the slowly melting fine ice maintains safe temperatures and preserves the important moisture content of the produce. As many as sixteen cakes of ice per minute can be sent through the ice crusher-slinger and converted into fine snow-ice.

A feature of the operation, providing necessary flexibility and control, makes it possible for the inclined pickup conveyor leading from the dock up to the icing machine to accumulate and hold the big ice blocks that it picks up from the dock conveyor at ten-foot intervals. The apron conveyor that feeds the crusher can also hold ice blocks when necessary, and crushed ice can be held on the reversible distributing conveyor while the car-icer is traveling between bunker cars.

Although the operation appears to be an intricate and complex engineering feat, it is actually a carefully thought out combination of a number of types of Link-Belt conveyors, crushers, and transmission machinery, all of which have been carefully planned, skillfully engineered, and ingeniously integrated for smooth, rapid performance.

By placing the controls for all these integral parts in one compact unit located right in the cab of the car-icer, Chicago Great Western has made it possible for one man to run the entire operation. From his control platform, riding above the level of the dock, the operator can see not only the dock and its conveyor load of ice blocks riding toward him, but the salt trailer, the discharge chutes, and the bunker cars he is servicing. With simple push-button controls located directly at his fingertips he moves the machine along the dock, starts and stops the dock ice conveyor belt and all the conveying devices on the icing machine, operates the crusher rolls, raises and lowers the discharge chutes and the pickup conveyor, controls the hydraulic gates over the bunkers, and regulates the flow of salt from the bins.

Completely in control of this entire operation, he can bunker-ice a refrigerator car in less than two minutes. Thus the installation of this remarkable icing dock, with its manufacturing plant, storage room, and finely adjusted mechanical controls, makes it possible for Chicago Great Western's Oelwein hub to service its refrigerator cars with utmost speed. This rapidity of movement, guaranteeing that the cars will be rolling on to their destinations with only the shortest possible delay, adds to the protection offered by proper icing in getting fresh meat and perishable farm products to the market place or to the slaughter house in prime condition.

At Oelwein the CGW has set up a most modern center of railroad operations, of which this fabulous car-icing process is but one.

Industrial Development

During recent years the general growth in the industrial facilities of the nation, and more particularly the continuous trend toward the decentralization of industry, has resulted in a marked expansion in the industrial capacity and potential of the entire area traversed by the Chicago Great Western. This industrial development, coupled with aggressive efforts by the company to attract industries to its area, has resulted in the location on its lines of 350 new permanent industrial plants within the last five years.

The company is using its best efforts to continue and to increase this industrial growth by establishing industrial districts at Roseport, Minnesota; Des Moines, Fort Dodge, and Mason City, Iowa; Saint Charles, Illinois; and Saint Joseph, Missouri; in which areas available industrial property is scarce.

The newly opened district at Roseport, situated about fourteen miles south of Saint Paul, Minnesota, along the west bank of the Mississippi River, contains approximately 6,000 acres of highly desirable industrial property, zoned for heavy industry, served exclusively by the main tracks of the Chicago Great Western and trunk highways 52, 55, and 56. While the property is adjacent to the main channel of the Mississippi River, affording water transportation, the area is entirely free from flood hazard.

Recently the Great Northern Oil Company completed and placed in operation on a 950-acre site at Roseport a $25,000,000 oil refinery, processing crude oil transported by pipeline from

Saskatchewan fields. There is presently under construction in the Roseport District by the St. Paul Ammonia Products, Inc., a $15,000,000 ammonia plant. Other nationally known companies are investigating the possibility of establishing plants at Roseport.

The railway company is engaged in the construction of, and will soon have completed, industrial trackage encircling the entire Roseport District, off which spurs can be taken to serve any additional industries locating in the area.

A tract of 140 acres of the Roseport District, ideally suited and located, has been set aside for the development of small industry. The area has been cleared, graded, and platted and is complete even to the construction of roadways. Track layouts for any plant arrangement are already drawn and can be constructed immediately to meet the most exacting requirements.

A modern freight station building with dock and ramp facilities has been erected to serve Roseport patrons.

Development of the new industrial district at Des Moines containing 425 acres has started. Paving of trunk highway along the property has been completed, and other state and Federal planned highways across and adjacent to the area should prove very beneficial in early development of the district. A large plant for the manufacture of paper and burlap bags was recently erected on the land, and negotiations are under way with several other concerns for plant sites at Des Moines.

New industries at Fort Dodge include a large grain elevator and feed mill erected by Farmers Elevator Service and a $6,000,000 plant under construction by Celotex Corporation. Additional land has been acquired to expand the industrial district and care for expected industry at Fort Dodge.

The recently acquired Mason City District, containing seventy-four acres, is already being utilized by one new large industry, the North Iowa Cooperative Processing Association, processors of soy beans, and early development of the balance of the property is expected.

The Chicago Great Western has acquired property at both Saint Charles, Illinois, and Saint Joseph, Missouri, for industrial development and is presently engaged in readying the districts for anticipated industry with whom it is now in contact.

The establishment of these strategically located new industrial districts holds high promise of early development of substantial industry and production of additional traffic for the CGW.

CHAPTER XLIII

SANTA FE

New Freight House and Retarder Yard at Corwith, Chicago

Right in the heart of America's second-largest city stands one of the country's most modern and efficient freight-station operations—the new freight house of the Santa Fe's Corwith yard. Located at Forty-seventh Street and Hamlin Avenue, Chicago, within easy reach of that great railroad hub's shippers, the new facility has six tracks, permitting roofed accommodations for a total of 160 cars and uninterrupted freight-handling operations no matter what the weather.

L.c.l. handling is speeded here by a modern communications system, by auxiliary handling equipment, and by a special towing system that expedites cargo ranging from a small carton to a five-ton load.

The new freight station looks something like an elongated letter "E," with the lengthy crossbars running north and south. The vertical staff of the letter would be the office building, in back of which is a platform; the three horizontal bars would be concrete platforms, running parallel to Hamlin Avenue, each of which is 1,235 feet long. At the north (the open end of the "E") there is a ramp 80 feet long leading from each of the platforms to a concrete driveway ribbon on which trunks can circle the entire building.

The headhouse is one-story high. Made of concrete and brick, it is 25 feet wide by 248 feet long and includes a complete basement, offices for the foreman and his staff, washrooms, locker rooms, a lunchroom, a cold room, a "hold" room, and a cooper's room. The platform back of it is also of concrete; it is 50 feet wide and 204 feet long, and it connects the three long working platforms.

On the extreme western side the platform is used for outbound freight. Tailboard space for some seventy trucks is provided. That portion of the platform used by the trucks is 45 feet wide, after which it narrows to 25 feet for the remainder of its length. A total of fifty trucks picking up inbound cargo can be accommodated on a similar concrete platform that forms the easterly platform, or the lowest crossbar of the long "E." The center platform serves four tracks—two on each side—while the northern and southern platforms serve one track each; three of the total of six tracks lie on each side of the center platform.

In the floor of each of the three platforms is the unusual feature that makes this Santa Fe freight house a model of freight-handling efficiency: the Towveyor system. It is the first installation of its kind in any railroad freight station, and was designed by Santa Fe engineers in conjunction with experts of the Jervis-Webb Company of Detroit.

Used for the movement of merchandise on platform trucks from unloading to stowing points, the Towveyor is a roller-type continuous-chain conveyor installed right in the floor of the platforms. At about 15-foot intervals in the chain are catch devices that engage tow pins attached to the platform trucks; the pins extend downward through a continuous slot about an inch wide in the surface of the platforms. The chain moves at speeds variable between 110 and 160 feet per minute and is in continuous use during working hours.

In the Santa Fe freight house, the Towveyor system consists of two separate and independent units. One of these is 2,685 feet long and serves only the outbound freight platforms. It circles the first three tracks, running along both the western and the center platforms, while the other makes a complete 2,330-foot circuit on the eastern platform and serves inbound business only. Each of the two circuits is driven by a caterpillar roller-chain drive powered by a 30-horsepower electric motor, and each is equipped with a counterweight device designed to keep the

298

chain taut regardless of the amount of load it is moving at any given time. At intervals along its length each of these long chains has ten brushes, which constantly push any dirt or paper that may fall into the slot toward small pits that are placed at intervals of about 240 feet along the course of each of the two circuits.

The trucks themselves are of the four-wheel type, with caster-type front wheels. There are five hundred of them in use here, all of which were built to specifications for this installation by the Mercury Manufacturing Company, Chicago.

Each truck has a special towing device, known as a "Santa Fe pin," at its front end. Connected to a foot pedal operated by the handlers, this pin can be locked in raised position or dropped to the platform surface, where it will slide along until the platform slot is reached. The pin will then drop into the slot and will automatically engage the next catch device to come along. The trucks also have the regular railroad front and rear coupling devices so that they can be made up into trains for mass hauling.

The longer circuit, operating around two platforms, will accommodate about 175 trucks at a time. In crossing from one platform to another it uses the headhouse platform at the southern end, but at the open end of the "E" it must cross under three tracks and operate up and down two 6-degree ramps. This presented a special problem, since the crossing designs had to incorporate sufficient strength for the railroad's tracks to support switch engines and loaded freight cars, even while being cut and undermined by the chain slot of the Towveyor. The problem was solved through the use of special crossings made of manganese steel designed to meet this need.

The shorter circuit carries 165 trucks at a time, but since its complete run is limited to a single platform, no crossing or ramp runs are involved.

Allowing 500 pounds as the empty weight for each truck, and giving consideration to the average number of empty trucks that would be likely to ride the system at any one time, Santa Fe officials came up with an average load requirement of 1,000 pounds per running truck. A limit switch has been installed on each of the two circuits, and it serves to cut power to either line should the total haul at any time exceed the total computed load; thus no damage can be done to the power units of the twin systems by creating overload conditions.

There are seventy-five blocks at the Corwith freight house, and to keep the conveyor system in continuous operation, it has been necessary to plan carefully the movement, timing, and track assignment of these blocks so that track switching will not interfere with the operation of the Towveyor at those points where it crosses tracks. For this reason it is customary to assign to the eastern three tracks cars containing overflow merchandise that arrives too late for the night switch. Occasionally it is necessary to halt the Towveyor for purposes of switching a cut out, but service is normally not interrupted for an interval of any more than four minutes.

The middle track between the western and middle platforms (Track No. 2) is depressed for use of refrigerator cars that are usually loaded at this station with "dry" cargo scheduled for movement to California. This places the higher floor level of those cars more nearly on the same elevation as that of the standard freight cars. Although the difference between the two floor levels of the different car types is fourteen inches, this track is depressed only seven inches. This was decided upon because at times standard boxcars are spotted on the track, to be loaded by means of steel aprons connecting them to cars on the adjoining track. The full fourteen-inch depression would have provided too steep an angle to make possible the movement of heavy items between the cars on the two tracks.

A two-way communications system between the headhouse and various points on the three platforms, as well as pneumatic tubes connecting the headhouse office with offices located on both inbound and outbound aprons, provides for increased efficiency through maximum use of man power. Checkers no longer work on the platforms, but, by using the intercommunications setup, are able to be stationed in offices where each can handle the work of three callers. Each working unit formerly consisted of a checker, a caller, and a trucker; now, with the Towveyor system and the communications circuits, there are more callers, but there are fewer checkers and there are no longer any truckers at all.

There are two distinct circuits that make up the communications plan at Santa Fe's new Corwith freight house. First there is a two-way-wiring connection between checkers in an office and callers in the cars. Then there is a circuit connecting headhouse office consoles and the two platform offices with talk-back and paging speakers. Through a console and switchboard arrangement in the headhouse office, both circuits can be interconnected at will.

There are nine checkers located at desks in the headhouse office, each of whom is equipped with a boom-type microphone and a console fitted with toggle switches and indicator lights. Each desk is fitted on three sides with a 30-inch-high soundproofing panel, permitting each checker to concentrate on his own conversation and reception without undue interference from other business going on around him. Each checker works with three callers—there are five switches on each console, but experience has shown that working with three callers provides optimum conditions with maximum results for each checker—and handles his waybills with both hands free, since his console is operated by a conveniently placed foot switch.

There are 132 plug-in points at various spots around the platforms, and a central switchboard makes it possible to hook up any checker with any one of these points. The plug-in locations are at intervals of about 45 feet, which is approximately the length of a boxcar, and there are outlets for extension light cords located near each of the plug-in points.

Each caller is equipped with a portable talk-back speaker which has a 25-foot extension wound around a reel. The caller merely has to plug into the outlet nearest the car in which he is going to work, carry the speaker into the car with him, and press a button when he is ready to talk to the checker. This operation flashes and buzzes a signal on the board of the checker who has been hooked into him by means of the central switchboard; when the checker is free to talk to the caller, he presses his foot

301

switch and throws the proper toggle switch, and the two are in direct telephonic connection.

The other circuit permits the assistant foreman in the headhouse office to talk through any combination or all of the twenty talk-back speakers and twenty-eight paging speakers located around the platform areas. Other assistant foremen in the platform offices can talk to the one in the headhouse office or to any or all of the six talk-back speakers on their own platforms.

The interconnection feature of the two units provides a communications flexibility that can meet any emergency that might arise. Either the foreman in his private office or the assistant foreman in the headhouse office can be connected to any plug-in spot, any paging speaker, or any combination with which he may wish to communicate. The checkers—any or all of them—can easily be connected with any desired speakers, or a general announcement can be made by the foreman to all personnel over the entire range of plug-in points and speakers, some of which are located in off-platform areas such as the lunchroom, cooper's room, etc.

Long, time-consuming walks are completely eliminated for the delivery of receipts, bills of lading, and waybills by the installation of pneumatic tubes that connect the inbound and outbound platform offices with the headhouse office.

Light and spaciousness are striking features of Santa Fe's new freight house in the heart of Chicago. One roof covers all platforms, with its steel supporting columns so located as to present a minimum of obstruction to platform operations. The outer lines of these columns are at 25-foot intervals along the outer edges of the platforms, and they are the only columns on those platforms. No columns have had to be located on the center platform, since the two intermediate lines fall between lines of track separating the center platform from each of the other two.

Along the truck tailboard loading spaces there are cantilevered visors 8 feet wide, which give protection to those areas during bad weather. Transite siding was applied to the upper portions of the building sides to add further protection against the elements.

Daylight that might reach the tracks near the center platform is often cut off by cars standing on adjourning tracks, so a clerestory, glazed with deep-angle white corrugated glass, is built into the roof along its entire length above the center platform. There are mercury-vapor lights all along the three platforms, whose illumination is bolstered by 750-watt incandescent lamps at regular intervals. These latter are left on during nonworking hours for policing purposes.

To assist in handling heavy items there is a 5-ton hoist at the south end of the outbound platform, and a 35-ton gantry crane has been constructed in an area next to the east side of the new freight station.

Construction of this new Santa Fe freight house is merely a part of an over-all plan to enlarge and improve operations in the Corwith yard. Tracks have been rearranged in a more efficient layout to take full advantages of the added facilities afforded by the new freight house.

Before the new station was constructed, all l.c.l. cargo was handled in a long, narrow transfer house that was served by four tracks for half its length and by three transfer tracks, with the remaining portion devoted to spaces for truck tailboards. Another transfer dock used for l.c.l. was separated from this house by two through tracks.

Narrow platforms made congestion the rule rather than the exception, and made it impossible to take advantage of the economies and time-saving attributes of modern materials-handling equipment. Much hand trucking through the cars was necessary too.

But all that is in the past. The well-designed, efficiently constructed new freight house at the Corwith yards, right in the middle of a bustling city, now provides the Santa Fe Railroad and its shippers with the most modern, efficient, and time-saving methods of handling l.c.l. freight loads, and it is appropriate that a great rate and traffic expert like Gerald E. Duffy, traffic vice-president of the Santa Fe, should have this modern installation so near his office in Chicago, eastern headquarters of the Santa Fe.

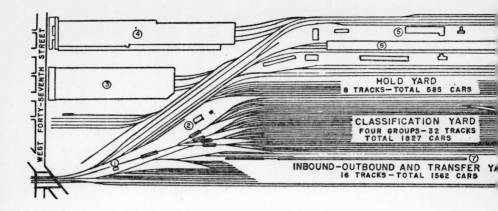

Installation of Santa Fe Railway's new Corwith "push-button" freight yard marked the completion of a nine-year, $20,000,000 master plan for modernization of the company's Corwith yard facilities.

Corwith yard handles traffic not only from Chicago industries located on the line but a heavy freight-house traffic as well, and also very substantial traffic coming from eastern and other connections, all of which must be expedited through the yard in order to keep the route a free-flowing artery. The purpose of improving and modernizing the yard was to make this densely confined area capable of accepting and expediting expanded traffic so that the yard itself would be able to keep pace with Chicago's continuing industrial growth.

Before reconstruction the Corwith yard had a storage capacity of 4,596 cars and a working capacity of 1,500 cars per day. The new yard has a storage capacity of 5,881 cars (an increase of approximately 28 per cent) and a working capacity of 3,000 cars (an increase of 100 per cent). The new arrangement gives the Chicago area faster, more efficient freight service and reduces car delays and car handling time.

Another remarkable feature of the yard is the high degree of utilization of available space. On only 190 acres of ground, the railroad's engineers have located a 32-track automatic retarder

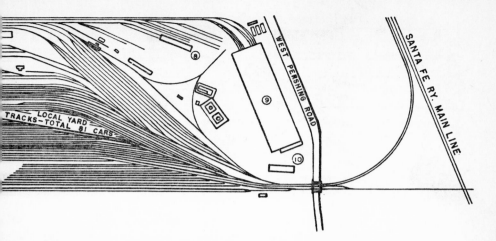

yard of 1,800 cars capacity, three modern spacious freight houses equipped with Towveyor systems, a 1,362-foot car repair shed, an inbound-outbound and transfer yard of 16 tracks with 1,350 cars capacity, an eight-track hold yard of 520 cars capacity, a nine-track local yard of 110 cars capacity, a two-stall diesel locomotive shop and related facilities, a two-story terminal office building, store department facilities, a 70-car icing dock, a piggyback loading setup and other improvements.

The successful completion of the project is a tribute to the ingenuity of the company's engineering, operating, mechanical and communications-signal departments who were confronted with the problem of entirely reconstructing one of the busiest railroad yards in the country while at the same time maintaining normal service through the yard.

The Santa Fe Railway entered Chicago from the west in 1888 and acquired a freight yard at Corwith, about six miles southwest of the Loop District. Additions to the yard were made over the ensuing years, and eventually the layout consisted of a roundhouse, store department building, car repair and other facilities located in the center of 190 acres of ground and surrounded by yard tracks.

The old arrangement served its purpose well during the days of steam railroading, but with the coming of the diesel era and

305

the tremendous increase of traffic during World War II problems developed. The old layout did not lend itself to efficiency of operation and was proving inadequate to handle the growing traffic properly. Short tracks caused considerable doubling and delays, and inadequately designed lead tracks increased the limitations for freight handling and added to the congestion.

Studies were instituted for entirely reconstructing the Corwith yard based on making the best possible use of the land area by clearing out old buildings in the center of the yard and erecting new ones along the west side and corners. Under this plan, longer tracks could be provided and the associated yards could be grouped together.

Construction work under the master plan began in February, 1949, with erection of a new diesel shop in the northwest corner of the Corwith yard, and was climaxed with completion of the "push-button" retarder yard in February, 1958.

Utilizing radar and an electronic "brain," Santa Fe's new Corwith classification yard comprises 32 tracks and is equipped with electropneumatic car retarders and VELAC automatic classification system.

An outstanding feature of the VELAC equipment is its inherent accuracy in measuring frictional and other characteristics of rolling freight cars. The system can handle four cars per minute over the hump and includes automatic switching, electronic speed control, electronic computers and various intricate measurement devices. In addition, Type CY cab signals are used to direct the movements of engines from the receiving yard to the crest of the hump.

In a two-story office building at the crest of the hump, the hump conductor on the second floor has charge of a route selection panel containing one push button for each of the 32 tracks. Operation of these buttons successively aligns the electro-pneumatic switches at the proper time to direct the cars to the desired track. This machine is capable of "storing up" 5 movements in advance of their actual arrival at the retarder. From this station the signals directing the pusher locomotive also are controlled.

Cars approaching the hump pass over an underground inspection pit and through a journal oiling station. As cars are released from the crest of the hump, their speed is controlled by automatic action of the car retarders, depending upon the weight of car and lading, car-rolling capability for the particular track to be entered and the space remaining on this track. The speed of cars is continuously measured by radar equipment in the retarder area. Information gathered by the various measuring devices is assimilated by electronic computers which predict the car speeds and automatically preset the retarder apparatus. When the correct speed of a car through a retarder is achieved, the braking effect is released by the speed control apparatus. This results in cars leaving the final retarder to a yard track at proper coupling speed to prevent damage to equipment and lading. The automatic features of the layout are geared to govern a coupling speed of not more than four miles per hour.

A four-story tower is located at the bottom of the hump. The first floor houses the electronic "brain" equipment. Communications equipment is on the second floor. The retarder operator is on the third floor, and the hump yardmaster's office is on the fourth floor. The retarder operator's office contains a control console on which is a complete track diagram, equipped with indicating lights reflecting operation of the entire system. In an emergency, the operator can instantly assume control of any part of the system by individual levers which supersede the automatic features. The hump yardmaster and the hump conductor jointly control a cab-signal system which operates by electronic equipment in the control center and on the locomotive to direct the enginemen. Four such engines are equipped at Corwith.

Grade of the track from the crest of the hump through the retarders is designed to handle easy and slow-rolling cars and keep them rolling until they take their proper place on the classification tracks. The hump retarder setup consists of one master retarder which slows the easy rollers and four "group" retarders, one for each group of eight tracks, which give the final retardation.

Construction of the automatic classification yard involved

providing approximately 22 miles of new track and relocation and rebuilding of 34 existing miles. A second entrance to the yard was provided between the main line and the north entrance, which necessitated crossing the GM&O and the I & M Canal.

On the fourth floor of the hump tower the yardmaster has a console which controls 36 talk-back speakers located throughout the south end of the yard, two-way radio communications with all yard engines, including a separate channel for the humping operation, and the general yard frequency, and intercommunication with the superintendent, trainmasters and the yardmaster at 38th Street (the north end of the yard).

An intercommunicating circuit designated "common hump" links together the yardmaster on the fourth floor, the retarder operator on the third floor, the hump conductor at the crest and the inspection pit. This circuit is so arranged that talk from any one of the stations is heard by the other three stations, facilitating rapid communication between the people actually involved in the humping operation. The hump conductor at the crest also has a talk-back speaker to the pin-puller who works alongside the cars at the crest of the hump as well as a remote control unit on the hump radio station for instant contact with the pusher loco-motive.

Consists of inbound transfers and road trains are transmitted by teletype from the bill office at 38th Street to receiving machines located in the north end yardmaster's office, and the offices of the yardmaster, retarder operator and conductor at the hump. Car inspectors working in the train yard are provided with light, portable, two-way radio sets for instant communication with the yardmaster and the general car foreman's office. A combination paging speaker and telephone system is used for communication at the new car repair facility.

At each end of the yard receptacles are provided for plugging in a telephone handset which the yard clerk uses to call off car numbers on trains or transfers entering the yard. These receptacles will be connected to tape recorders in the bill office where the by-check is recorded. Portable two-way radios also are provided for car checking within the yard, and reception from these may be connected to a tape recorder. Waybills are carried between No. 1 yard office at 38th Street and the hump area by a four-inch pneumatic tube system.

This retarder installation was built and installed by the Union Switch and Signal Company in cooperation with the Santa Fe engineering and signal department.

Three of Chicago's most up-to-date freight houses are located in the Corwith yard area—Freight House No. 1 (handling National Carloading Company traffic), Freight House No. 2 (handling Republic Carloading Company traffic) and Freight House No. 3 (Santa Fe l.c.l. and New Kress traffic). Not located within the 190-acre Corwith tract but served by the new Corwith yard is a fourth new freight house handling Clipper-Carloading Company traffic. This house, located about one and one-half miles northeast of Corwith, was completed in 1954 and has four tracks with a 63-car capacity.

Each has a fully enclosed warehouse where all cars are loaded and unloaded under roof cover. Roof structures were designed to require a minimum of supports to leave all platforms clear for efficient freight handling. All houses are equipped with Towveyor systems and with comprehensive communications systems including centralized freight-checking facilities and talk-back and paging speakers.

House No. 1 has six tracks with a capacity of 160 cars. House No. 2 has six tracks with a capacity of 108 cars. Santa Fe l.c.l. has eight tracks, capacity 128 cars. In addition to handling Santa Fe l.c.l. freight, House No. 3 also is handling freight for the New Kress, a division of Chicago Furniture Forwarders.

Speedy repair of bad order cars, another important part of maintaining a fast freight service for shippers, is accomplished in a new car repair shed completed in November, 1957. This building, of prefabricated steel on concrete foundation, is 1,362 feet long, 75 feet wide, and 20 feet high. It contains three tracks with a capacity of 72 cars. Outdoor car repair platforms at this location have an additional capacity of 72 cars.

The Terminal Office Building is a two-story brick and concrete structure topped by a glassed-in cupola for yardmaster's use, located at the north end of the 190-acre tract. It was completed in 1952 so that the terminal superintendent's force and the agent's force could be moved to Corwith from their old location in Chicago and consolidated with the yard office force to provide more centralized, efficient supervision.

Communications facilities in this building include a telegraph office, an interoffice communicating system, and a two-way radio and talk-back speaker installation for the yardmaster. From here, the yardmaster has two-way radio contact with switch engines and talk-back contact with 50 speakers located at strategic points throughout the north half of the yard.

Prior to the yard reconstruction, the crossing at 38th Street was at grade and all switching and in and outbound movements moved over it, causing considerable interference with automobile and pedestrian traffic. The company decided to separate the grade and built this subway. The street is carried under the tracks and provides for four lanes of highway traffic, with sidewalk facilities for pedestrians. Elimination of this grade crossing did not cost the taxpayers a cent. Entire cost of the project was borne by the railroad.

A few of the other improvements at the new Corwith Yard include: Yard lighting by mercury vapor and sealed-beam lamps mounted 60 to 70 feet high to minimize glare for switchmen. Lights are controlled automatically and are served by underground wiring to eliminate overhead lines; a piggyback loading setup at the south end of the yard consisting of four spur tracks (two with portable steel ramps which are under construction and two with wooden ramps) and a one-story office building for clerks and drivers; a 1,400-foot icing dock with 70-car capacity; a two-stall diesel locomotive servicing shop, a heating plant and fueling facilities; and a main store building, truck garage and nonferrous metal sorting building and storehouse platforms.

This $20,000,000 terminal improvement is another example of how the Santa Fe and other railroads of the United States put their own money into facilities to provide transportation service—facilities on which the railroads pay substantial taxes for the support of schools and general government, as exemplified by the following statement showing 1955 property taxes paid by the railroads and other transportation in the state of Illinois:

The railroads operating in Illinois paid 1955 property taxes in Illinois amounting to $32,000,000.

Two hundred forty-four truck lines operating in Illinois paid 1955 property taxes in Illinois amounting to $730,000.

The certificated airlines paid 1955 personal * property taxes in the State of Illinois amounting to $65,000.

Sixty-five barge and towing lines operating on the navigable rivers and canals in and adjoining the State of Illinois paid 1955 personal † property taxes in Illinois amounting to $12,000.

Following is a comparison of these taxes paid for the support of schools and general government:

	Schools	General Government	Total
Railroads	$18,240,000	$13,760,000	$32,000,000
Truck Lines	416,000	313,900	730,000
Certificated Airlines . .	37,050	27,950	65,000
Barge and Towing Lines .	6,840	5,160	12,000
Percentage	57.0%	43.0%	100.0%

* Includes all flying equipment, floating equipment, rolling equipment, maintenance and operating equipment, office equipment, tools, supplies, money, and all other movable property, but does not include any real estate which might be owned. Taxes on unknown owned real estate are very difficult to secure because of real estate being listed by legal descriptions on the tax books, but it is the considered opinion of the tax men who obtained this information that taxes on the owned real estate would be comparatively insignificant.

† Apportioned to schools and general government in the same proportion as total taxes of all railroads.

CHAPTER XLIV

LACKAWANNA FIGHTS A FLOOD, WINS, AND PAYS FOR IT

So Have Many Other Railroads Overcome Catastrophes at Their Own Expense

On August 18, 1955, the weather experts told the nation that hurricane Diane had just about blown itself out. It rested innocently off the eastern seaboard of the United States, and no further damage was expected from it.

But in its course from its spawning place in the Caribbean Sea, the wild wind had gathered hundreds of tons of moisture-laden air, and when the hurricane center gradually began moving again, its own winds carried this heavily saturated air to the interior of many of the states in the Northeast. When this massive movement of air hit the Appalachians, its great load of water was dumped with terrific fury in a matter of a few hours.

In upper Pennsylvania, for example, one resident reported that a tub standing in his back yard gathered more than 10 inches of rainfall in about six hours. Normally peaceful mountain streams were soon transformed into raging torrents, and Brodhead Creek, near Stroudsburg, Pennsylvania, on the main line of the Lackawanna, rose 30 feet in a matter of fifteen minutes. The unprecedented increase in pressure caused small dams to give completely, letting loose many thousands of gallons of water to ravage the countryside.

Over 50 miles of Lackawanna's main line between East Stroudsburg and Scranton were cut by almost one hundred washouts and landslides, and a double-track, four-span bridge near East Stroudsburg was completely demolished. Two passenger trains were stranded at Tobyhanna and Cresco, and three freight trains were also caught in the unexpectedly sudden rise of the waters.

These severe damages were suffered not only along the road's main line. Possibility of immediate rerouting on branch lines was almost completely eliminated as tracks were washed out at no fewer than eighty-eight locations along both main and branch routes. Altogether a total of seven bridges and large culverts were swept away by the torrents, and at seven other points huge landslides blocked the trackage with thousands of tons of earth and rock.

The rains that washed away the railroad tracks, of course, inflicted equal or greater damage upon highways and vehicular bridges, so that access to the stranded trains was impossible until daylight came to aid in the exploration for alternate routes by which passengers could be taken to safety.

The story of how the Lackawanna organized to repair these great ravages, to bring aid to thousands of homeless persons, to restore its lines, and to renew its service is a story of typical American ingenuity, imagination, organization, and hard work.

Immediately Lackawanna officials began the vast job of mobilizing repair crews, equipment, and materials, but only a token effort could be undertaken, since in many areas it was not possible even to estimate how much damage had been done until the high flood waters receded, at least enough to enable engineers to examine the scene.

But even the stalled milk train at Tobyhanna was pressed into emergency service. Its six cars of milk and cream, a total of more than 48,000 quarts en route to New Jersey points, were made available to a local depot of the Army Signal Corps, so that the needed dairy products could be distributed for the relief of destitute individuals in the area. Even when blocked by washouts and landslides, No. 44 was able to provide a needed service!

Before beginning any repair work at all, the first task was to work out details of rerouting, using branch lines that had not been damaged and entering into cooperating arrangements with other railroads that had not been so seriously hurt. It took twenty-nine days of intensive, round-the-clock reconstruction work to bring the main line back into full service, but within twenty-four hours of the disaster freight was being moved in considerable quantity by detouring Lackawanna trains over tracks of the Pennsylvania Railroad between Elmira, New York, and Kearny Junction, New Jersey; between Binghamton and Schenectady, New York, over lines belonging to the Delaware & Hudson; and between Schenectady, New York, and Jersey City, New Jersey, over New York Central trackage.

By Sunday afternoon, August 21, some passenger service was already restored between Hoboken and Buffalo. This was done over Lackawanna trackage for the most part, with a detour arranged for between Phillipsburg, New Jersey, and Pittston Junction, Pennsylvania, over Lehigh Valley tracks. Westbound trains operating under this arrangement included No. 3, the Phoebe Snow; No. 7, the Westerner; and No. 15, the Owl—all of which began running on Tuesday, August 23. A day earlier, regular service through the Lehigh Valley railroad detour had begun for three eastbound trains: No. 6, the Phoebe Snow; No. 10, the New York Mail; and No. 2, the Pocono Express.

The first known instance in American railroad history in which an exclusively passenger streamliner was used to haul freight occurred on the first run of the Phoebe Snow that day. Emergency conditions in the Pocono Mountains, normally scenic, peaceful hills where many of New York's millions spend restful vacations, required immediate delivery of materials for the construction of temporary bridges over the raging streams. The ability of the authorities to deliver much-needed food, clothing, and medical supplies to the thousands of stranded inhabitants and vacationists in the mountains was seriously impeded by the destruction of bridges that had been important links in the area's network of highways and secondary roads.

Cooperating with the Army Corps of Engineers, Lackawanna moved thirteen carloads of Bailey bridges—the spans developed during World War II for crossing streams—from East Buffalo to Scranton. Using railroad cranes, flatcars were loaded and attached to the regular consist of the Phoebe Snow.

314

Shortage of motive power was another factor that had to be taken into account in any attempt to restore something approaching normal service, even with the quickly organized detour routes available. Additional time was taken up on each run because of the extra mileage involved in moving over trackage of other lines. With seventeen of its diesel units marooned on the Stroudsburg-Scranton break, the Lackawanna quickly made arrangements to rent sixty-one road-switcher units; twenty were leased from the New York Central and the same number from the New York, New Haven & Hartford Railroad, fifteen from the United States Army, and six from the Erie.

Because of the additional traffic on routes that remained open, some trains were on the line more than sixteen hours on their runs, requiring the placing of double crews. But the emergency aspect of the situation resulted in concentrating upon detouring freight trains and temporarily curtailing passenger service.

It is virtually impossible to estimate in terms of dollars the amount of damage that was entailed by the Lackawanna or by any of the other affected railroads in the area. Certainly it would run into a total of many, many millions of dollars, if some method were ever discovered of adding it all up.

With detours arranged for, some service restored, and the heavy rains over, the work of rebuilding began in earnest. Passengers who had remained on marooned trains overnight were removed with the advent of daylight by Army helicopters, and by buses where road transportation was not too severely interrupted. Crews of the stranded freight trains were also taken to safety. As they were transported away from their blocked engines and cars, they saw engineers and work crews already beginning the overwhelming task of assessing the damages, working out methods of bringing in materials and equipment, and planning to overcome the great problems brought on by the ravaging floods.

In the key 50-mile area that marked the most serious damage to Lackawanna operations, engineers faced tremendous problems. Many of the washed-out or blocked locations were completely inaccessible either by highway or by rail. Within two miles of each end of the 50-mile stretch, heavily damaged track made it impossible to approach the area or to start rebuilding inward from the edges of the stretch.

The four-span girder bridge over Brodhead Creek that had been destroyed prevented access to the eastern end of the ruined area; on the west 800 feet of trackage had been washed out to a depth of 60 feet and about one-third of a stone-arch culvert and its northern wall had been demolished, so that the section could not be entered until that gap had been repaired.

Lackawanna engineers and officials saw only one possible solution to this dilemma. It was to flank the entire 50-mile stretch and come to the railroad at key points with a sufficient number of men and enough materials and equipment to begin repair work on all washed-out sections at the same time. In this way, they believed, it would be possible to support weakened track and to build up culverts as well as subgrade and trackage, so that work trains would then be able to enter the area to unload ballast and additional fill material without actually waiting for new tracks to be built across the breaks.

Lackawanna hired fifteen contractors, who brought in an army of workmen, along with several hundred pieces of equipment, such as earth-moving machinery, cranes, pile-drivers, and dump trucks. These men were set to work on the primary problem of restoring subgrade and bridge structures. In some cases no roads were available to reach the track area, so that contractors built their own roads over which to move machinery and materials. Hundreds of additional men were hired at various local spots to assist in the tremendous job of rebuilding line, unloading ballast, and surfacing track.

At the 800-foot washout section alone, seven contractors were at work. New roadbed was laid, crews built a single line of temporary track across it almost as soon as it was packed down, and entire hillsides disappeared as gigantic machines chewed into the surrounding country to obtain earth for fill.

Reconstruction work went on along the line for twenty-four hours of each day, with portable generators and floodlighting equipment brought in from all over the railroad or being bought or rented to provide sufficient light for night operations.

Special 25-foot and 35-foot steel girder spans were made on rush order by American Bridge Company. Sheet piling was driven in to form the sides of new culverts. Dynamiting operations went on all along the line to clear wrecked spans and debris.

Under the direction of G. A. Phillips, chief engineer of the Lackawanna, the intense, gigantic repair job went on night and day. Supervising reconstruction from the west end of the 50-mile stretch was J. P. Hiltz, Jr., formerly engineer maintenance of way for the Lackawanna, whose services the railroad secured through the friendly cooperation of the Delaware & Hudson, where he was now operating vice-president. Working with him was R. F. Bush, who was the railroad's current engineer maintenance of way, while B. L. Beier, engineer maintenance of structures, supervised the bridge-rebuilding tasks over the entire area.

The Scranton and Stroudsburg track supervisors were given much welcomed assistance by their colleagues brought in from track supervisor posts at Buffalo, Elmira, Syracuse, and Binghamton. To expedite progress, these supervisors were given wide authority to hire workers and equipment and to purchase materials as the need arose right on the job.

Mining operations at nearby Scranton proved a valuable and convenient source of important fill material by providing tons of mine rock, which is a waste material that emerges from strip-mining operations. Stream beds throughout the area were dredged to supply roadbed material, rock bluffs were blasted off, and material for fill was gathered from every conceivable source.

So-called "pioneer gangs" were set to work laying single-track sections, under the watchful eyes of the track supervisors, just as quickly as subgrade was sufficiently restored all along the line. Rail and ties were secured from adjacent main-line tracks on both sides of the washouts, with the material having been ripped up and collected at needed points even before subgrading was complete. Thus the track was at hand, along with all necessary materials, to be laid as soon as the subgrade was prepared for it.

317

Work trains followed this operation, moving over the new single-track lines, dumping ballast around the clock. Power jacks were brought into play to raise trackage to grade, and track-liners went into action.

Temporary switches were installed at selected intervals to provide for storage space and switching connections between the new through track and disabled main-line trackage.

Thousands of feet of rail were either completely lost or so badly damaged as to be unusable. To replace this loss, 3,000 tons of emergency rail were ordered by the Lackawanna from the Bethlehem Steel Company. It was delivered to the road's Buffalo division to be laid there, while the rail it released was used to repair second and third main tracks in the damaged areas.

Although emergency repairs were pushed through with such energy, stamina, and ingenuity that full service on the damaged lines was restored within a very few weeks, the complete repair job was clearly a long-time project. Much of the material that was used as fill during the twenty-nine-day reconstruction project was of too unstable a nature to be considered for permanent use, according to Lackawanna engineers. A large-scale riprapping program was therefore undertaken immediately after the resumption of service, and some 20,000 carloads of rock were ultimately to be used in replacing the temporary fill.

To anyone viewing the almost hopeless devastation that greeted the dawn of August 19, 1955, it must have seemed that no railroad could run through the mountains of northern Pennsylvania again for many years. But the Lackawanna, enlisting the cooperation of friendly roads, bending its energies, its total efforts, and its determination to the seemingly impossible task, was back in business in less than a month. The floods of 1955 provided a test for America's railroading men, and they met it with flying colors.

Thus more than 5,000,000 hard-earned Lackawanna dollars went out to repair this damage, just as many other U.S. railroads spent millions of their own money, not government funds, to fight the elements, including blizzards, floods, and earthquakes.

As recently as the winter of 1958 the Southern Pacific spent over $2,300,000 repairing damage along its lines. Yes, the American railroads, officials, men, and money are always there in the pinches.

INDEX

A

ACBX-8 air conditioning, 132
Addison, W.Va., 26, 55
Adlake sash units, 105
Advance 91, 90
Advance Motor Special, 53
Advertising, 19, 20
AGS, 93
Air-brake charging, 17
Alabama State Docks, 186
Alamogordo, N.M., 86
Albany, N.Y., 253, 255
Albuquerque, N.M., 103
Alco locomotives, 281
Alco transfer units, 283
Alexander, Idaho, 160
Alexandria, La., 111
Alford, B. J., 59
Alhambra, Calif., 108
Allegheny Mts., 284
Allentown, Pa., 65, 69
Altar of Sacrifice, 37
American Bridge Co., 317
American Thread Co., 8
Amarillo, Tex., 138, 139
Ampex hi-fi equipment, 238, 239
Andover Junction, N.J., 64
Angel's Landing, 37
Appalachia, Va., 186
Appalachian Mts., 312
Arizona, 107
Arkansas, 172
Army Corps of Engineers, 314
Army Signal Corps, 313
Aroostook County, Me., 8, 9, 200, 207, 208
ASF disc-tread brakes, 139

Ashland, Ore., 111
Asheville, N.C., 16
Astra-dome coaches, 129, 130
Atlanta, Ga., 17, 18, 20, 21, 96, 173, 183, 184, 191, 241, 244, 245, 246, 247, 250, 252
Atlantic Coast Line, 135
Atlantic communities, 183
AT&SF, 26
Auburn, Wash., 220, 225
Audigage units, 85
Aurant, Calif., 231
Austin, Minn., 46
Austin, Tex., 111, 230
Automatic block signals, 72
Automatic classification, 306-309
Automation, 33, 219
Automotive Special, 183

B

Badger, 76
Bailey bridge, 314
Bakersfield, Calif., 262
Baldwin locomotives, 72, 281
Ball, R. B., 143
Baltimore & Ohio R.R., 203, 210, 214, 255
Bancroft, Idaho, 160
Bangor, Me., 6, 8
Bangor & Aroostook R.R., 5-9, 113-117, 206; Diesel engines, 114; Diesel motor generators, 114; Radio maintenance, 113-114
Barngrove, Jr., James L., 92
Bartlesville, Okla., 175
Bath, N.Y., 256

321

324

Fargo, N.D., 224, 227, 228
Farmers Elevator Service, 295
Farr intake hoods, 132
Farr filters, 132
Farr filter-cleaning machines, 199
Federal Express, 70, 71
Federal-Farnsworth radio telephone, 117
Federal Telephone & Radio Corp., 117
Ferryboats, 76, 77
Firestone Park, Calif., 231
Fishkill-on-the-Hudson, 69
Flannery, Olive B., xvii
Flatcar service, 57
Flatonia, Tex., 81
Flood-lighting, 17
Florida, 94, 95, 187
Fontana, Utah, 39
Forest Park, Ill., 44
Formica bulkheads, 130
Formica dressing tables, 131
Formica panels, 104, 128
Ft. Dodge, Iowa, 46, 157, 294, 295
Ft. Kent, Me., 6, 113
Ft. Worth, Tex., 23, 26, 27, 29, 30, 53, 54, 56, 111, 172, 230
Fossil, Wyo., 160
Franklin, N.J., 64, 67, 69
Fraser Paper Co., 8
Fresno, Calif., 230

G

Gadsden, Ala., 16
Gallatin River, 51
Galveston, Tex., 111, 230
Garfield, Utah, 255
Garrison, Mont., 51
Gateville, Tex., 172
Geier, B., 146, 147
General Electric Co., 21, 22
General Electric locomotive, 281
General Electric switch-heaters, 163
General Foods, 8
General Motors, 110
General Motors, London, Ont., plant, 281
General Steel Castings Corp., 131, 139
Geneva, Utah, 39
Georgetown, Idaho, 160

Georgia, 187
Glacier Point, 142
Glendive, Mont., 220, 221, 228, 268
GM & O, 308
Gold Creek, Mont., 51
Golden Rod, 241
Golden State Route, 230
Gold Spike ceremony, 130
Grand Rapids, Mich., 76, 281, 282, 283
Granger, Wyo., 159, 160
Granger-to-Pocatello project, 160
Granite Peak, 51
Grant, U. S., 51
Grants Pass, Ore., 111
Grauman's Chinese Theater, 128
Gray, Carl, 39, 40
Great Lakes, 94, 119
Great Northern Oil Co., 294
Great Northern Paper Co., 8
Great Northern R.R., 44, 111
Great Plains, 140
Great White Throne, 37
Greenbrier Clinic, 284
Greenbrier Hotel, 284, 285
Green Mountain potatoes, 206, 207
Greensboro, N.C., 21
Greenville, Me., 7
Greenville, S.C., 21
Greycliff, Mont., 51
Greycourt, N.Y., 64, 69
GS&F, 26, 93, 246
Guadalupe, Calif., 255
Gulf, Colorado & Santa Fe R.R., 25
Gulf port communities, 182
Gurley, Fred G., 23

H

Hammond grinders, 199
Harlem River, 69
Harlingen, Tex., 111
Harvey, Fred, 141
Hayne, S.C., 94, 98, 196, 197, 199
HB-3, 90
Healdsburg, Calif., 111
Hearne, Tex., 81
Helena, Mont., 51
Heliarc welders, 199
Helicopters, 315

325

L

Lackawanna Dispatch, 66
Lackawanna Limited, 257, 258
Lackawanna R.R., 10-13, 64, 69, 72,
  87-91, 144-149, 210, 253-260, 312,
  313, 314; Maintenance of Way and
  Structures, 146
Lafayette, La., 111
LaGrange, Me., 7
Lake Charles, La., 111
Lake Erie, 77, 119, 145
Lake Michigan, 75, 76
Lake Pend Oreille, 52
Lake Superior, 266
Lancaster, Tex., 111
Laramie, Wyo., 160, 162, 166
Las Vegas, Nev., 41, 42
Leavenworth, Kan., 44
Leece-Neville alternator-rectifier, 225
Leefe, Wyo., 160
Lehigh & Hudson River Railway, 63-
  73, 254; passenger traffic, 70, 71;
  train schedules, 65-67
Lehigh Valley R.R., 68, 314
Levee District, 169
Lewis and Clark expedition, 49, 50
Lewis and Clark Traveler's Rest Car,
  50
Lewiston, Idaho, 123
Lewisville, Tex., 23, 26, 29
Lexington, Ky., 282, 283
Limestone, Me., 6
Limestone Air Base, 7
Link-Belt Co., 291, 293
Linton, N.D., 224
Livestock shipping, 286-289
Livingston, Mont., 51
"LNSW," 109
Loewy, Raymond, 50
Logan, Mont., 51
Logan, W.Va., 282
Long Beach, Calif., 39, 103, 231
Long Island R.R., 70, 88
Loop district, 305
Los Angeles, Calif., 41, 42, 102, 103,
  108, 109, 111, 140, 173, 175, 177,
  229, 230, 231, 261, 262
Los Angeles Harbor, 111
Los Angeles River, 231
Los Nientos, Calif., 109, 231

Louisiana, 80, 81, 83, 85, 108, 110,
  111, 230, 235, 261
Louisville, Ky., 21, 22, 75, 76, 185,
  246, 248, 255, 282, 283
Ludington, Mich., 76
Ludlow, Ky., 245, 246
Lufkin, Tex., 56, 111
Luminator Inc., lighting fixtures, 132
Lynchburg yard, 243

M

MacFarlane, Robert S., 126
Macon, Ga., 241, 246
Madawaska, Me., 113
Magnaglo test benches, 199
Magnus Ajadip parts cleaners, 199
Maine, 8, 206; agricultural industry, 8
Maine Line, a magazine, 8
Maine potatoes, 206-208
Manitowoc, Wis., 76, 255
Manson, Idaho, 160
Marconi, Guglielmo, 257
Mars warning lights, 132
Marse, Wyo., 160
Marsh, Ernest, 106
Marshalltown, Iowa, 46, 157
Mason City, Iowa, 294, 295
Massachusetts, 254
Matisa-Schlatter butt welding process,
  178, 179
Maybrook, N.Y., 63, 64, 65, 69, 72
McCammon, Idaho, 160
McKenzie, H. J., 174
McKenzie, N.D., 224
Medford, Ore., 111
Memphis, Tenn., 15, 16, 53, 56, 94,
  184, 244
Mercury Manufacturing Co., 299
Meridian, Miss., 183, 241
Michigan, 75, 76
Michigan Central R.R., 255
Milk, 71
Miller, Edgar, 50
Millinocket, Me., 6, 113, 116
Millinocket Summit, Me., 7
Milwaukee R.R., 42
Milwaukee, Wis., 76
Mine Hill R.R., 68
Minneapolis, Minn., 44, 150

327

328